ANCIENT INDIAN TRADITION & MYTHOLOGY

Translated by
A BOARD OF SCHOLARS

And Edited by
Prof. J. L. SHASTRI

VOLUME 21

ANCIENT INDIAN TRADITION AND MYTHOLOGY SERIES

[PURĀṆAS IN TRANSLATION]

Volumes Released

ŚIVA 1-4
LIṄGA 5-6
BHĀGAVATA 7-11
GARUḌA 12-14
NĀRADA 15-19
KŪRMA 20-21
BRAHMĀṆḌA 22-26
AGNI 27-30
VARĀHA 31-32
BRAHMA 33-36
VĀYU 37-38
PADMA 39-48
SKANDA, PARTS I-XXI, 49-69

Volumes Under Preparation

SKANDA, PARTS XXII-XXIII, 70-71
VĀMANA 72-73
BHAVIṢYA
BRAHMAVAIVARTA
DEVĪBHĀGAVATA
KĀLIKĀ
MĀRKAṆḌEYA
MATSYA
VIṢṆU
VIṢṆUDHARMOTTARA

THE
KŪRMA-PURĀNA

PART II

Translated and Annotated by

DR. G.V. TAGARE

MOTILAL BANARSIDASS PUBLISHERS
PRIVATE LIMITED • DELHI

Reprint: Delhi, 1997, 2010
First Edition: Delhi, 1982

ISBN: 978-81-208-0353-1

MOTILAL BANARSIDASS
41 U.A. Bungalow Road, Jawahar Nagar, Delhi 110 007
8 Mahalaxmi Chamber, 22 Bhulabhai Desai Road, Mumbai 400 026
203 Royapettah High Road, Mylapore, Chennai 600 004
236, 9th Main III Block, Jayanagar, Bangalore 560 011
Sanas Plaza, 1302 Baji Rao Road, Pune 411 002
8 Camac Street, Kolkata 700 017
Ashok Rajpath, Patna 800 004
Chowk, Varanasi 221 001

UNESCO COLLECTION OF REPRESENTATIVE WORKS—*Indian Series*
This book has been accepted in the Indian Translation Series of the UNESCO Collection of Representative Works, jointly sponsored by the United Nations Educational, Scientific and Cultural Organization (UNESCO) and the Government of India

Printed in India
By Jainendra Prakash Jain at Shri Jainendra Press,
A-45 Naraina, Phase-I, New Delhi 110 028
and Published by Narendra Prakash Jain for
Motilal Banarsidass Publishers Private Limited,
Bungalow Road, Delhi 110 007

PUBLISHER'S NOTE

The purest gems lie hidden in the bottom of the ocean or in the depth of rocks. One has to dive into the ocean or delve into the rocks to find them out. Similarly, truth lies concealed in the language which with the passage of time has become obsolete.

But he has neither the means nor the leisure to embark on that course. We have, therefore, planned to help him acquire knowledge by an easier course. We have started the series of *Ancient Indian Tradition and Mythology* in English Translation. Our goal is to universalize knowledge through the most popular international medium of expression. The publication of the Purāṇas in English translation is a step towards that goal.

PREFACE

The present volume contains the *Kūrma Purāṇa*, Part II (Chapters 1-46) completing the second half (*Uttarārdha*) of the text in English translation. This is the Twentyfirst Volume in the series of fifty volumes which we have planned on *Ancient Indian Tradition and Mythology*.

The project of the series was envisaged and financed in 1970 by Lala Sundar Lal Jain of Messrs Motilal Banarsidass. Hitherto twenty volumes of the series, (comprising English translation of *Śiva*, *Liṅga*, *Bhāgavata*, *Garuḍa*, *Nārada and Kūrma* have been published and released for sale.

This volume, (*Kūrma* pt. II,) like all other volumes, is encyclopaedic in character. It deals with miscellaneous topics such as the Pāśupata Yoga, the Vibhūti Yoga, the Yoga of Īśvara as the means of crossing the ocean of Worldly existence. In Religion and Ethics, it places emphasis on the performance of duties of one's own profession (*Varṇa-dharma*) in relation to one's stage of life (*Āśrama*). In Philosophy it follows the Sāṅkhya system of thought in regard to the concept of Puruṣa and Prakṛti and the evolution of Universe by the union of both. In Geography it describes the holy centres situated in the different parts of the country, on the Narmadā river in particular. It comments upon the topics of creation, sustenance and dissolution. As a special feature, the present part mentions some expiatory rites for the person who fails to observe duties prescribed for him in the Dharma-śāstra. For further specialities of this Purāṇa, the reader is referred to Introduction prefixed to Part I of this Purāṇa.

The present translation is based on the Sanskrit text of the *Kūrma Purāṇa* as published by Messrs Kṣemarāja Śrīkṛṣṇadāsa, Veṅkaṭeśvara Press, Bombay. This text constructed on the collation of mss. and supported by the evidence of citations found in the Smṛti granthas, is fairly accurate.

The present Part, the second half includes besides translation and notes of Kūrma, the Preface, Abbreviations, Contents and the General Index to the complete Purāṇa.

Acknowledgment of Obligation

It is our pleasant duty to put on record our sincere thanks to Dr. R. N. Dandekar and the UNESCO authorities for their kind encouragement and valuable help which render this work very useful. We are extremely grateful to Dr. G. V. Tagare who has meticulously and delightfully accomplished this onerous task. The critical Introduction, the lucid translation and explanatory notes are, in fact, his monumental contributions to the studies in Indology. We must also thank Shri T. V. Parameshwara Iyer for his valuable assistance in the preparation of translation. We express our gratitude to all those who have offered suggestions for improving the same.

— Editor

CONTENTS

A. PREFACE vii

B. ABBREVIATIONS xi

C. TRANSLATION AND NOTES

Chapters	Part II	Pages
1.	The Dialogue between Sages and Vyāsa	337
2.	The Yoga of Īśvara	342
3.	Prakṛti and Puruṣa	348
4.	The Glory of Śiva	350
5.	Śiva's Dance—Śiva eulogised by Sages	354
6.	The Glory of Śiva	359
7.	The Vibhūti-Yoga of Śiva : Fundamentals of Pāśupatism	364
8.	The Means of Crossing the ocean of Worldly Existence	367
9.	The unsullied form of Śiva	370
10.	The form of the Supreme Brahman Śiva—the Parabrahman	372
11.	The Path of liberation of the individual soul from bondage	374
12.	The Path of Action—Duties of celibate students	388
13.	The Usages of Śiṣṭas. Good Conduct	395
14.	Duties of Brahmacārins	400
15.	The Duties of the Householder	410
16.	The Duties of the Householder. Rules of Good Conduct	415
17.	Decision about Acceptable and Prohibited Food	424
18.	Daily Duties of a Householder	430
19.	Daily Duties of a Householder : Mode of taking meals	443
20.	Procedure of Performance of Śrāddha	447
21.	Rules governing Śrāddha	453

22. Rules for performance of Śrāddha 460
23. Rules regarding Impurities caused by Birth or Death 471
24. The Duties of Agni-hotrin 482
25. The Means of Livelihood of a Brāhmaṇa Householder 485
26. Rules of offering religious gifts 487
27. Duties in Vānaprastha (Hermit's) Stage 495
28. Duties of Yatis (recluses) 500
29. Duties of an Ascetic 504
30. Rules of Expiation 509
31. Importance of Kapāla-mocana Tīrtha 512
32. Expiatory rites 522
33. Expiatory rites (continued) 524
34. Expiatory rites (continued) 529
35. Greatness of Gayā and other sacred places 544
36. Glory of Sacred Places : the death of Kāli 551
37. Glory of Mahālaya and other holy centres 555
38. The Description of Dāruvana 562
39. The Entry into the forest of Devadāru 570
40. The Glory of Narmadā 577
41. Glory of different sacred places on the Narmadā river 581
42. Greatness of holy centres on the Narmadā river 591
43. Greatness of Naimiṣāraṇya and Japyeśvara 596
44. Description of sacred places (continued) 599
45. Description of four types of Dissolution 602
46. Dissolution of subsidiary creation 608
INDEX 623

ABBREVIATIONS

Common and Self-evident abbreviations such as ch(s)—chapter(s), p—page, pp—pages, v—verse, vv—verses, Ftn—footnote, Hist. Ind. Philo—History of Indian Philosophy are not included in this list.

ABORI	*Annals of the Bhandarkar Oriental Research Institute*, Poona.
AGP	S. M. Ali's *The Geography of Purāṇas*, PPH, New Delhi, 1973.
AIHT	*Ancient Indian Historical Tradition* F. E. Pargiter, Motilal Banarsidass (MLBD), Delhi.
AP	*Agni Purāṇa*, Guru Mandal Edition (GM), Calcutta, 1957.
AV	*Atharva Veda*, Svadhyaya Mandal Aundh.
Bhā. P.	*Bhāgavata Purāṇa*, MLBD, Delhi 1973.
Bh. P.	*Bhāgavata Purāṇa*, Bhagavat Vidyapeeth, Ahmedabad.
Bm. P.	*Brahma Purāṇa*, GM. 1954.
Brn.	*Bṛhannāradīya* Pt. Hrishikesh Shastri, Chowkhamba, 1975.
Bs. P.	*Bhaviṣya Purāṇa*, Vishnu Shastri Bapat, Wai.
Bv. P.	*Brahma Vaivarta Purāṇa*, GM, 1955-57.
CC	*Caturvarga Cintāmaṇi* by Hemādri.
DB	*Devī Bhāgavata*, GM, 1960-61.
De or GDAMI	*The Geographical Dictionary of Ancient and Mediaeval India*—N. L. De, Orienta Reprint Delhi, 1971.
Dh. S.	*Dharma Sūtra* (preceded by the author's name such as Gautama).
ERE	*Encyclopaedia of Religion and Ethics*—Hastings.
GP	*Garuḍa Purāṇa*, Ed. R. S. Bhattacharya, Chowkhamba, Varanasi, 1964.
GS	*Gṛhya Sūtra* (Preceded by the name of the author such as Āpastamba)

HD	*History of Dharma Śāstra* by P. V. tane, G.O.S.
IA	*The Indian Antiquary.*
IHQ	*The Indian Historical Quarterly.*
KP	*Kūrma Purāṇa*, Venkateshwara Press Edt. Bombay, also Kashiraj Trust Edt., Varanasi 1971.
LP	*Liṅga Purāṇa*, GM, 1960.
Mbh.	*Mahābhārata*, Gītā Press, Gorakhpur Vs. 2014.
MK	*Mārkaṇḍeya Purāṇa.*
MN	*Mahābhārata Nāmānukramaṇī*, Gītā Press, Gorakhpur VS 2016.
Mt. P.	*Matsya Purāṇa*, GM, 1954.
MW	*Monier Williams* Sk. English Dictionary, MLBD, Delhi, 1976.
NP	*Nāradīya or Nārada Purāṇa*, Venkateshwar Press, Bombay.
PCK	*Bhāratavarṣiya Prācina Caritra Kośa*, Siddheshwar Shastri, Poona, 1968.
Pd. P.	*Padma Purāṇa*, GM., 1957-2959.
PE	*Puranic Encyclopaedia* by V. Mani, English, MLBD Delhi, 1975.
PJ.	*Purāṇa* (Journal of the Kashirāj Trust) Varanasi.
PR or PRHRC	*Puranic Records on Hindu Rites and Customs* R. C. Hazra, Calcutta, 1948.
RV	*Ṛg Veda*, Svadhyaya Mandal, Aundh
Śat. Br	*Śatapatha Brahmaṇa.*
SEP	*Studies in Epics and Purāṇas* by A.D. Pusalkar Bharatiya Vidya Bhavan(BVB), Bombay.
SG or SGAMI	*Studies in the Geography of Ancient and Mediaeval India*—D. C. Sircar MLBD, Delhi, 1971.
SKD	*Śabda-Kalpa-Druma*—Raja R. K. Dev., Chowkhamba, Varanasi.
Sk. P.	*Skanda Purāṇa*, GM. 1960-65.

SM	*Sādhana Mālā*—B. Bhattacharya, GOS, Baroda, 1928.
SMC	*Smṛti Candrikā*—Devanna Bhaṭṭa.
Smṛ	*Smṛti* (preceded by the author's name or simply the author's name e.g. Manu Smṛti or Manu. All GM editions in the Smṛti-Sandarbha. 1952-57.
Sv. P.	*Śiva Purāṇa,* Pandit Pustakālaya Kashi, V.S. 2020.
Va. P.	*Vāyu Purāṇa*, GM, 1959.
VP.	*Viṣṇu Purāṇa*, Gītā Press, Gorakhpur, V.S. 2026.
VR	Vālmīki Rāmāyaṇa, Gītā Press, V.S. 2020.
VRK	*Vālmiki Rāmāyaṇa Kośa*—Ramkumar Rai, (Chowkhamba Varanasi.)
Yaj	*Yājñavalkya* (Smṛti), etc.
YSP	*The Yoga System of Patañjali*—J. H. Wood. (MLBD)

CHAPTER ONE[1]

The Dialogue Between Sages and Vyāsa

The Sages said:

1. O holy Lord ! The creative activity of the self-born god Brahmā has been duly recounted by you; so also the earlier extent of the Cosmic Egg and the ascertainment of (the nature and extent of) the Manvantaras (periods of different Manus).

2. It has been mentioned by you in that connection that the Lord of Lords, the Supreme god, should be propitiated by persons of all castes who are exclusively devoted to Dharma and are always engaged in the paths of knowledge and Yoga.

3. You have expounded to us the excellent knowledge which has Brahman as its only object and which leads to the complete annihilation of all the miseries of Saṁsāra (worldly existence) and where-with we can perceive that Supreme Brahman.

4. O holy lord, indeed you have acquired the entire perfect wisdom from Kṛṣṇa Dvaipāyana who is Nārāyaṇa himself. Hence we ask you again.

5. On hearing that request of the sages, the holy lord Sūta who had heard the Purāṇas from Kṛṣṇa Dvaipāyana, just began to narrate.

6. In the meanwhile, at that juncture, Vyāsa, Kṛṣṇa Dvaipāyana, himself, arrived there where the excellent sages were performing the satra (sacrificial session).

7. On seeing Vyāsa who was a deep scholar of the Vedas, whose lustre was like that of a black cloud and whose eyes

---

1. Chapters 1 to 11 of this part (Uttarārdha) of KP. constitute *Īśvara-gītā*—the song of Īśvara (god Śiva) just as the BG (Bhagavadgītā) is "the song of the Lord (Kṛṣṇa)". The similarity is not merely in titles but in the contents as well. The *Īśvaragītā* has incorporated a number of verses mainly from the BG. and next to that from Upaniṣads like Kaṭha, Śvetāśvatara.

were like the petals of a lotus, the leading Brāhmaṇas bowed to him (out of respect).

8. On seeing him, Lomaharṣaṇa fell on the ground like a staff. After bending down the head, he dedicated himself unto him (*v.l.* circumambulated Vyāsa and sat by his side) with the palms joined in reverence.

9. Śaunaka and other Brāhmaṇas were duly enquired after their health. Thereupon they assured the great sage (about their health) and offered him a befitting seat.

10. Then the holy lord, the son of Parāśara, addressed these words to them, "I hope there is no deficiency or difficulty in your penance, in your learning and in your practice of the self-study of the Vedas".

11-13. After bowing down to his preceptor, the great sage Sūta said:—"It behoves you to recount to the sages the perfect knowledge pertaining to Brahman. Indeed, these sages are quiescent. They are ascetics solely devoted to Dharma. They have the keen desire to hear. It behoves you to explain (everything) precisely, the divine knowledge that bestows liberation, that has been directly taught to me by you and that had been formerly narrated to the sages by Viṣṇu in the form (incarnation) of Kūrma (Tortoise)".

14. On hearing the words of Sūta, the saintly son of Satyavatī, bowed down his head to Rudra and spoke these pleasing words of discourse.

This chapter presents the setting for the proposed dialogue. The sages in the Naimiṣāraṇya wanted to get from Sūta, the supreme knowledge of the Brahman which leads to the annihilation of Saṁsāra. Sūta was about to tell when his preceptor Vyāsa came there. Sūta requested him to explain to the sages the knowledge about Brahma which Vyāsa taught him as it was explained by Lord Kūrma to the sages of old (Verse 12.)

Vyāsa now attributes the knowledge to Śiva who explained it to ten sages like Sanatkumāra and others (V. 15), who at Badarikāśrama appealed to Nārāyaṇa for this spiritual knowledge (vv. 16-30). While Nārāyaṇa was about to speak god Śiva came there (v. 31). Nārāyaṇa conveyed the request of the sages to him (v. 40) and god Śiva co-seated with Nārāyaṇa began to speak. The Pāśupata twist in this episode is obvious.

Vyāsa said :

15. I shall now narrate to you what formerly Lord Mahādeva was asked by the leading Yogins, the chief of whom was Sanatkumāra and what he himsalf has expounded it.[1]

16-18. The following sages viz. Sanatkumāra, Sanaka, Sanandana (and Sanātana), Aṅgiras, Bhṛgu, the knower of the supreme Dharma and accompanied by Rudra, Kaṇāda, Kapila, Garga, the great sage Vāmadeva, Śukra and lord Vasiṣṭha—all of them had perfectly controlled their minds. They consulted one another. *With full self-control on their minds, they performed terrible penance in the holy Badarikāśrama.

19. They saw the sage Nārāyaṇa of great Yogic power, the son of sage Dharma, devoid of beginning and end, and accompanied by Nara.

20. They eulogised him with various hymns taken from the Vedas. The Yogins, endowed with devotion, bowed down to the deity, the most excellent among the knowers of Yoga.

21. After knowing their desire, the omniscient lord spoke in a majestic tone : "Why is this penance being performed by you ?"

22. With delighted minds, they bowed to the eternal (lord), the Ātman of the universe, lord Nārāyaṇa himself who had arrived, indicating the *Siddhi* (achievement of their desires).

23. "We have adopted the attitude of self-control** even though all of us are expounders of the Brahman. We have sought refuge in you, the only Puruṣottama.

24. You are Lord Nārāyaṇa, the ancient sage, the unmanifest Being. You know the entire Supreme esoteric doctrine.

25. Excepting you, the great Īśvara, there is no other knower. It behoves you, of such a nature, to dispel our formidable doubts.

---

1. As Hazra points out, this irrelevance of Vyāsa's answer is a Pāśupata interpolation (PRHRC pp. 62.63) Sūta has requested Vyāsa to narrate the spiritual knowledge which he (Vyāsa) heard from Lord Kūrma and taught him (Sūta).

*In view of V. 25 below, a better v.l. is *Saṁśaya* instead of *Saṁyata*. v.l. means, 'but had their minds engrossed in doubt.'

**v.l. *saṁśayam āpannāḥ* (Although all of us are expounders of Brahman) we are entangled in a doubt.

26. What is the cause of all these (things in the world)?* Who undergoes worldly existence for ever? What is the Ātman? What is salvation? What causes the rebirth or recurring worldly existence?

27. What is (the nature of this) worldly existence? Who is Īśāna, who perceives everything? What is the supreme Brahman? It behoves you to explain everything".

28. After saying this, the sages stood looking at Puruṣottama, who shedding off his guise as an ascetic, was stationed there in his own brilliance.

29-30. He was shining free from impurity. He was embellished with a halo of brilliant splendour. He was the lord having the lustre of molten gold. He was marked by the Śrīvatsa mark on his chest. He was holding Śaṅkha, Cakra, mace and the Śārṅga bow in his hands. He was enveloped by glory and splendour. Thanks to his brilliance, Nara was not even seen from that moment.

31. In the meanwhile, Maheśvara, the great lord, whose coronet was marked with the (crescent of the) moon, Rudra (the deity) appeared before them disposed to bestow Grace upon them.[1]

32. On seeing the three-eyed moon-bedecked lord of the universe, Parameśvara (Śiva), they were delighted in their minds. With devotion they eulogised the great lord:

33. "O Īśvara, be victorious, O Mahādeva, O Śiva, the lord of the goblins, be victorious; Glory unto you, O Lord of the sages, O lord worshipped by means of penance.

34. O Ātman of the universe, O God of thousands of forms, O activiser of the machine of the universe, O Infinite one, be victorious. Glory to you, O cause of the origin, sustenance and annihilation of the universe.

35. Be victorious O Īśāna, O Śambhu, O thousand-footed one, O deity bowed down by leading Yogins, O consort of Ambikā. O lord Parameśvara, obeisance to you."

---

*or 'What is the (nature of this) entire cause?

1. This uninvited entry of Śiva is a ruse to Pāśupatise this text.

36. On being thus eulogised, the three-eyed lord Īśa, favourably disposed towards the devotees, embraced Hṛṣīkeśa (lord Viṣṇu) and addressed him in a majestic tone :

37. "O Puṇḍarīkākṣa (lotus-eyed god), why have these leading sages, the expounders of Brahman, come to this place. O Acyuta, what is to be done for them by me ?"

38. On hearing those words of his, Janārdana, the lord of Devas, spoke to Mahādeva who was standing there well-disposed to confer grace.

39-40 "O lord, these sages and ascetics have shed off their sins. If the lord be delighted with the sages who have sought refuge in you, who are desirous of your perfect vision and whose Ātmans are purified, it behoves you to impart to them that divine wisdom in my presence.

41. O Śiva, indeed, you know your own Ātman. No one else does so. You explain your own Ātman yourself. Reveal your Ātman to the leading sages".

42. After saying thus, Hṛṣīkeśa (Nārāyaṇa) looked at the bull-bannered Deity (Śiva) and exhibiting his accomplishments in Yoga, instructed the great sages (as follows) :

43. "It behoves you to realise precisely that you are all blessed by the vision of the Trident-bearing Śaṅkara, the great Īśa. You now deserve to know precisely (the divine knowledge).

44. It behoves you to see the lord of devas who stands in front and who is visible in form. He alone is capable to say precisely everything in my presence".

45. After hearing the words of Viṣṇu and bowing down to the bull-bannered deity, those sages the chief of whom was Sanatkumāra, asked Maheśvara :

46. In the meanwhile, a holy auspicious divine seat shone there for the sake of Īśvara. It appeared from the sky in an unimaginable way (lit. was beyond the ken of imagination).

47. The creator of the universe, the Yogic Ātman, occupied it along with Viṣṇu. Lord Maheśvara shone there filling the universe with his brilliance.

48. Then the expounders of the Brahman saw Śaṅkara, the overlord of the chiefs of Devas, shining brilliantly on the faultlessly pure seat.

49-50. They saw the lord of the Bhūtas (goblins or living beings) seated on the throne, the lord, within whom all the universe exists, and from whom the universe does not exist separately. They saw Īśāna, the great Īśa accompanied by Vāsudeva. On being asked, Parameśvara spoke to the sages about the excellent Yoga of the Ātman, after glancing at Puṇḍarīkākṣa. "O sinless ones ! Listen ye all, with calm minds the knowledge (as it is) recounted by me. It is the pure knowledge pertaining to Īśvara. Be ye all calm in minds."

CHAPTER TWO

The Yoga of Īśvara.

Īśvara said :

1. This perfect knowledge of mine is an eternal mystery and secret. It cannot be adequately expressed. Devas do not know it even though they strive for it, O twiceborn ones.

2. Resorting to this perfect knowledge, excellent Brāhmaṇas have become identical with Brahman. They, the earlier expounders of Brahman, do not undergo worldly existence i. e. Saṁsāra (cycle of births & deaths consequent to sufferings).

3. It is the secret of secrets. It must be strenuously guarded. I shall explain it to you who are expounders of Brahman and endowed with devotion.

4. This Ātman is absolute, pure, clean (v. l. quiescent) subtle and eternal. It exists within everything. It is the pure consciousness itself. It exists beyond the darkness of ignorance.

5. According to Vedas He is the immanent Being, the Puruṣa, the vital Breath, Maheśvara, Kāla (Time). Here he is unmanifest but He knows.

6. The universe is born of him. In him alone it gets dissolved. He is the master of the Māyā but unfettered by it (the Māyā), he assumes various bodies (or forms).

7. He does not undergo the process of worldly existence (i. e. birth and death). The lord is not identical with the physical world, He is neither the Earth nor the water nor the fire nor the wind nor the Ether.

8. He is not the Vital breath, nor the mind nor the Pradhāna nor the unmanifest. It is neither the sound nor the touch nor the colour nor the form nor the taste nor the smell nor the ego nor the Agent of an act or speech.

9. O excellent Brāhmaṇas, the Ātman is (not a sense organ as he is) nor the foot, neither the anus nor the genitals. He is neither the doer (the agent of an action) nor the enjoyer, neither the Prakṛti nor the Puruṣa.

10-11. As a matter of fact, Caitanya* (consciousness) or the Ātman is neither Māyā nor the Vital Breath. Just as the relation between light and darkness cannot be deemed possible, so is the relation between Prapañca (the visual illusory world of diversity) and the supreme Soul.

11b-12a. Just as shade and the sunlight are mutually distinct and different in this world, in the same manner, the world and the puruṣa are intrinsically and factually different.

12b-13a. Should it be argued that the Ātman is innately soiled or dirty, created and changeable, it can never be liberated even in hundreds of births.

13b-14a. The liberated sages visualize that their Ātman is intrinsically devoid of aberrations or change, free from Dvandvas (mutually chasing opposites). They realise that the Ātman is blissful in form and unchanging.

14b-15a. The ideas that "I am the doer"; "I am happy", "I am unhappy", "I am lean", "I am stout" etc. are caused by the ego. They are superimposed on the Ātman by the people.

15b-16a. Vedic scholars assert that the Ātman is the witness, beyond the range of Prakṛti. It is the enjoyer, imperishable, enlightened and permeating everything. Hence, the worldly existence or Saṁsāra of all embodied beings originates from ignorance.

---

*v.l. accepted as *mā caiva* of the veṇkṭ. Edt. gives no subject to the predicate.

17-19. Due to ignorance and erroneous conception the reality gets mingled with Prakṛti. The ever-rising self-luminous Puruṣa is the greatest and omnipresent. Due to the thoughtlessness, non-discrimination of the ego, one considers himself, "I am the doer". But the sages realize the unmanifest soul as eternal and Prakṛti of the nature of *sat* and *asat* (existence and non-existence). He takes Pradhāna to be Puruṣa and begins to argue that it is the Brahman that is the cause. Thereby the Ātman, though steady and unsullied becomes (associated with it) by contact.

20. He (therefore) does not comprehend that his own Ātman is in reality the imperishable Brahman. (What he has then) is the (erroneous) notion of the Ātman in what is the non-Ātman. Hence it is misery.

21. All defects such as passion, hatred etc., are brought about due to wrong notions. Its greatest defect is performance of actions meritorious or otherwise. This is the state.

22. It is due to that cause that everyone is invested with different kinds of physical bodies. The soul, however, lies concealed within, yet it is everywhere, eternal and free from blemishes.

23. It stands* single by his Māyā power and not by its nature. Hence the sages say that non-dualism is the ultimate truth.

24-25a. The difference is due to the nature of *Avyakta* (the unmanifest). That Māyā has the Ātman for its support. Just as the sky does not become dirty or soiled due to the contact with smoke, so also the Ātman is not vitiated due to the effusions of the *Antaḥkaraṇa* (the inner sense-organ or mind).

25b-26a. The unattached (pure) crystal piece shines by dint of its own lustre, without any conditioning cause, so also does the pure Ātman shine untouched by any conditioning causes.

26b-27a. Clever people call this universe as being of the

---

*As this statement is contradictory, the other reading *ekaḥ sa bhidyate* is preferable. It means "Although the Ātman is one, it appears as many through his Māyā Power and not due to his inherent nature".

form of knowledge. Other people with vitiated vision* (followers of heretic paths) see it in the form of matter or the objects.

27b-28a. The Ātman or spirit is by nature steady, devoid of Guṇas, omnipresent and of the nature of consciousness. But it is looked upon as matter by men of wrong (heretical) outlook.

28b-29a. Just as the pure crystal when in contact with a red object like Guñjā seeds appears to be red, so also the great Being is seen (in the form of the objects or Guṇas).

29b-30a. Hence the Ātman should be worshipped, pondered over and heard by the seekers of liberation, as being in the form that is imperishable, pure, eternal, omnipresent and unchanging.

30b-31a. When consciousness ever appears everywhere in the mind of a faithful Yogin, he attains the knowledge of the self.

31b-32a.** When one observes all living beings as abiding in the Ātman and the Ātman in all living beings, the Brahman is realised.[1]

32b-33a. When the Ātman is in the state of *Samādhi* (Trance), he does not perceive the living beings. Then he has become one with the Supreme Soul. The Ātman is absolute then.

33b-34a. When all the passions that stick to the heart, drop off, the scholar becomes immortalised and attains welfare (*mokṣa*)†.

34b-35a. When he realizes the whole variety or the separate states of the living beings as stationed in the One and as evolved from just that One—he attains the Brahman.

---

*The word *jñāna-dṛṣṭibhiḥ* in the text is unsuitable. It should be *sajñāna-dṛṣṭibhiḥ*)

**BG. 6.29

1. The Yoga of Īśvara is based on Sāṅkhya philosophy. Īśvara explains the nature of Ātman (vv. 3-29) and exhorts that Ātman should be meditated upon. He (Ātman) is in all beings. When this specialised knowledge is realized, one becomes identical with Śiva. This is the Sāṅkhya Philosophy (vv. 30-41). Concentration on this knowledge is Yoga. Yoga and knowledge are interdependent.

†BG. 13.30

35b-36. When he observes the absolute Ātman factually, and the entire universe only an illusion, he experiences the greatest bliss.

37. When one derives the perfect knowledge of the absolute Brahman, the sole panacea for the miseries of births and old age as well as ailments, he becomes Śiva.

38. Just as the rivers and rivulets get mingled with the ocean and become one, so also the Ātman becomes one with the imperishable and the unsullied Brahman.

39. Hence perfect knowledge alone exists. Neither the universe nor its existence is real. Perfect knowledge is enveloped by ignorance in this world, thereby the world gets deluded.

40. Perfect knowledge is blemishless, subtle, free from doubts and unchanging. Everything else is *Ajñāna* (Ignorance). This entire (thorough) realisation is considered *Vijñāna* (perfect knowledge).

41. Thus the Sāṅkhya which is called excellent knowledge has been recounted unto you. It is certainly the essence of all Vedānta (Upaniṣads). Yoga is the single-minded concentration on this knowledge.

42. Knowledge originates from Yoga and Yoga functions due to knowledge. There remains nothing unaccomplishable to one endowed with both Yoga and Knowledge.

43. That which the Yogins attain is also attained by Sāṅkhyas. He who sees Sāṅkhya and the Yoga as one, is the knower of the real principle*.

44. O Brāhmaṇas, other Yogins, very much attached to *Aiśvarya* (prosperity and glory), get submerged in those different activities. So also those whose intellects are impeded and blunted.

45. At the end of the body (i. e. on death), one who is endowed with *Jñāna* and *Yoga* shall attain the great, pure and divine *Aiśvarya* (prosperity and glory of Brahmahood) which is approved by all.

46. This Ātman is I myself, the unmanifest Master of

---

*BG. 5.5.

Māyā, the great Īśvara. I am glorified in the Vedas, as being the Ātman of all and having faces in all directions.

47. I (i. e. the Ātman) have within me all forms, tastes fragrances. I am free from old age and death. I have hands and feet all round. I am the eternal immanent soul.

48. Though handless and feetless I am the speediest grasper, and am stationed in the heart of all. (Though) eyeless I observe and (even if) earless, I do hear.*

49. I know all these. No one knows me. Persons of truthful vision call me as being one, the only great Puruṣa.

50. Sages of subtle visions see the cause of the Ātman (?) They see the excellent *Aiśvarya* of the Nirguṇa form which is blemishless.

51. I shall mention to you what Devas, deluded by my Māyā, do not know. Ye all the expounders of Brahman, listen with concentration of your minds.

52. I am by nature beyond the ken of Māyā. Hence I cannot be praised** (?) by all. I, however, urge it the reason of which the wise sages know.

53. Hence, the Yogins who have visualised Reality get into my secretmost (inner) personaliy which is omnipresent, and attain complete identity with me.

54. Those who have crossed my Māyā which is of universal forms, attain the great and pure Nirvāṇa (beatitude) along with me.

55. They have no return (to saṁsāra) even in hundreds and crores of Kalpas, thanks to my favour. O leading Yogins, this is the injunction of the Vedas.

56. The (perfect knowledge) should be imparted (only) to sons, disciples and Yogins. Thus the perfect knowledge which is a synthesis of Sāṅkhya and Yoga (lit. Sāṅkhya based on Yoga) has been expounded by me.

---

*Śvet. Up. 3.19 : apāṇipādo javano grahītā paśyatyacakṣuḥ sa śṛṇotyakarṇaḥ.

**If *Praśastaḥ* in the text is amended as *Praśāstā* (as in the Crt. Ed.) it means, "I am not the ruler of all the world)".

CHAPTER THREE

Prakṛti and Puruṣa

Īśvara said :

1. Kāla (Time), Pradhāna or Prakṛti and the supreme Puruṣa originated from the unmanifest (Brahman). All these (objects of the universe) were born of them. Hence the universe is identical with Brahman.

2. All round it has (the extremities of) hands and feet; it has eyes, heads and mouths on all sides; all round, it has ears; it exists enveloping the world*.

3. It appears to possess the attributes of the sense organs but it is devoid of all sense-organs. It is the support of all; it is perpetual bliss, unmanifest and devoid of duality. **

4-5. It is non-comparable. It is beyond all means of valid knowledge and is yet comprehensible; it is devoid of all alternatives; it is free from appearances (?); it is the abode of all; it is the supreme deathless one. It is non-different (from the universe) yet it is stationed separately on a different footing). It is constant, unchanging and eternal. It is devoid of Guṇas. It is the highest brilliance. Sages know that to be perfect knowledge.

6. It is the Ātman of all living beings; he is both within and without; he is the supreme (beyond all). I am that Ātman, the omnipresent, quiescent, the great Īśvara and the embodiment of knowledge (consciousness).

7. All this universe consisting of the mobiles and immobiles has been pervaded by me. All beings exist in me.† He who has realized this knowledge is the real knower of the Vedas.

8. That entity is said to be both Pradhāna and Puruṣa. Kāla, manifesting through their union, is said to be the greatest and beginningless.

9. All these three are devoid of beginning and end; they are stationed in the Unmanifest Brahman, but the wise sages

*BG. 13.13, Śvet. 3.16.

**BG. 13.14, Śvet. 3.17.

†BG. ix. 4.

knew that my form (person) is both identical with as well as different from them.

10. That which is said to be Prakṛti gives birth to the entire universe beginning with *Mahat* and ending with *Viśeṣas* (the particularised forms). It deludes all embodied beings.

11. Stationed in the Prakṛti, the Puruṣa enjoys the attributes of Prakṛti.* Since it is devoid of the ego, it is called *Pañcaviṁśaka* (the total of twenty-five Principles or the twenty-fifth Principle).

12. The first evolute of Prakṛti is called *Mahat.* Through its knowledge of being endowed with knowledge, *Ahaṁkāra* (ego) was evolved out of it.

13. The principle called Mahat is one and it is (also known as) Ātman. He is also called Ahaṁkāra (the principle individuation). It is called *jīva* (the individual self) and the inner soul by the thinkers of the real principles.

14. It is through it (ego) that (the soul) experiences pleasure and misery in the (various) births. It is of the nature of *Vijñāna* (knowledge) and the *Manas* (mind) is its accessory.

15. Puruṣa identifies himself (with the world) even due to that (ego) and is involved in Saṁsāra. That ignorance originates due to the union of Prakṛti and Kāla.

16. Kāla (Time) creates the living beings, Kāla annihilates the subjects. Everything is dependent on Kāla; Kāla is not under the control of anyone.

17. He is eternal and restrains everything from within. He is called Prāṇa (the vital breath), omniscient, Lord Puruṣottama (The Supreme Puruṣa).

18. Learned men say that *Manas* (mind) is superior to and beyond the sense-organs. *Ahaṁkāra* is greater than and beyond *Manas,* and the principle *Mahat* is greater than *Ahaṁkāra.***

19. *Avyakta* (the unmanifest *Prakṛti*) is greater than and beyond *Mahat, Puruṣa* is Superior to and beyond *Avyakta*; Lord

---

*BG. xiii. 21

**BG. III. 42; also Kaṭha Up. VI. 7, 8 and III. 10, 11.

Prāṇa, the vital breath, is greater than and beyond *Puruṣa*; all this universe belongs to and is controlled by him.

20. *Vyoman* (the ether) is greater than and beyond *Prāṇa*; the fire-god is beyond *Vyoman*; I am that unchanging Brahman; the quiescent one. This universe is beyond *Māyā* (v.l. I am the embodiment of knowledge, the supreme lord).

21-22. There is no other living being greater than I. By realising me, one is liberated. The living beings including the mobile and the immobile ones in the universe are not eternal with the exception of me, the unmanifest, Maheśvara of the form of the *Vyoman*, (the universe has no separate existence). I create everything; I annihilate the universe for ever.

23. The lord, master of Māyā and identical with it, is united with Kāla. Due to my presence this Kāla, the infinite Ātman, creates the entire universe and controls it (by propelling it to work). This is the injunction (teaching) of the Vedas.

CHAPTER FOUR[1]

The Glory of Śiva

Īśvara said :

1. I shall recount the greatness of the God of the gods from whom everything is produced (or functions). Ye, expounders of the Brahman, listen with concentration of the mind.

---

1. In this chapter full of quotations from the BG., the author describes the greatness of Śiva in Vedantic epithets emphasising the path of Bhakti for god-realisation. The description of his own self by Īśvara constantly reminds one of Kṛṣṇa's discourse in the BG. He explains how the process of this universe goes on due to his potencies called Māyā, Vidyā, and Tāmasī or Kāla (18-23). He classifies the devotees according to the path of Karma, Jñāna, Bhakti and Dhyāna (meditation or Yoga ?) followed by them (24-26). He proclaims his identity with Hari by stating that devotees of Hari also propitiate him.

2. I cannot be realised by men, by means of the various kinds of penances or by means of charitable gifts or by means of sacrifices.* Without ardent and excellent devotion it is impossible to know me.

3. Indeed I abide within all living beings, all round. But the leading sages, people do not know me, the cosmic witness.

4. I am the *Dhātṛ* (creator) and *Vidhātṛ* (the dispenser of destiny), Kāla (Time), the Fire-god with faces all round. All this universe exists in me and I am the transcendental annihilator of all (v.l. and I, the supreme deity inherent in all).

5. The sages, the *Pitṛs* and the heaven-dwellers do not see me. Nor do the others of well-known prowess such as Brahmā, the Manus, and Śakra (the king of gods) know me.

6. The Vedas perpetually eulogise me as the only Supreme Lord (*Parameśvara*). The Brāhmaṇas worship me with various kinds of Yajñas and Vedic *Makhas* (sacrifices).

7. All the worlds, god Brahmā, the grand-sire of the world, do not perceive me. The Yogins (however) meditate on me, the luminous God, the lord of all creatures.

8. As everything gets submerged in me and as I am the *Ātman* of all, I assume the bodies of all the gods and become the enjoyer (recepient) of all *Havis* (sacrificial offerings §) and the dispenser of the fruits thereof.

9. Pious scholars, the expounders of the Vedas see me here itself. I am always present near them who always worship me devoutly.

10. Virtuous Brāhmaṇas, Kṣatriyas and Vaiśyas worship me. On them I bestow that supreme abode that is the bliss of Ātman itself.

11. Even the others (such as) Śūdras, other persons of low birth, who observe duties and are endowed with devotion are liberated even though they are united with Kāla (v. l. liberated in due course and become one with me).

---

*BG. 11.48.
G. 9.24.

12. My devotees do not perish. My devotees are devoid of sins. It has been promised by me at the very outset that my devotees do not perish.*

13. The fool who censures my devotee actually censures me the lord of Devas. He who worships him with devotion, perpetually worships me.

14. Whether it be a leaf, a flower or a fruit or mere water, if any devotee of mine regularly offers it by way of propitiating me, is beloved of me.**

15. At the beginning of universe, I created Brahmā, Parameṣṭhin and handed over to him the Vedas that came out of myself.

16. I alone am the unchanging (eternal) preceptor of all Yogins; I am the protector of the virtuous and the slayer of those who hate the Vedas.

17. I am the liberator of Yogins here from all worldly bondage. I am the cause as well of worldly existence though I am bereft of all worldly ties.

18. I alone am the annihilator, the creator and the protector of the universe. Māyā, the enchantress of the worlds, is my own potency.

19. What is called as *Vidyā* (knowledge) is my own transcendental power. Stationed in the hearts of Yogins, I annihilate that Māyā.

20. I am the originator and restrainer of all powers. I am the support of all potencies. I am the storehouse of nectar (or immortality).

21. Presided over by me, one of my powers which inheres in all and is identical with me assumes the form of god Brahmā and creates this world which is full of variety and diversity (O Brāhmaṇas who have resorted to the supreme Yoga, I am not the prime mover or propeller (of the universe).

22. Another immense power of mine becomes Nārāyaṇa, the infinite, the Lord of and the pervader of the world, and sustains (with stability) the universe.

---

*BG. 9.31.

**BG. 9.26.

23. The third great *Śakti* annihilates the entire universe. It is mine and is called *Tāmasi* as well as Kāla. It is in the form of Rudra.

24. Some perceive me through meditation, others through the path of spiritual knowledge; others through the path of devotion and still others through the path of action.

25. Among the devotees, he who always propitiates me through spiritual knowledge and not otherwise, is my most beloved devotee.

26. Others who are the devotees of Hari but who (thereby) propitiate me also, attain to me. They do not return again to *Saṁsāra*.

27. This entire universe constituted of Prakṛti and Puruṣa is pervaded by me.[1] The *Citta* or mind (v.l. *Viśva* or the universe) is stationed in me alone. The universe is impelled on (or directed) by me.

28. O Brāhmaṇas ! I am not the (direct) impeller but by adopting the highest Yoga, I urge on the entire universe. He who realizes this is immortal (i.e. is liberated from Saṁsāra).[2]

29. I (hereby) observe this entire universe as if existing of itself (naturally). It is Lord Kāla, the master of great Yogins who creates, maintains and destroys it.

30. It is I who am mentioned as Yogin and Māyin (Master of Māyā) in the scriptures by wise sages; (I am) He, the master of Yogins, Lord Īśvara of the great Yoga himself.

31. The greatness of parameṣṭhin is due to his being the most excellent of all *Sattvas* (living beings). Lord Brahmā is mentioned as identical with the great Brahman. He is free from blemish.

32. There is no doubt in this that he who knows me like this as the overlord of all the masters of Yoga is united with me through the sure path of Yoga (or by *nirvikalpa* meditation).

33. Such am I the impelling God. Resorting to the supreme bliss, I, the Yogin, dance on for ever. He who knows it is the knower of Yoga*.

---

1. BG. 9.4; 18.46.
2. Śvet. Up. 3.1; 3.13.

*v.l. I impel the entire universe. He who knows it, is the knower of the Vedas).

34. This secret-most knowledge is the decision enshrined in the Vedas. This should be imparted to one of pure mind, to one who is virtuous, and to one who maintains the sacrificial fires (as an *Āhitāgni*).

CHAPTER FIVE[1]

Śiva's Dance—Śiva eulogised by Sages

Vyāsa said :

1. After saying this much to the Yogins, Lord Parameśvara began to dance demonstrating his supreme divine nature.

2. They saw Īśāna, the greatest treasure-house of splendour, the sovereign lord, dancing along with Viṣṇu in the clear firmament.

3. In the firmament, they saw that lord of all living beings whom the Yogins, the knowers of the principles of Yoga who have their minds under control, realize.

4. The sovereign Lord of the universe who impels the world into action which is the creation of his Māyā, was verily seen dancing by Brāhmaṇas.

5. They saw the lord of *Bhūtas* (creatures or elements) dancing, the lord by remembering whose lotus-like feet a man can eschew the fear originating from ignorance.

6. Those who have conquered their sleep and controlled their breath, who are quiescent and endowed with devotion, see him as full of brilliance, that is how Śiva the Yogin was seen.

7. In the firmament, they saw the great Rudra, the liberator, the delighted lord, favourably disposed to his devotees and who instantaneously liberates the devotees from ignorance.

8. They saw the lord with a thousand (i.e. innumerable) heads, a thousand feet, a thousand shapes, and a thousand arms,

1. This chapter describes the Cosmic dance of Śiva but takes care to emphasize the identity of Śiva and Viṣṇu (V. 17).

with matted hair and with his coronet embellished with the crescent Moon.

9. The lord was wearing the tiger's hide; his mighty hand was holding the trident; he had a staff in his hand; he had the sun, the moon and the fire as three eyes.

10. By his brilliance he had enveloped the whole of the cosmic egg; he was standing with a refulgence equal to that of a crore of suns; he appeared terrible due to his fearful large teeth and was unthwartable.

11. They saw the Lord, the creator of the universe dancing and emitting flames of fire and thereby burning (as it were) the entire universe.

12. They visualised the great God, the veritable great Yoga incarnate, the divinity of celestial beings, the lord of all Paśus (individual souls), the supreme Ruler, the imperishable bliss and Light.

13. They saw the Pināka-bearing Lord of large eyes : the antidote for those who ail from worldly existence (saṁsāra), the lord who was the soul of Kāla, the lord of Devas; the slayer of Kāla.

14. They saw the consort of Umā, the great deity of large eyes and full of Yogic bliss; the lord who is the abode of knowledge and detachment; the eternal lord of the path of knowledge.

15-17a. The sages who were well-versed in Vedas, saw the lord of eternal prosperity and glory; the lord who is difficult to approach yet is the support of Dharma; who is bowed to by Upendra (Viṣṇu) and Mahendra who is honoured by groups of great sages; who abides in the hearts of Yogins who become united with Īśvara in a trice; and was enveloped by Yogic Māyā; who was the source of the origin of the universe; who was identical with Nārāyaṇa and free from all ailments.

17b-d. Having seen that Lordly form in which Rudra was identical with Nārāyaṇa (or which showed the identity of gods Śiva and Viṣṇu), the sages who were the propounders of the Vedas felt that they had achieved their ultimate goal in life.

18-20. Sanatkumāra, Sanaka, Bhṛgu, Sanātana, Sanandana, Aṅgiras, Vāmadeva, Śukra, Atri the great sage, Kapila and Marīci saw Rudra, the lord of the universe with his left side being occupied by Padmanābha (Viṣṇu). They meditated on him who was enshrined in their hearts. With palms joined in reverence, they bent down their heads again and again. Having uttered the sacred syllable OM, they saw the lord abiding in the cavity of the heart. Their minds were filled with bliss. They eulogised the lord in the words of Vedic Sūktas.

The Sages extolled : Eulogy of Śiva

21. All of us bow down to you, the only supreme Ruler, the ancient Puruṣa, the lord of the Prāṇas (vital breaths), RUDRA of infinite Yogic Power. You are stationed in the cavity of the heart, you are Pracetas (of lofty mind), holy and identical with Brahman.

22. After meditating within their self in their (physical) bodies on the absolutely immovable or unagitated *Kavi* (the seer or the wise) who is supremely superior to the greatest, the quiescent sages of perfect self-control perceive you, the pure, gold-complexioned God originating from the Brahman (or the creator of God Brahmā).

23. The mother of the universe (*Prakṛti*) is born of you; though minute like the atom, you experience (perceive) everything. You are minuter than the minute atom and greater than the greatest being.* Sages say that you alone are all.

24. Hiraṇya-garbha, the inner soul of the universe, the ancient Puruṣa was born of you; even as he was being born, he was immediately enjoined by you to create everything in accordance with the injunctions.

25. The Vedas are born of you; and ultimately they find stability in you alone. We see that you are the cause of the universe. We see that you who abide in our own hearts, are dancing.

26. This wheel of Brahman (the creation etc. of Brahmāṇḍa) is made to revolve by you alone. You are the master of Māyā and the only lord of the worlds. We seek refuge in you and bow into you; the very soul of Yoga, who dance the divine dance.

---

*Kaṭha Up. 2.20; Śvetā. Up. 3.20

27. We perceive you who dance in the middle of the highest firmament and we remember your grandeur. Experiencing constantly the supreme bliss of the Brahman, you who abide in the souls of all, permeate the universe on all sides.

28. The syllable OM, the seed of liberation, is your (expressive) symbol. Imperishable though you are, you lie concealed in the primordial Nature (Prakṛti). Such as you are, saints here aver that you, the self-luminous one of such prowess are the Reality.

29. The Vedas perpetually eulogise you. The sages whose blemishes have been wiped off, bow unto you. Ascetics engrossed in Brahman, with quiescent souls and truthful as well enter unto you, the excellent one.

30. You are the destroyer of the earth; you are without beginning. You have the universal form. You are Brahmā the Parameṣṭhin and Viṣṇu the most excellent. Those who are not unsteady and those who are ever liberated, experience the bliss of their Ātman and enter into you, the self-luminous one.

31. Though one as Rudra you are, you create the universe; you protect the entire universe; with all its forms; all these (visible worlds) attain to you as their ultimate abode. We seek refuge in you and make obeisance unto you.

32. The Veda which has many branches and is infinite is one. It reveals you alone who are of a single form. Those Brāhmaṇas who seek refuge in you who are worthy of being respected, cross the Māyā in this very world.

33. They call you the only poet (kavi), the Supreme Rudra, eulogising the Veda, Hari, fire and Īśa; they call you the eternal Rudra, the wind-god, the consciousness, the creator, the sun-god of many forms.

34. You are the supreme imperishable one that should be realised, You are the ultimate receptable of this universe. You are the unchanging one, protecting the eternal Law (dharma). You are the most excellent Puruṣa, the eternal one.

35. You alone are Viṣṇu; you are the four-faced deity (Brahmā); you alone are Rudra, the lord Īśa as well; you are verily the lord of the universe; you are Prakṛti, the basis of all. You are the lord of all, the supreme Īśvara.

36. The sages say that you are the ancient Puruṣa, one without a second, of the brillance of the sun beyond the darkness (of ignorance). They call you, the consciousness itself the unmanifest, of infinite forms, the void, the firmament, the Brahman, the Prakṛti and the Guṇas (v. l. above i. e. transcendental to the Guṇas).

37. This form of yours is something that cannot be conceived of; within it all these (visible worlds) appear; it is unchanging and blemishless, but is one single form; it is beyond the ken of thought and indescribable; all that appears within it is you alone, (or : your form is so wonderfully indescribable that the Reality shines in it).

38. Seeking refuge in you, all of us make obeisance to you, the gracious lord of Yogas, the greatest goal of infinite power, the ancient one with the body of Brahman, O Lord of Bhūtas, O Maheśa, be gracious unto us

39. By remembering your lotus-like feet, the seed (cause) of the entire worldly existence becomes dissolved. After controlling the body and concentrating the mind, we propitiate you, the only Supreme Lord.

40. Obeisance to Bhava, the source of origin of the worlds; to Kāla, to Śarva, to you the annihilator; obeisance be to Rudra with matted hair. Obeisance to you. O Lord, who are the fire; obeisance to Śiva."

41. Thereafter, the bull-vehicled Lord with matted hair delightedly withdrew his great cosmic form. Bhava (Śiva) manifested his normal (usual) form.

42. On seeing Bhava, the lord of everything past and future, remaining as before and lord Nārāyaṇa (also in that state), the sages were struck with wonder and they spoke these words.

43. "O eternal lord, O lord of the past and future, O deity marked by the emblem of the bull ! On seeing your grand form we are delighted. (v. l. attained quiescence).

44. Thanks to your grace, there is born our unswerving devotion to you, the great Supreme lord, the blemishless one.

45. O Śaṅkara, now we wish to hear about your greatness as well as the eternal reality about Parameṣṭhin".

46. On hearing their words the lord, the bestower of Yogic siddhi on the Yogins, glanced at Mādhava and said in a majestic voice.

CHAPTER SIX[1]

The Glory of Śiva

Īśvara Said :

1. O Ye sages, listen all of you, I shall recount the greatness of the supreme Lord (Parameṣṭhin) precisely as it is known by those who know the Vedas.

2. I am the sole creator of the entire universe, the sole protector of all peoples and the sole annihilator of all worlds. I am the eternal universal Ātman.

3. I, Maheśvara, am the *Antaryāmin* (the Immanent soul) of all subjects. Everything is stationed within me, but I am not everywhere in the universe.

4. A wonderful form of mine which has been seen by you is my similitude. O. Brāhmaṇas, verily my Māyā has been demonstrated by me.

5. Stationed within all beings, I propel the entire universe. This is my *Kriyāśakti* (the power of action).

6. This universe stirs and moves due to me. That follows my will. I am Kāla and I urge the entire universe consisting of the elements.*

7. O leading sages, with one single part of mine, I create the entire universe; by another form I annihilate, neverthless, my sameness (stability) is unchanged.

8. I am devoid of beginning, middle and the end; I am the activisor of the principle of Māyā; at the beginning of creation, I make both *Pradhāna* and *Puruṣa* co-agitate.[2]

---

1. Īśvara explains his immanence and describes the working of his Kriyā Śakti (Power of action).

*According to Pāśupatas, Kāla signifies the elements of the gross or material world (vide *Sarva-darśana-Saṅgraha*)

2. KP. subscribes to theistic Sāṅkhya.

9. When the pair of them become mutually united, the universe is born in the order of *Mahat* etc. My splendour and glory become menifested therein.

10. Hiraṇya-garbha, the Sun-god, who is the witness unto all worlds and who makes the wheel of Time function, is also born of my body.

11. O Brāhmaṇas, in the beginning of the Kalpa, I who am perfectly self-possessed, gave unto him the four Vedas, my own divine glory and the eternal path of knowledge.

12. It is at my behest that god Brahmā who has been created out of me permanently understood (v.l. always carries) my sovereign divine glory.

13. That self-born omniscient god, the creator of all the worlds, becomes a four-faced deity and brings forth the creation (of the universe) as per my command.[1]

14. He who is called Nārāyaṇa, the infinite one, the immutable source of all worlds and who is only another form of mine, performs the duty of protection.

15. Lord Rudra, of the nature of Kāla (Death), who is the annihilator of all living beings (is also) a manifestation of mine. At my behest, he will annihilate the universe for ever.[2]

16. It is due to his being charged with my divine energy that the Fire (god) carries (sacrificial) oblations to gods and food (*Kavya*) etc. to its consumers (viz. Pitṛs) and carries out the function of cooking etc.

17. At the behest of *Īśvara* the firegod Vaiśvānara (the fire of digestion) digests the food eaten by day or by night.

18. The leading god Varuṇa, who is the source of origin of all waters shall enliven everyone at the bidding of Īśvara.

19. Lord Prabhañjana (Wind god) who stays within and without the bodies of living beings, sustains the physical bodies of all living beings at my command.

---

1. VV. 13-15 describe how creation, maintenance and destruction of the universe is due to Śiva.

2. In the remaining portion of the Chapter, Īśvara tells that all deities function in their respective spheres due to his energy and at his behest. Nay everything that happens is at his command.

20. Soma (the Moon god) who is the enlivener of men and the storehouse of nectar for Devas, is activated through my bidding.

21. The sun who illuminates the entire universe everywhere through his own refulgence, brings about the rainfall through his own rays (at the bidding) of the self-born deity.

22. God Śakra, the lord of all immortal beings, who rules over the entire universe and who is the bestower of fruits on those who perform sacrifices, functions at my bidding.

23. Yama, the son of Vivasvān, the god who chastises the wicked ones, abides regularly at the bidding of the Lord of Devas.

24. Even Kubera, who is the presiding deity of all riches and who is the distributor of all wealth, behaves so at the behest of Īśvara.

25. God Nirṛti who is the lord of all Rākṣasas and who is the bestower of benefits on those who are Tāmasaic by nature, always behaves so at my command.

26. Īśāna who is the lord of the groups of Vetālas (ghosts) and Bhūtas (goblins) and who is the bestower of the fruits of enjoyment of pleasures on his devotees, also abides at my bidding.

27. Vāmadeva who is the disciple of Aṅgiras, who is the leader of groups of Rudra and who is the protector of Yogins does so far ever through my behest.

28. Vināyaka who is worthy of the worship of all the worlds and who is the leader of obstacles (i.e. one who dispels them) is engaged in piety evidently at my instance.

29. The self-born god Skanda who is the most excellent among the knowers of the Brahman, and who is the lord of Devasenā (Goddess of that name or the army of Devas) behaves so always, on being urged by my command.

30. Marīci and other great sages who are progenitors of the world create different kinds of worlds, only through the bidding of the supreme Deity.

31. Śrī the Goddess of Wealth who is the spouse of Nārāyaṇa and who bestows large fortune on all living beings, behaves so through my blessings.

32. Goddess Sarasvatī who bestows ample fluency, functions, so, on being urged by the bidding of Īśvara.

33. Sāvitrī,[1] who, on being remembered will redeem all men from the terrible hell, is one who carries out my behests.

34. The supreme goddess Pārvatī who, on being specially meditated upon, is the bestower of the spiritual love (Brahmavidyā) is also one who follows my utterances.

35. Ananta, the serpent Śeṣa who has infinite greatness, and is the lord of all immortal beings and who holds the worlds on his hoods does so at the bidding of the lord.

36. The Fire-god Saṁvartaka (destroyer of the universe at the time of dissolution of the worlds) who is stationed in the form of submarine fire eternally drinks up the entire ocean at the order of Īśvara.

37. The fourteen Manus whose prowess is well-known, protect all subjects at his bidding.

38. Ādityas (sons of Aditi or the sun-god), Vasus, Rudras, Maruts and two Aśvinī-Kumāras and all other divinities are created (v.l. are appointed) at my command.

39. Gandharvas, Garuḍa and others, Siddhas, Sādhyas Cāraṇas, Yakṣas, Rākṣasas and Piśācas are created by and established there as per order of the self-born deity.

40. The (divisions of Time such as) Kalās, Kāṣṭhās, Nimeṣas, Muhūrtas, days, nights, seasons, fortnights and months abide by the commandment of Prajāpati.

41. The Yugas and the Manvantaras remain within my control. So also the Paras, Parārdhas and other varieties of time-units.

42. The four categories of living beings, both mobile and immobile, do abide by the bidding of the lord, the supreme Ātman.

43. All the nether worlds, the upper worlds and the Brahmāṇḍas do follow the injunctions of the self-born deity.

44. The innumerable universes of the past which were all over endowed with floods (multitudes) of objects functioned at my command.

---

*Known popularly as Gāyatrī Mantra (RV. III. 62.10).

45. The future Brahmāṇḍas, along with the Ātmans present in them, will carry out the injunctions of the greatest Ātman.

46. The Earth, the Waters, the Fire, the Wind, the Ether, the mind, the intellect, the Ahaṅkāra and the primordial Prakṛti stay within my injunction.*

47. Māyā which is the source of origin of the entire universe and which fascinates all embodied beings, transforms itself for ever at the bidding of Īśvara.

48. Puruṣa who is the lord of all embodied beings, and who is cited as the supreme Ātman, eternally exists and functions as per instruction of Īśvara.

49. The intellect too, through which one observes that region, (i.e. the supreme self), after eschewing all the confused delusions, invariably abides by the will of the great god (Maheśa).

50. What need there is of prolixity, the entire universe is constituted of my potency (*Śakti*). The whole of the universe is urged on by me and in me does it dissolve in the end.

51. I am the lord Īśa, the eternal entity that is self-luminous. I am the great Ātman, the supreme Brahman. There is nothing other than I.

52. Thus, this greatest knowledge has been communicated to you by me. After knowing this, a creature is liberated from the bondage of births and worldly existence.

*BG. VII. 4.

CHAPTER SEVEN[1]

The Vibhūti-Yoga of Śiva : Fundamentals of Pāśupatism

Īśvara Said :

1. Ye Sages, listen all of you to the prowess of Parameṣṭhin on realising which man becomes liberated and does not fall into the worldly existence again.

2. That is my greatest abode, the Brahman, which is greater than the greatest, eternal, steady and immutable, of perpetual bliss, devoid of doubts and alternatives.

3. Among the knower of Brahman, I am god Brahmā the self-born deity with face all round. Among the wielders of Māyā, I am the ancient, imperishable god Hari.

4. Among Yogins, I am Śambhu, among ladies I am goddess (Pārvatī), the daughter of the lord of mountains. I am Viṣṇu among sun-gods and am the fire-god among Vasus.

5. Among Rudras, I am Śaṅkara; among those who fly (i.e. birds), I am Garuḍa; among the leading elephants, I am Airāvata and among those who bear weapons (warriors), I am Rāma.

6. Among the sages, I am Vasiṣṭha; among Devas, I am Śatakratu (one who has performed a hundred sacrifices i.e. Devendra); among craftsmen I am Viśvakarman and among the enemies of Devas, I am Prahlāda.

7. Among ascetics I am Vyāsa; among the Gaṇas (attendants of Śiva) I am Vināyaka; among heroes, I am Vīra-Bhadra; and among the Siddhas, I am ascetic Kapila.

8. Among the mountains, I am Meru; among constellations, I am the Moon; among the weapons of striking potentiality I am the thunderbolt; and among holy rites, I am truthfulness.

---

1. This chapter corresponds to Ch. X of the BG. The list of the best person, deity or thing is claimed to be Himself by Śiva here, as was done by Lord Kṛṣṇa in BG. X.

This chapter includes also the fundamentals of Pāśupatism. The explanations of the technical terms like Paśu, Pāśa, Kleśa are given in the latter part of the chapter.

As most of the Vibhūtis are practically borrowed from the BG., it is not necessary to give reference to their parallels in the BG.

9. Among serpents, I am Ananta (Śeṣa); among generals of armies, I am lord Pāvaki (son of the firegod i.e. Skanda); among the stages of life, I am the householder's stage and among Īśvaras (Rulers) I am Maheśvara.

10. Among Kalpas, I am Mahākalpa (the greatest Kalpa); among the Yugas, I am Kṛtayuga; among the Yakṣas, I am Kubera and among grasses, I am Vīrudha (plant which grows after being cut) (v.l. am Vīruka among Gaṇeśas)

11. Among the Prajāpatis (progenitors of the world), I am Dakṣa; among the Rākṣasas I am Nirṛti; among powerful persons, I am Vāyu, and among the continents, I am Puṣkara.[1]

12. Among the leaders of beasts, I am the lion; among mechanical devices (weapons), I am the bow; among the Vedas, I am Sāmaveda and among Yajur Mantras I am Śatarudrīya (Vaj. Saṃ. XVI. 1-66).

13. Among the Japyas (Mantras for the purpose of Japa), I am Sāvitrī, (RV. III. 62. 10); among mystic secret Mantras, I am Praṇava (*Om*), among the hymns, I am the Puruṣasūkta (RV. X. 90) and among the Sāman Mantras I am Jyeṣṭha Sāman.

14. Among the scholars of Vedic topics, I am Svāyambhuva Manu; among territories, I am Brahmāvarta[2] and among holy centres, I am Avimuktaka (Vārāṇasī).

15. Among Vidyās (lores), I am the Ātmavidyā (spiritual science, leading to realization of Ātman). Among types of knowledge, I am the greatest knowledge pertaining to Īśvara; among the elements, I am the Ether, and among the entities (or realities) I am Mṛtyu (Death).

16. Among the nooses and fetters, I am Māyā, and among the Calculators, I am Kāla (Time), among goals I am

1. M. Ali identifies Puṣkara dvīpa with the region now called Japan, Manchuria and South-eastern Siberia (*The Geography of the Purāṇas*, p. 44), while De (p. 163) locates it in Central Asia commencing from the north of the Oxus including Western Tartary. He believes Puṣkara is derived from Bhushkara (Bokhara).

2. Brahmāvarta—The country between the Sarasvatī and Dṛṣadvatī later on known as Kurukṣetra (DC. p. 40). KP. does not imply Brahmāvarta Tīrtha near Bithur Cawnpur Dist. (U.P.)

liberation (from saṁsāra) and among the greatest ones, I am Parameśvara (the supreme) God.

17. Whatever else be in the world that stands most prominent by means of Sattvaguṇa, brilliance of power, you can vouchsafe for it that it is a manifestation of brilliance.*

18. All the Ātmans existing in the world are said to be *Paśus*. I am remembered as their lord, Paśupati by the wise sages.[1]

19. In my sportive activity, I bind all these Paśus by means of the noose of the Māyā. Expounders of the Vedas say that I am the liberator of the Paśus (Individual souls).

20. Excepting me, the great Ātman, the unchanging overlord of the Bhūtas, there is no other liberator of those who are bound with the noose of the Māyā.

21. The twenty-four principles, the Māyā, the Karman and the three Guṇas—these are the nooses (in the hands) of Paśupati; and distresses are the bondages of individual souls (Paśus).

22. The mind, the intellect, the ego, the firmament, the wind, the fire, the water, and the Earth—these eight are Prakṛtis (causes) and the other things are Vikāras (effects).

23-24. The ears, the sense of touch, the eyes, the tongue and the fifth one the nose (these are the sense-organs of knowledge), the anus, the genitals, the hands, the feet and the organ of speech (these are the organs of activity), sound, touch, colour, taste and smell (these are the five objects of pleasure)—these fifteen together with the eight objects mentioned before (Verse 22) constitute the twenty-three Prākṛtas or Products of Prakṛti.

25. The twenty-fourth principle is the *Avyakta* (unmanifest), Pradhāna characterised by its Guṇas. It has neither beginning nor middle nor destruction. It is the supreme cause of the universe.

---

*BG. x. 41.

1. From v. 18 to the end is the discussion on Pāśupatism. Though the sect poses to be independent, the influence of the Sāṅkhyas is obvious (vide vv. 18-27).

26. Sattva, Rajas and Tamas—these are called the three Guṇas. The state of equilibrium of these, they know to be the *Avyakta Prakṛti* (the unmanifest *Prakṛti*).

27. Sattva is knowledge; the Rajaś and the Tamas are ignorance (*Ajñāna*) (v.l. Rajas is) a mixture of knowledge and ignorance. The wise sages know that the inequality of the Guṇas is due to the disequilibrium in intellect.

28. What are called Dharma and Adharma (Virtue and Evil) are the binding nooses called Karmans. But those Karmans dedicated unto me are conducive to liberation and not to bondage.

29. *Avidyā* (Ignorance); *Asmitā* (Egotism), *Rāga* (Passion) *Dveṣa* (hatred) and *Abhiniveśa* (attachment) are called the *Kleśa* (miseries).[1] They are themselves the bonds that fetter the Ātman.

30. Māyā alone is called the cause of these Pāśas. It is the original unmanifest Prakṛti. That Śakti (divine power) stays in me.

31. He alone is the primordial nature or Pradhāna as well as Puruṣa and the product such as Mahat etc. He is the eternal God of gods.

32. He alone is the bondage and the maker of bondage; He alone is the Pāśa and the sustainer of the Paśus. He knows everything but no one knows him. They call him the Primordial and ancient Puruṣa.

CHAPTER EIGHT

The Means of Crossing the Ocean of Worldly Existence.

Īśvara said :

1. O leading Brāhmaṇas I shall tell you another esoteric knowledge whereby the creature (the Jīva) can cross the terrible ocean of worldly existence.

1. The same as in the Pātañjala Yoga Sūtra II. 3. They are regarded as 'bonds' or 'fetters' (Pāśa) in Pāśupatism.

2. This Brahmā is quiescent thanks to penance(v. 1 I am the same as the Brahman, eternal etc.). He is eternal unchanging and blemishless. He is one without a second and is the absolute supreme Lord.

3. My womb is the great Brahman (Prakṛti). I sow my seed therein and that is named Mūlamāyā (Original Māyā). This universe is born thereof.

4. All these were born viz. Pradhāna, Puruṣa, Ātman, Mahat, Bhūtādi (ahaṁkāra) the Tanmātras (subtle elements), the mind, the (gross) elements and the sense organs—all these were born from it viz. (Mulamāyā).

5. Thence a golden Egg having the luster of a crore of suns was born; the great Brahmā was born of it. He was invigorated through my Śakti.

6. Innumerable other Jīvas are all identical with him. Deluded by my Māyā they do not perceive me their father.

7. The sages know that (Māyā) is the supreme source (Mother) and I alone am the father of the various species in which all those forms (creatures) are born in this world.

8. He who thus knows me as the sower of the seed, the lordly father, is a hero in all the worlds and he does not get deluded.

9. I am the lord of all lores, the supreme controller of all creatures, the veritable Praṇava (the sacred syllable OM) incarnate, the master endowed with six divine powers, god Brahmā, the lord protector of all beings.

10. He who perceives Parameśvara present equally in all living beings, but as imperishable when they perish, perceives factually.[1]

11. Inasmuch as he perceives the lord equally present everywhere, does not injure his real self (Ātman by his (lower) self, he therefore attains the greatest goal.[2]

12. He who, having realized the seven subtle principles[3] and the great God with his six limbs[4] (potencies), knows the role

1. The same as BG., XIII. 27.
2. BG. XIII. 28.
3. vide v. 13 below.
4. vide v. 14 below.

assigned to Pradhāna (understands the distinction between the material principles and the self) reaches the highest Brahman.

13. Omniscience, joy of satiety, eternal knowledge, independence, ever-inexhaustible power and infinite strength—these are the six 'limbs' of the great God for realization.

14. They (the knowers) call the following as seven subtle principles viz. the five subtle elements, mind and the soul. That which is the cause (of this creation) is the Primordial Matter (Prakṛti). It is also called Pradhāna, the bondage by moral discipline (a better v.l. *viniyoga* - application).

15. There is a Śakti (power) latent in form in the Prakṛti. It is mentioned in the Vedas as the cause (of the world) and the source of origin of Brahmā. In front of her is her Puruṣa, Parameṣṭhi, the great God, the very embodiment of the Reality.

16. He alone is Brahmā, the great Yogin, the supreme Ātman, the huge one pervading the sky, the ancient one comprehensible only through the Vedas. He alone is the only Rudra, the cause of annihilation, the unmanifest, the sole seed, the universe itself.

17. Some say he is one : Others say that he is many. Some say that you are the self. Some say that he is another. The great God (Mahādeva) is proclaimed as minuter than an atom and greater than the greatest and omniformed (with the universe as his form).

18. The intelligent person who realizes that supreme Master, immanent in the cavity of the heart, that ancient Puruṣa, whose form is the manifested universe and is the highest goal of the wise and the intelligent, transcends the sphere of *Buddhi* (intelligence).

CHAPTER NINE

The unsullied (Niṣkala) form of Śiva

The Sages said :

1. O Mahādeva, the Supreme God is unsullied, pure, eternal and devoid of activities. Hence, explain to us how you become identical with universe in form.

Īśvara replied :

2. O Brāhmaṇas, I am not the Universe (in reality). Nor does the universe exist without me. In this respect Māyā is the cause and she is supported by me in my Ātman.

3. Māyā is a Śakti (a potency) which has neither beginning nor destruction. It is supported in the *Avyakta* (the unmanifest). This world is caused by it and is indeed born of Avyakta.

4. They (the sages) say that the unmanifest which is bliss luminous and imperishable is the cause. I am the Supreme Brahman and nothing else exists without me.

5. In my unity and diversity (or apparent identity and separateness from the universe) the expounders of the Vedas have decisively concluded my being universe-formed.

6. I am that greatest Brahman, the eternal supreme Ātman. O Brāhmaṇas. As I am said to be the non-cause, no fault can be attributed to Ātman.

7. The divine powers are infinite, unmanifest, permanent and established by Māyā. The absolute Avyakta (unmanifest) which is abiding in the heavenly region (beyond the reach of this world) shines eternally.

8. The unmanifest eternal Brahman which is without any beginning or end and which is permanent is united with Māyā and thereby is called diverse and divided though it is an undivided whole.

9. Just as the manifestation of the Puruṣa's one power is not concealed or obscured by another, he functions through the power of knowledge without beginning, middle and the end.

10. That is the supreme unmanifest, embellished with a halo of lustre. That is the imperishable light. That is the supreme abode of Viṣṇu.

11. Therein the entire universe is woven as if in the warp and woof of cloth. That alone is the entire universe. Having realised this, one is liberated.

12. Brahman is that entity from which words along with mind recede due to their inability to reach it. He who has realized the joy of the Brahman entertains no fear from anywhere at any time.[1]

13. I know this supreme Puruṣa with the refulgence of the sun in front of me (v.l. beyond the darkness of ignorance). Having realized him as such, the knower is liberated (from Saṁsāra). Becoming identical with the Brahman, he enjoys perpetual bliss.[2]

14. Realizing that is his self from which there is nothing that is greater, and that is the supreme light of the luminaries stationed in the heaven, the knower becomes identical with the Brahman and attains perpetual bliss.

15. Knowers of the Brahman (or Brāhmaṇas) who are established in the Brahman, proclaim that I am however impenetrable, subtle-bodied, joy of the Brahman and the immortal abode of the universe, and after attaining whom one never reverts to Saṁsāra.

16. The lustre that appears to shine in heaven is the principle of the highest firmament of golden colour. The sages visualize it in their own supreme knowledge as the resplendent, pure (spotless) abode of heaven.

17. Thereafter, the bold (self-possessed) men observe it, after experiencing the (cosmic) Ātman directly in their individual Ātman. Parameṣṭhin, the lord himself, is the greatest one. The Lord has the bliss of Brahman.

18. That one Lord is lying hidden in all living beings. He is omnipresent, the immanent soul of all living beings. The self-possessed men who see him as one (without a second) enjoy permanent bliss and not the others.

19. He has heads and necks on all sides. He is the ultimate goal of all. He abides in the cavity of the heart of all

---

1. Taittirīya Up. II. 9.
2. Śvetāśvatara Up. III. 8 also, III. 21.

living beings. That lord is omnipresent. There is nothing other than he.

20. O leading sages, thus the knowledge pertaining to Īśvara has been related to you. It should be particularly guarded, as it is very difficult even for Yogis to attain.

CHAPTER TEN

The form of the Supreme Brahman Śiva—the Parabrahman

Īśvara said :

1. It has been concluded definitely that Brahman is *Liṅgas* (Symbols) ; it is one (without a second) and unmanifest is its characteristic feature. It is self-luminous, supreme, premier. It is established in the sky (transcending the phenomenal world).

2. The unmanifest which is the cause (of the phenomenal world) is the imperishable supreme region. Learned men perceive it as devoid of Guṇas and perfect knowledge.

3. The Vedas declare that to be the *Liṅga* viz. the supreme Brahman which is perceived by the sages whose concept of egotism (and other doubts) is resolved (destroyed) and who are perpetually merged in its meditation.

4. O leading sages, it is not possible to see me otherwise. There is no knowledge whereby that great Ātman is realized.

5. Only sages can know this supreme abode (v.l. knowledge). Since the universe is the product of Māyā, knowledge about it is enveloped by the darkness of ignorance.[1]

---

1. v.l. *ajñānam itaraj jñānam* for *ajñāna-timiraṁ jñānaṁ* is better. Combined with the previous v.l. *jñānam* for *sthānam* in the Veṅk. Text, the verse would mean : "This is the supreme knowledge which only sages knew. The other knowledge (about the phenomenal world etc.) is really ignorance, as this world is composed of illusion (Māyā).

6. The knowledge that is immaculate, pure, free from doubts, and unsullied is my soul. The sages declare that (supreme knowledge) to be this (my soul).

7. Even those who see that greatest region as multifarious understand the unity of the unchanging principle after resorting to the greatest adherence to principles.

8. Those devotees who perceive me, the greatest principle, the Īśvara either as one or many, should be known as identical with that (Principle).

9. They directly perceive their own soul (Ātman), the supreme lord full of perpetual bliss, above doubt, Reality incarnate. This is the exact position (truth).

10. They who are established in their own self which is beyond Avyakta, are quiescent, resort to enjoy the supreme bliss which permeates everything and is identical with the universe.

11. This is the greatest liberation. This is my excellent *Sāyujya* (Identity with me). Poets know this as Nirvāṇa, identity with Brahman and Kaivalya (absolute oneness).[1]

12. Hence, the only entity devoid of beginning, middle and end and the supremely auspicious one, is Lord Mahādeva. After realising him, one is liberated.

13. The sun does not shine there, nor does the moon, nor the group of stars nor the lightning. Illuminated by it the entire universe shines. It shines with great refulgence and is devoid of impurities.*

14. That which is called 'The All' (or universe) which is indivisible, immutable, pure, great, shines (brilliantly). The immovable principle which the knowers of the Brahman (or the Vedas) permanently visualize within themselves is the Īśa (the Lord).

15. All the Vedas say that the Puruṣa is pure, nectarean, perpetual bliss and embodiment of truth. Those who have come to a definite conclusion through the study of the Vedas

---

1. This is a synthesis of Sāṅkhya, Bauddha and Vedantic concept of Liberation.

*Kaṭha Up. iv. 15; Śvetāśvatara Up. vi. 14.

meditate on the lord by means of the Praṇava, as their vital breath.

16. Neither the Earth, nor the waters, nor the mind, nor the fire, nor the vital breath, nor the wind, nor the sky, nor the intellect, nor the consciousness, nor does anything else shine in the firmament. Only the Lord Śiva alone shines in the great sky.

17. Thus has been communicated to you this topmost supreme secret, the knowledge that is sung in all the Vedas. The Yogī alone knows this. One should incessantly practise Yoga in a secluded place.

CHAPTER ELEVEN[1]

The Path of liberation of the individual soul from bondage.

Īśvara said :

1. Henceforth, I shall explain a Yoga that is very difficult of access and whereby the devotees visualize the Ātman, the Īśvara (brilliant) like the sun.

2. The fire of Yoga quickly burns the entire cage of sins. Pure and perspicuous knowledge which directly accords the attainment of Liberation (from Saṁsāra) arises thereby.

3. Knowledge originates through Yoga; Yoga functions through knowledge. The great God (Maheśvara) is delighted with one devoted to the practice of Yoga and knowledge.

4. Those who practise the great Yoga once, twice or thrice everyday or continuously should be known as Maheśvaras.

5. Yoga should be known as one of two kinds. The first one is called as Abhāva Yoga. The other one is known as the Mahāyoga (the great Yoga). It is the most excellent among all Yogas.

6. The Yoga wherein one's own soul is meditated upon

1. This chapter deals with Pāśupata Yoga (for details *vide* Introduction: Section on Pāśupatism).

as void and devoid of all false appearances is proclaimed as Abhāva Yoga whereby one realizes thoroughly one's own self.

7. The Yoga wherein one sees one's own self as immaculate, eternal bliss and identical with me is called by me as the highest Yoga.

8. Those other paths of Yogas practised by other Yogins and those Yogas which are heard (described) in other extensive works (on Yoga) do not deserve to be even one-sixteenth part of the Brahma-Yoga (Yoga leading to the realization of the Brahman).

9. The Yoga in which the liberated souls directly perceive the universe as one with Īśvara, that Yoga is considered to be the greatest of all Yogas.

10. Thousands and numerous Yogins of controlled minds who consider themselves as excluded or different from Īśvara do not perceive me as one without a second.

11. O excellent sages, (the following are the essential adjuncts of Yoga) viz. Prāṇāyāma, Dhyāna (meditation), Pratyāhāra (withdrawal of the sense-organs), Dhāraṇā (retention), Samādhi (trance), Yama (control), Niyama (Restraint and observance), Āsana (posture).

12. The adjuncts of the same Yoga have been narrated to you. Yoga is the concentration of the mind in me alone along with control of the intermediary urges.

13. *Ahiṁsā* (non-violence), *Satya* (truth), *Asteya* (non-stealth), *Brahmacarya* (celibacy) and *aparigraha* (non-possession or non-acceptance of monetary gifts). These are the Yamas (controls). They have been succinctly mentioned. They bestow purity of mind upon men.

14. It has been declared by the great sages that Ahiṁsā (non-violence) is non-causation of distress to any living being at any time physically, mentally and verbally.

15. There is no greater Virtue than Ahiṁsā; there is nothing more conducive to happiness than Ahiṁsā. The Hiṁsā (violence) that is committed according to the injunctions (of the Vedas) is indeed glorified as Ahiṁsā.[1]

---

1. This exception in the case of animal sacrifices is stoutly defended by Mīmāṁsakas.

16. The act of stating precisely in conformity to what is factual is called *Satya* (truthfulness) by the twice-born ones. One obtains everything through *Satya.* Everything is founded on *Satya.*

17. Removal of another man's wealth or property either by stealth or through force is called *Steya,* (stealth). Refraining from doing it is *Asteya.* It is a means of Virtue of merit.

18. Eschewing copulation either physically, mentally and orally in all stages, at times, and in all places is called *Brahmacarya* (celibacy).

19. Nontaking of monetary gifts voluntarily even during adversity is called Aparigraha. One should maintain it strenuously.

20. *Tapas* (penance), *Svādhyāya* (self-study of Vedas), *Santoṣa* (contentment), *Śauca* (purity), *Īśvara-Pūjana* (worship of God) these are mentioned as *Niyamas* (observances) succinctly. They are the bestowers of Yogic perfection (*Siddhis*).

21. Ascetics call it the excellent penance if the body is dessicated by means of fasts and observances of religious vows like Parāka, Kṛcchra, Cāndrāyaṇa etc.

22. Learned men say that this is Svādhyāya if one performs the Japa of the Vedantic passages, *Śatarudrīya* (Vaj. Saṁhitā XVI. 1-66), *Praṇava* (Om) etc. It brings about the achievement of Sattva Guṇa in men.

23. There are three types of *Svādhyāyas* viz. *Vācika* (verbal), *Upāṁśu* (inaudible muttering) and *Mānasa* (mental), those who know the meanings of the Vedas say that the latter ones are better than the earlier ones.

24. The Svādhyāya (recitation or study of the Vedas) the words of which are clearly audible (understandable) to other listeners is called *Vācika* (vocal).

Now the characteristic of *Upāṁśu* (inaudible) Svādhyāya is as follows :

25. That which involves only the throbbing of lips but the words of which are inaudible to others is designated as *Upāṁśu* (inaudible Svādhyāya). It is better (more efficacious) than vocal Japa.

26. The contemplation of all the words (of the text of (prayer) in the proper sequence of words and syllables

without throbbing of the lips, is called *Mānasa Japa* (mental Japa).

27. Sages say that the praise-worthy attitude of the man who regards whatever wealth is acquired through luck (without striving for it)as sufficient(to him), is called contentment and it is characterised by a feeling of happiness.

28. O excellent Brāhmaṇas, *Śauca* (cleanliness) is said to be twofold—the external and the internal. The external cleanliness is by means of clay and water, while the internal one consists of the purity of the mind.

29. The extremely steady devotion to Śiva through the Verbal, mental and physical activities such as singing eulogy, recollection (of His Name etc.) and worship (of Śiva) is called *Īśa Pūjana* (Worship of God).

30. The *Yamas* and the *Niyamas* have been expounded. Now understand the *Prāṇāyāma*. Prāṇa is the air circulating within one's own body. Its restraint is called Āyāma.

31. Prāṇāyāma is three-fold, the *Uttama* (excellent), *Madhyama* (the middling) and the *Adhama* (lowly). Another twofold classification of Prāṇāyāma is *Sagarbha* and *Agarbha* (i.e. Prāṇāyāma with the repetition of Om or any other *Mantra bīja* is *Sagarbha* and without it is called *Agarbha*).

32-33. The lowly type of Prāṇāyāma is *Manda* and the duration (of retention of breath) is twelve Mātrās; the middling is of the duration of twenty-four Mātrās while the last type of restraint of Prāṇa is of thirtysix Mātrās. In these three types, perspiration, shivering and gasping are generated in due order. This is the most excellent of the Yogas to even ordinary men due to bliss) [v. 1. The excellence of these should be judged by the bliss caused thereby].

34. That Yoga is called *Śunaphā*[1] and is the triumph of *Sagarbha* type of Prāṇāyāma. O learned ones, the sages say that this is the characteristic of the breath-control of Yogins.

---

1. *Śunaphā* is a particular configuration of the planets (when any one of the planets except the Sun, occupies a secondary position to the moon). This configuration is called *Śunaphā-Yoga*. But it is not clear why this astronomical term is brought in here. The crt. Edt. reads : *Sagarbham āhuḥ sajapam agarbhaṁ vijapaṁ budhāḥ* 'the Prāṇāyāma which is accompanied by muttering (of *bīja mantras*) is called *sagarbha* and that which is devoid of *japa* (muttering of mantras) is known as *agarbha*, O learned ones'.

35. Controlling one's breath, one should repeat three times the Gāyatrī Mantra along with its Vyāhṛtis (OṀ Bhūḥ, Bhuvaḥ, Svaḥ) and its head. This is called the breath-control.

36. It is mentioned in all scriptures by Yogins of fully controlled minds, that the Prāṇāyāma consists of three stages *Recaka*, *Pūraka* and *Kūmbhaka*.

37. *Recaka* is exhalation of breath while its retention (inhalation) is called Pūraka. The state of equilibrium (between the two) is spoken of as Kuṁbhaka.

38. O excellent men, it is said by good men that the restraint of the sense-organs which are naturally straying over the pleasurable objects is called *Pratyāhāra*.

39. *Dhāraṇā* is the fixation of the mind in the lotus of the heart, umbilical region, cerebral region limbs, forehead and such other spots.

40. Learned men called *Dhyāna* (contemplation) as the continuous concentration of mind which is fixed on particular spot (part of the body) and is undistracted by any other object nearby.

41. The perception of one form (object of contemplation) alone is *Samādhi* (trance) wherein the awareness of the surrounding place is absent. Only the object is perceived. This is the excellent injunction in the Yoga.

42. Twelve Prāṇāyāmas lead up to the Dhāraṇā; twelve Dhāraṇās lead into *Dhyāna*. Twelve such *Dhyānas* are said to constitute a Samādhi.

43. *Āsanas* (bodily postures) are (mainly three) *Svastika*, *Padma* and *Ardha*. This is the most excellent of all means.

44. O leading Brāhmaṇas, the soles of both the feet are placed over the thighs. Sitting thus is called the excellent *Padma* posture.

45. Both the soles of the feet are placed in between the knees and the things; seating oneself in this excellent posture is called *Svastika*.

46. O excellent Brāhmaṇas, when one sits placing one's foot on the other thigh (e.g. right foot on the left thigh), it becomes *Ardhāsana*. It is an excellent posture for the accomplishment of Yoga.

47. Yoga is not seen practised at in the improper time or in an unsuitable place; nor should it be practised near fire, in water or on dried leaf-stack.

48-49. The following places are also to be avoided for Yogic Practice: places where vermins abound, cremation ground, dilapidated cowpen, the quadrangle or place where four roads meet, a crowded noisy place or where there is an ant-hill or a *Caitya* (Buddhist place of worship), an unauspicious place full of wicked men, and places where mosquitoes are in plenty. Nor should one practise Yoga when the body is ailing or when the mind is dispirited.

50-51. With his mind devoted to Him (Lord Śiva), one should always practise Yoga* in a secluded place in an auspicious well-guarded place, in the cave of a mountain, on the banks of a river, in holy place, in a temple or in a clean place in the house, or in an isolated place devoid of worms or vermins.

52. After bowing down to leading Yogins,[1] their disciples, Lord Vināyaka, his own preceptor and me, the Yogin shall begin the practice of Yoga with full concentration of the mind.

53-54. He should sit in any of the postures—Svastika** Padma or Ardhāsana with his equi-poised gaze fixed on the tip of his nose and eyes partially opened. He shall be free from fear and calm; the illusory worries of worldly nature should be eschewed. One should then meditate on Parameśvara abiding in one's own soul.

55-56. The mystic lotus should be conceived at the tip of the tuft of hair (on the crown of one's head) twelve Aṅgulas in length. Dharma is its bulbous root from which it is originated. It is extremely beautiful and has spiritual knowledge as its stalk and eight divine potencies as its petals. It is white and has *Vairāgya* (Detachment) for its pericarp. One should contemplate

*BG. VI. 10.

1. Possibly a reference to *Supra* I. Ch. 53 where the incarnations of Śiva (all yogīndras) and their disciples are listed. A bow to these at the beginning of the practice of Yoga is probably advised.

**BG. VI. 13-14.

gold-coloured calyx (the greatest Kośa) in the pericarp of that lotus.

57-59. Within it one should meditate on the Lord whom they call divine and unchanging, the Lord who is endowed with all *Śaktis* (divine potencies), who is directly expressed by Oṁkāra, is unmanifest, enveloped in flames of rays (v.1. full of brilliance); one should meditate on the great brilliance, the imperishable one. He should deposit the bliss in that brilliance.[1] He should meditate on Īśa the great cause stationed in the middle of the *Kośa* (heart). Having become (identical) with its Ātman which is omnipresent, one should not think of anything else.

60-61. This is the secret-most knowledge. Now another type of meditation is described. After having contemplated as before on the excellent lotus in the heart, the Ātman should be thought of as a doer,[2] with the lustre equal to that of fire. In the middle of that lotus, Puruṣa, the twentyfifth principle should be thought of as being of the form of the flame of fire.

62-63. He should meditate upon the supreme Ātman in its middle—The Paramātman as the supreme firmament, the principle expressed by Oṁkāra and called eternal, auspicious, the unmanifest, latent in Prakṛti and the supreme light, the inner highest principle, the basis of Ātman and unsullied.

64. One should meditate on it with concentration and think of Maheśvara as a single form, after purifying all the principles through Praṇava.

65. Or the Ātman should be fixed in the greatest region which is free from impurity, after purifying one's own body with the self-same water of perfect knowledge.

66. One should dedicate one's soul unto me and concentrate one's mind in me and take up the *Bhasma* from the

1. v.l. In meditation he should establish his own soul in that brilliance as being perfectly identical with that lustre.

2. *Kāntāram* in Veṅkt. Ed. is obviously unacceptable.

Agnihotra fire. He should then dust all his limbs with it repeating the mantras of Agni[1] etc. and Āditya.

67. Then one should meditate upon Lord Īśāna in the form of the supreme light within one's own Ātman. This is the Yoga, pertaining to Paśupati. It is conducive to the liberation of the *Paśu* from the *Pāśa*.

68. This is the path of all the Vedāntas. The Śruti says that it is beyond all Āśramas (stages of life). This is the greatest esoteric truth that should be concealed as it bestows *Sāyujya* with absorption in me.

69-70. The observances for the twice-born celibate devotees have been recounted.[2] (Now I shall mention the observances) : Celibacy, non-violence, forgiveness, cleanliness penance, self-control, contentment, truthfulness, faith in Vedas, etc. These are the special ancillaries of the religious vows. Even if one of the holy vows is lacking it does not[3] affect it.*

71-72a Hence, one endowed with the attributes of the Ātman deserves to take up my *Vrata* (holy vow)—Many people who are devoid of lust, fear and anger have identified themselves with me, have resorted to me and have been purified by this Yoga and have reached my state of being.**

72b As men approach me, so do I accept them.‡

73. Hence, you all should worship me, the supreme Lord, by means of the path of knowledge or the path of devotion or by means of the greatest *Vairāgya* (detachment).

---

1. *agnir āditya-mantrataḥ*—no such mantra is traced in Bloomfield's *Vedic Concordance*. It may be in some *Āgama*. I feel it is better to take it as *agnir ityādi mantratah* as in the crt. ed. of the Kp. the MS. evidence supports that reading.

2. Though I have followed Veṅk. Edt., I think it better to take this line along with the above verse (no. 68). It would then mean : '(This esoteric doctrine) has been conveyed to the twice-born, devotees and Brahma-cārins.'

3. vv. 70-90 are borrowed from the BG., as can be seen from the footnotes.

*This is obviously a mistake v. l. the *lupyate* 'is lost or violated' is better than *na* in Veṅkt. Edt.

**BG. IV. 10.

‡BG. IV. 11.

74. Ever pure, one should worship me with the mind endowed with enlightenment. He should renounce all Karmas, accept no monetary gift and should partake of the alms (voluntarily given).

75-76a. He then attains identity with me. This secret has been communicated by me. He who does not hate any living being, who is friendly and sympathetic with all beings, who is devoid of myness and egotism and who is my devotee, is beloved to me.*

76b-77a.** A Yogin who is ever contented, is always endowed with self-control, is firm in his resolution, who is my devotee, who has dedicated his mind and intellect unto me, is my beloved.

77b-78a. He, by whom the world is not afflicted, he, who is not afflicted by the world, and he who is devoid of gaiety, anger, fear and anxiety is dear to me.

78b-79a. He who has no expectations, is pure, prompt and efficient, unconcerned and devoid of troubles and who has renounced all undertakings and is thus devoted to me is my beloved.***

79b-80a. One who equally reacts to censure and praise, who is silent, who is contented with whatever comes to him (he gets), who has no fixed abode, whose mind is steady and who is my devotee will attain me.†

80b-81a. One who performs all rites always doing continually all action but taking refuge in me, he reaches by my grace the eternal supreme abode.‡

81b-82a. One should seek refuge in me alone after mentally dedicating all actions unto me, after becoming devoid of hopes and myness (?) and considering me as the ultimate goal.§

82b-83a. By eschewing over-attachment to the fruits of actions and being ever contented and depending on nothing, one is enlightened by the action in which he is engaged.

---

*BG. xii. 13.
**BG. xii.14-16
***BG. xii.14-19.
†BG. xviii. 56.
‡BG. xviii. 57 ab III. 30.
§BG. IV. 20 and 22.

83b.-84a. One who is devoid of hopes, has his mind and self controlled and has abandoned all possession, attains to that supreme region by performing Karma by the body alone.

84b-85a. If one is contented with what he obtains* without efforts, if one is beyond the scope of mutually opposed pairs, the action performed by him for propitiating me is destructive of worldly existence.

85b-86a. 'Fix your mind on me; be devoted to me;** offer sacrifice to me; be solely absorbed in me, knowing me as the supreme Deity, the Lord of Yoga, propitiate me.

86b-87a. They call me the supreme Light. Thus enlightening each other and always speaking about me, they attain *Sāyujya* (union with me).

87b-88a. By means of the shining lamp of knowledge I destroy the entire darkness of those who are continuously attached to me.***

88b-89a. Those who have concentrated their mind† in me and are always worshipping me, I supply them what they need and preserve what is already possessed by them.‡

89b-90a. Others seeking enjoyment of pleasures may worship other deities. Their fruit should be known to that extent according to the capacity and power of that deity.§

90b-91a. Those who are devoted to other deities but are endowed with conceptions of me, are also liberated.

91b-92a. Hence, after abandoning all other transient deities, one should resort to me, the Lord. He attains the greatest region.

92b-93a. One must abandon love for sons and others. One should be devoid of sorrow and possessions. One should be detached and worship the Liṅga of Parameśvara until death.

---

*BG. IV. 22.
**BG. xviii.15.
***BG. x.10-11.
†BG. ix. 22.
‡BG. vii. 20.
§BG. ix. 23.

93b-94a. I give unto them the greatest region within a single birth, if they worship the Liṅga always, after eschewing all sensual pleasures.

94b-95a. The Liṅga of the great Ātman is the only Real (?) silver-line in lustre (v.l. stainless). The Liṅga is spiritual knowledge and is stationed in the hearts of Yogins.

95b-96. Regular devotees worship Maheśvara in the Liṅga anywhere, after sanctifying it duly. They may worship it in water, in the middle of fire, in the sky, in the sun or in other places.

97. Liṅga pertaining to Īśvara must be conceived of in jewels etc., and the Lord may be worshipped. All this is one with Liṅga and everything is within Liṅga.

98-99a. Hence one should worship the Eternal Lord anywhere in the Liṅga. The performers (of sacrifices and rituals) regard it as existing in the fire, the wise ones in water, the sky and in the sun, the fools in wood (i.e. idols made of wood) but with Yogins the Liṅga is in their hearts.

99b-100a. Even if the spiritual knowledge has not dawned, if one is detached, if one has sufficient love, one should perform the Japa of Praṇava as long as one lives. Since it is Brahmā's physical body.

100b-101a. Or a Brāhmaṇa should perform the Japa of Śatarudrīya until death. He should have full control over the mind and remain single. He attains the greatest region.

101b-103a. O Brāhmaṇas, one should remain at Vārāṇasī with full concentration until death. By means of the grace of god Śiva, he attains the greatest region. There, the lord grants the greatest knowledge to all the embodied beings at the time of departure (passing away.) Thereby they are liberated from bondage.

103b-104a. If a devotee fully dedicates himself unto me and performs the entire duties of the four castes and stages of life, he obtains perfect knowledge in the very same birth and attains the auspicious region.

104b-105. O Brāhmaṇas, all those people of lowly birth and sinful origin who reside there, cross the ocean of worldly existence, thanks to the grace of Īśvara. But obstacles befall those persons whose minds are affected by sins.

106. Hence, O Brāhmaṇas, one should always resort to virtuous activities for the sake of liberation. This is the secret of the Vedas. It should not be given (indiscriminately) to any one and everyone.

107-108. It should be given only to a virtuous one who is a devotee observing the vow of celibacy.

Vyāsa Said :

After imparting this excellent Yoga, the eternal Lord spoke to Nārāyaṇa who was seated there and who was free from ailments. "This knowledge has been explained by me for the welfare of the expounders of Brahman.

109. This auspicious knowledge of Brahman should be imparted by you to the disciples of quiescent minds". After mentioning this matter, the unborn Lord spoke to the leading Yogins.

110-111. "O excellent Brāhmaṇas, for the sake of the welfare of devotees of the twice-born caste, you too should impart to all devoted disciples, my perfect knowledge at my instance. There is no doubt in this that he who is Īśvara (Śiva) is Nārāyaṇa. This greatest knowledge should be imparted to those who do not see any difference (between the two) viz. Śiva and Viṣṇu.

112-113a. He who is called Nārāyaṇa is my Supreme personality. It abides in the soul of all beings, is quiescent and established imperishably.

113b-114a. The people who see difference (in me and Viṣṇu) and perceive me otherwise, do not see liberation. They are born again and again in the world.

114b-115a. Those who see this unmanifest Viṣṇu and me, Lord Maheśvara as identical are not born again (in Saṁsāra).

115b-116a. Hence observe and worship Viṣṇu, the unchanging Ātman without beginning and end as the same as me.

116b-117a. Those who see otherwise and think about the difference in the deities pass on to terrible hells. I am not present in them.

117b-118a. I liberate the person who does not censure Nārāyaṇa whether he is a fool or a scholar, or a Cāṇḍāla or a Brāhmaṇa depending on me.

118b-119a. Hence this great Yogin, the supreme person (Viṣṇu) should be worshipped and bowed to by my devotees in order to generate my pleasure."

119b-120a. After saying this and embracing Vāsudeva, the Pināka-bearing Lord vanished even as all were observing.

120b-121a. Lord Nārāyaṇa eschewed his excellent body and took up the excellent guise of an ascetic.

121b-122a. He said to the Yogins — "By the grace of Parameṣṭhin (Śiva) the blemishless perfect knowledge has been acquired by you all. The perfect knowledge of Lord Maheśa is destructive of worldly existence.

122b-123a. O Lordly sages, go forth without mental affection. All of you propagate the perfect knowledge of Parameṣṭhin to virtuous disciples.

123b-124a. This perfect knowledge pertaining to Īśvara should be given to a quiescent devotee, the virtuous one who maintains the sacrificial fire and particularly to a Brāhmaṇa."

124b-125a. After saying this, Nārāyaṇa, the great Yogin, the Ātman of the universe, the most excellent among the knowers of Yoga and Yogins, vanished from the scene.

125b-126a. Those sages bowed to Maheśvara, the Lord of Devas and Nārāyaṇa, the cause of the Bhūtas and went to their respective abodes.

126b-128. Holy lord the great sage Sanatkumāra gave the perfect knowledge pertaining to Īśvara to Saṁvarta. Who imparted it to Satya-Vrata. The leading Yogin Sanandana gave it to the great sage Pulaha. Pulaha gave it to Gautama. Prajāpati Aṅgiras gave it to Bhāradvāja, learned in the Vedas.

129-130a. Kapila gave it to Jaigīṣavya and pañcaśikha. My father Parāśara, the seer of all principles, acquired that great perfect knowledge from Sanaka. Vālmīki got it from him.

130b-131a. The great Yogi Vāmadeva, Rudra, the controller of Kāla and wielder of Pināka, the offspring of Satī and Śiva imparted this knowledge to me formerly.

131b-132a. Lord Nārāyaṇa, Hari, the son of Devakī, himself gave this excellent knowledge to Arjuna.

132b-134a. Ever since I acquired this excellent (perfect knowledge) from Rudra Vāmadeva, I have had a special devotion to Giriśa (Śiva, the Lord of mountains). I have sought special refuge in Giriśa worthy of being the shelter, Giriśa the Lord of the Bhūtas (goblins), the trident-bearing Sthāṇu, the Lord of Devas.

134b-136a. Accompanied by your wives and sons, O Gentle Sirs, you too resort to Lord Śambhu, Śiva the bull-vehicled deity. Exist by means of his grace. Worship Śaṅkara through the path of activity, worship Mahādeva, the Lord of bulls (lord of speech) having serpents for his ornament."

136b-138a. When this was narrated, Śaunaka and others bowed to Maheśvara, eternal Sthāṇu. Delighted in their minds they spoke to Vyāsa, the son of Satyavatī the holy Lord Kṛṣṇadvaipāyana, who was Lord Hṛṣīkeśa himself and Śiva, the Īśvara of the worlds.

138b-140a. By your favour, steady devotion to the bull-bannered deity worthy of being a refuge, has arisen. This is inaccessible even to Devas. O excellent sage, please narrate the excellent path of action (Karma-Yoga)[1] whereby Lord Īśa has to be propitiated by those who seek salvation. In your presence, Sūta may hear the words of the holy Lord.

141b-143a. Hence, mention the epitome of virtue (Dharma) capable of protecting the entire worlds. This is what has been narrated by Viṣṇu the Lord of Devas, who had assumed the form of a tortoise, when he had been requested by Śakra along with the sages at the churning of the Nectar.

On hearing the words of the sages, the son of Satyavatī, explained the whole of the eternal path of Action.

143b-144a. He who always reads this dialogue of the deity clad in Elephant-hide with the sages the Chief of whom was Sanatkumāra shall be liberated from all sins.

144b-145a. He who narrates this to pure Brāhmaṇas devoted to celibacy and he who ponders over the meaning attains the greatest goal.

1. This is how *Vyāsa-gītā*, the next section is introduced.

145b-147. He who listens to this always with great devotion and steady adherence to holy rites shall be freed from all sins and honoured in the Brahmaloka. Hence, this must be read with all efforts by learned men. It must be heard and subsequently pondered over particularly in the company of Brāhmaṇas.

CHAPTER TWELVE[1]

The Path of Action Duties of celibate students

Vyāsa said :

1. All of you, sages, listen to the eternal Karmayoga (Path of action) that brings about the everlasting benefit to the Brāhmaṇas. It is being narrated now.

2. To sages listening attentively to him, Manu, the progenitor of the world formerly explained this (path of Karma) that has been established in the Vedas and all the details of which were taught to Brāhmaṇas.

---

1. The present chapter is the first in the Vyāsa Gītā which forms a part of KP. (II chs. 12-24). In this section, Vyāsa explains the duties of all *Varṇas* and *Āśramas* (the four main divisions of the society and the four stages in the life of an individual). About its interpolatory nature vide Intro.—Pāśupatisation of the KP.

This chapter describes mainly the duties of a religious student (*Brahmacārī*). The description of the duties of a Brahmacārin are detailed in Smṛtis like Manu II. 36-249, Yāj. I. 10-50 & Purāṇas like AP. 153. 1-16, Bh. P. VII.12.1-16, VP. III 9.1-6 and a number of verses are common to them and the KP. But the special feature of KP. is *that it has incorporated practically the whole of this chapter from Auśanasa Smṛ. ch. I.* Hence there is no propriety (as A.S. Gupta does it in his Edt of KP. p. 824) in referring to Manu simply because Vyāsa is made to state that he is reporting what Manu expounded to sages in the days of yore.

KP. however, had the status of a Smṛti and many verses from this chapter are quoted as authority in respectable works on Dharma-Śāstra, like SMC, CC, Vīra-mitrodaya, Nirṇaya Sindhu and others.

3. As this path dispels all sins and is meritorious and as it is resorted to by multitudes of sages, listen to it with attentive mind, even as I narrate it to all of you.

4. O excellent Brāhmaṇas, in the eighth year of his life from the day of conception or from the day of birth[1] one should be invested with the sacred thread in accordance with the injunctions of one's own Sūtra. He should then study the Vedas.

5. He should have a ritualistic staff, wear a girdle and a secred thread and the skin of a black antelope, subsist on alms, observe celibacy and should stay happily in his hermitage (or stage of life).

6. Cotton thread was created formerly by Brahmā for the purpose of Upavīta (sacred thread). It consists of thrice-spun yarn. It should be made of Kuśa grass or cotton.

7. A Brāhmaṇa should always wear the sacred thread and keep his tuft of hair (on the head) tied into a knot. Otherwise, whatever rite he performs shall be futile.

8. He should wear unmutilated (unsewn?) cloth of cotton (which may be) ochre-coloured. White cloth without holes (i.e. not torn) is the excellent wearing apparel.

9. The skin of the black antelope makes an excellent upper cloth. It is auspicious. If the hide of the antelope is not available, that of Ruru deer is prescribed.

10. If the thread is placed over the left arm and under the right arm it is called *Upavita*.[2] This is the way in which it is always worn. If it is worn round the neck (like a garland) it is called *Nivita*.

11. O Brāhmaṇas, if the thread is worn over the right arm and under the left arm it is called *Prācināvita*. It should be followed at the time of the performance of the rites for the Pitṛs.

---

1. *Vide* Āśvalāyana Gr. S. I. 19.1-6. This is endorsed by Āpastamba (10.2-3) and even Patañjali (Mahābhāṣya II p. 57).

2. VV 10-13 explain the three methods of wearing the sacred thread and the occasions on which they are to be so worn. This practice is as old as *Tait. Saṁhitā* (II.5.11.1) which states :

nivītam manuṣyāṇām prācīnāvītam pitṛṇām pavītaṁ devānām

The method of wearing the thread as *upavīta*, *prācināvīta* is given in Gobhila Gr. S.I. 2.2-4. KP. endorses the same.

12-13. One should always wear the sacred thread as *Upavita* in the following instances viz.—in the chamber of sacrificial fires, in the cowpen, while *Homa* is performed or *Japa* is undertaken, during the recitation of the Vedic Mantras, while taking food always in the presence of Brāhmaṇas, while respectfully worshipping the preceptors, at the two junctions (i.e. performing *sandhyā*-prayer at dawn and at dusk) and while meeting saintly men. This is the eternal injunction.

14. The girdle[1] of the Brāhmaṇa should be made of the Muñja grass twisted three times. It shall be soft and of equal thickness throughout. There may be one or three knots. O Brāhmaṇas, (if Muñja grass is unavailable), it may be made of Kuśa grass as well.

15. A Brāhmaṇa should hold a staff[2] made of Bilva or Palāśa tree. It should come up to his head (in height). It can be made of any other tree (prescribed as being) worthy of being used for sacrifices. It should be soft and devoid of crack in the middle.

16. A *Brāhmaṇa* should perform the *Sandhyā*-Prayers with full concentration in the morning as well as in the evening. By failure to perform it due to passion, covetousness, fear or delusion, he shall become fallen.

17. Thereafter, he should perform the rites of the fire-worship in accordance with the injunctions, both in the morning and in the evening. He should propitiate Devas, the sages as well as the *Pitṛs* only after taking bath.

18. He should worship the deities with flowers, leaves and water. He should invariably revere the elders, according to the prescription in *dharma*.

19. Desirous of* longevity and health but, excluding (request for) wealth, he should humbly bow down respectfully saying (at the same time his name). "Sir, this I am (so and so) by name".

---

1. Āśvalāyana Gr. S. I.19.11, Manu II.42; II.43 allows one, three or five which Kullūka attributes to family usage.

2. Baudhāyana Dh. S.II.5.17 is accepted here.

**anvicchan* is a better *v.l.* than *sānnidhyam* (vicinity to longevity and health) adopted in the Veṅkt. Text.

20. At the time of obeisance, the *Brāhmaṇa* should be told: O be longlived, O gentle one, at the end of his name, the long letter A should be added with the *Pluta* accent (of three mores) on the penultimate syllable (i.e. the vowel is prolated).

21. If a Brāhmaṇa does not salute in return when saluted, he shall not be honoured by learned men he is just like a Śūdra.[1]

22. The hands should be cross-wise when touching the feet of a preceptor. His left foot should be touched with the left hand and the right foot should be touched with the right hand.[2]

23. One should in the first instance make obeisance to that gentleman from whom one has acquired regular, Vedic or spiritual knowledge.

24. (While paying obeisance) one should carry in one's hands, water, alms, flowers, sacrificial twigs and such other things. Now (should he do so ?) when performing the rites of gods.

25. On meeting a Brāhmaṇa, one shall ask him about *Kuśala* (welfare), a Kṣatriya should be asked *Anāmaya* (non-ailment); Vaiśya should be asked about his *Kṣema* (prosperity and security) and Śūdra should be asked about his health.

26-28. The preceptor, father, eldest brother, king, maternal uncle, father-in-law, maternal grandfather, paternal grandfather, one belonging to a superior caste and paternal uncle—all these are remembered as *Gurus* (superiors). Mother, maternal grand-mother, teacher's wife, sisters of father and mother, the mother-in law, paternal grandmother and elder brother's wife—these are elderly ladies. Thus the elder ones on the side of mother and that of the father have been detailed.

29. Mentally, Verbally and Physically one should obey these. On seeing the preceptor, one shall get up and make obeisance with palms joined in reverence.

30. One should not sit along with these; one should not argue with these for the sake of money (over money matters).

---

1. Manu II. 126.
2. This method of clasping the feet of the preceptor is prescribed in Dh. S. of Viṣṇu (28.15), Baudhāyana (I.2.24) and Manu II.72.

Even for the sake of remaining alive, no one should speak harshly to these out of hatred.

31. Even a person who has risen up by dint of other good qualities, incurs downfall if he hates elders. Among all these elders, five are particularly to be revered.[1]

32. Among them the first three are the most excellent, (viz.) he who procreates, she who gives birth to and he by whom learning is imparted and among these three (at first) the mother (should be) highly respected.

33-36. (The three mentioned before and) thc eldest brother and husband—these five are remembered as *Gurus*. These five must be specially worshipped through every effort of oneself or even by sacrificing one's life, by one who wishes for prosperity. As long as the parents are devoid of observations the son should abandon everything else and should be solely devoted to them. If the mother and the father are very well pleased with the good qualities of the son, that son shall attain all *dharma* (religious merits) due to that holy rite. There is no deity equal to the mother; there is no preceptor equal to the father.

37. There is no way of fully repaying their debts (by helping them in return). One should continuously do everything physically, mentally and verbally that pleases them.

38. Without being permitted by these two, the son should not perform any other holy rite excepting what yields salvation as well as the *Nitya* and *Naimittika* rites.

39-40a. The essence of *dharma* that yields infinite benefit after death, has been related. After propitiating the expounder duly and dismissed by him with due permission, the disciple enjoys the benefit of learning. After death he is respected in the heaven.

40b-41a. The foolish person who disrespects the eldest brother who is on a par with his father, falls into a terrible hell after death, as a result of that sin.

41b. If one is to follow the path (of religion) the master (husband) should always be honoured.

1. VV. 31-37 enumerate the persons who are to be respected as *gurus* (preceptors). Manu II. 227-237 and Devala quoted in SMC I. p. 35.

42a. Even if service is rendered to one's mother, one attains greatness in the world.

42b-43a. Holy sage Manu has said that those men who lay down their lives for the sake of the master's doles attain everlasting worlds.

43b-44. The younger people should stand up and greet[1] the followidg by saying *Asau Aham* (this I)—the people, viz.—uncles both maternal and paternal, fathers-in-law, sacrificial priests and preceptors. The initiated, though he be younger shall not be addressed by name.

45-46. The knower of virtue should address him with the prefix *bho bhavān.* The Brāhmaṇa shall be honoured, worshipped and bowed to by Kṣatriyas and others, seeking fortune. They must be honoured with due respect. The Kṣatriyas and others are not to be greeted first by a Brāhmaṇa.

47. Those who have vast learning and are endowed with perfect knowledge, holy rites and good attributes, do worship. The Śruti says that the Brāhmaṇa should offer *Svasti* (Blessings, may it be well with you) to people of all castes.

48-49a. Between people of the same caste greeting and saluting is desirable. Fire-god is the preceptor unto the twice-born; a Brāhmaṇa is the preceptor unto the people of all castes. The husband is the preceptor unto the women and the guest is the preceptor unto all.

49b-50a. Learning, holy rites, penance, kinsmen and wealth the fifth in the series—they say that these five are things worthy of honour. The earlier one is better than the latter one.

50b-51a. Any man of three castes who possesses these both in number and superiority, is worthy of being recepient of honour. A Śūdra in the tenth decade of life is also worthy of respect.

51b-52a. Way should be given(priority should be accorded) to the Brāhmaṇa, to a woman, to the king, to the blind, to the aged one, to one bending down with burden, to the sick and to the weak.

---

1. VV. 43b-50 deal with the etiquettes of paying respects by a junior to a senior. It consists of declaration of one's name etc. (*upasaṅgrahaṇa* and *Abhivādana*)

52b-53a. (The religious student) should, with purity of body and mind, bring alms everyday from the houses of decent people, offer it first to the preceptor and then partake of it silently with his permission.

53b-55. The excellent Brāhmaṇa who has been invested with the sacred thread should beg for alms with the word *Bhavatī* in the beginning—(i.e. *Bhavati Bhikṣāṁ dehi*—O gentle lady give the alms); the Kṣatriya should use the word *Bhavati* in the middle (i.e. *Bhikṣāṁ bhavati dehi*—Alms O gentle lady, give) and a Vaiśya should use the word Bhavati in the end (i.e Bhikṣāṁ dehi Bhavati—give alms O gentle lady).[1] One should beg for alms, at the outset, of his mother, sister, mother's sister or one who does not disrespect him. He should go to the houses of the people of his own caste for begging or indiscriminately to the houses of any person of any caste taking care to avoid the house of the fallen man.

56. A Brahmacārin (a religious student) should beg for alms everyday from the houses of persons not devoid of Vedas and Yajñas and those who strictly adhere to their duties. He should be pure in mind and body.

57-58a. One should not beg for alms at the house of the preceptor or a cousin or near kinsman. If the other houses are not available, he should avoid the earlier houses, i.e. taking the last named first.

58b. Or if the houses mentioned before are impossible, he should roam the whole village with self control, exercising restraints over speech and not glancing at various quarters.

59-60a. Collecting the alms without any deceit, he should cook it (v.l. collecting alms just sufficient for his need) he should eat it always with self restraint, control over speech (i.e. silently) and with proper attention.

60b-61. An observer of the vow (of celibacy) should always subsist on alms and take food once a day. The subsistence of one who maintains himself on alms is remembered to be on a par with fast. He should honour the cooked food always and eat without despising it.

1. Baudhāyana Gr. S. II.5.47-53, also Manu II. 49-50.

62. Looking at it, he should be delighted and contented.

63. Gluttonous eating is ill for health and destructive of longevity, and it does not secure heaven. It is non-meritorious and reproached by the world. Hence, one should avoid it.

64-65. One should eat food facing the east or the sun. Hc should not take food facing the north. This is the eternal injunction. After washing the hands and feet he should perform *Ācamana* rite[1] twice. He should sit in a clean place and take food. After taking food he should perform *Ācamana* twice.

CHAPTER THIRTEEN

The usages of Śiṣṭas. Good Conduct.

Vyāsa said :

1-3. An excellent Brāhmaṇa should perform the *Ācamana*[1] rite (sipping water) in these circumstances (even though he had done so previously) : after taking food, after drinking any beverage, after sleeping, after bath, after walking in a street, on touching the lips without the hair, after wearing garments, after the discharge of semen, urine or faeces, on uttering an improper word, after spitting, at the beginning of Vedic study, at the time of hiccough or sigh, on coming from a quadrangle or a cremation ground and at the time of the two Sandhyās i.e. dawn and dusk. In the last case, he shall perform the *Ācamana* twice.

4-10. The *Ācamana* rite is to be performed in the following circumstances also :- After talking to a Cāṇḍala or a Mleccha;

---

1. Since ancient times *Ācamana* or sipping of water before, in and after certain acts, occasions etc. was regarded essential from the purificatory point of view. Elaborate rules for *Ācamana* rite are prescribed in Dharma Sūtras e.g. Āpastamba I.5.15.2-11; 16.1-16) and Smṛtis like Manu II. 58-62, Yāj. I. 18-21. The occasions for *Ācamana* detailed here, were already prescribed in Āpastamba Dh. S. 1.5.16.15-16, Manu V. 138 & 145 & Yājñavalkya 1.196.

after conversing with women, Śūdra and a person defiled by *Ucchiṣṭa* (stale leaving), after touching a person who is defiled by *Ucchiṣṭa* as well as food-stuff of that sort. When one sheds tears or spills blood, after taking food, performance of the *sandhyā* prayer at dawn and dusk, after taking a bath, after discharging urine and faeces and shall perform Ācamana twice; after sleeping, he should perform the rite only once; after touching fire, or cows. After touching women or after binding the knot of the waist-cloth, he should perform *Ācamana*. He should touch the grass, water or the earth, when he touches his hair or touches a cloth that is not washed; for the purpose of *Ācamana* the water should not be hot nor shall it contain foam. It should be pure. He should be silent at that time. A person seeking purity shall sit facing the east or the north at the time of Ācamana. If one performs *Ācamana* covering his head or neck with *dhotī* (waist-cloth) worn loosely without knot or tucking and the knot of the tuft of the hair united and without washing feet, one remains impure despite *Ācamana*. A wise person should not perform *Ācamana* with shoes on, standing in water, wearing a turban.

11-15a. No sensible man should perform *Ācamana* when the hand is defiled by *Ucchiṣṭa* (leavings of food) nor should he perform the *Ācamana* with the water by means of the shower, nor should he perform *Ācamana* with water supplied by a single hand. It should not be without the sacred thread. He should not be seated with shoes on (?) or on the knees. The hand shall not reach outside the knees. The water shall not be poured out by Vaiśya Śūdra etc. by means of their hands. Nor should they be defiled by *Ucchiṣṭa*. *Ācamana* should not be performed by touching water with fingers. One should not produce sounds (at the time of Ācamana). His mind should not be dwelling on other topics. The water should not be defective in colour or taste. The water should not be in short supply. The water should not be agitated with the hands. It should not be performed outside the room (?). A Brāhmaṇa is sanctified when the water (of the *Ācamana* rite) reaches his heart. A Kṣatriya is sanctified when the water reaches the throat. A Vaiśya is purified as soon as the water is drunk. A woman and a Śūdra are purified by merely touching the water.

15b-18. The *Tīrtha*[1] (holy place) on the line at the root of the thumb is called Brāhmya (Brāhma Tīrtha) (i.e. Brāhma Tīrtha is presumed to exist there). The root of the index finger is the excellent Pitṛtīrtha. The space after (beyond) the root of small finger is called Prājāpatya (Tīrtha). At the tip of the fingers is remembered Daiva Tīrtha. It is glorified for the sake of the Deva (?). Or it is enjoined at the root (of the fingers) that pertaining to Agni is remembered in the middle finger. The same itself is the Saumika (pertaining to Soma) Tīrtha. Realising thus one is not deluded. A Brāhmaṇa should always perform the *Ācamana* rite through the Brāhma Tīrtha.

19. He shall be pure if he performs the *Ācamana* rite by means of the body belonging to the divinity (i.e. Daiva Tīrtha) Pure at the outset, a Brāmaṇa should perform *Ācamana* three times.

20. He should touch the mouth with the root of the thumb well-covered.* (?) He should then touch the eyes by means of the thumb and the ring finger.

21. He should touch both the nostrils by joining together the tips of the index finger and the thumb. He should touch the ears by joining together the tips of the small finger and the thumb.

22. He should touch the arms with all fingers and the heart with palm. He should touch the umbilical region and the head, with all fingers. Or he shall touch both of them by means of the thumb.

23. He should drink water three times. Thereby the deities are well delighted. We have heard that Brahmā, Viṣṇu and Maheśa are delighted thereby.

24. By the wiping off (Parimārjana) of mouth the Gaṅgā and the Yamunā are pleased. When the eyes are wiped the moon and the sun are delighted.

---

1. The right hand (palm) used for holding water for Ācamana is regarded as a congregation of holy *Tīrthas* as given in VV. 15-18 here. The idea that holy Tīrthas are located at the roots and or tips of fingers is as old as *Dharma Sūtras* (e.g. Viṣṇu 62.1-4, Baudhāyana 5.14-18), though they differ regarding the location of certain Tīrthas.

*The Veṅk. Text reads *Saṁvṛta* but *Sammṛjya* 'having wiped out) will be a better reading.

25. When the two nostrils are touched, the Aśvin gods (Nāsatya and Dasra) are delighted. Similarly, when the two ears are touched the wind god and the fire god are delighted.

26. When the heart is touched, the deities are pleased. By touching the head, Puruṣa becomes delighted.

27. (While performing *Ācamana*) when the sprays (of water) touch the limbs they do not defile by means of Ucchiṣṭa. One shall be impure by touching the space between the teeth, when teeth are touched as well by means of the tongue and the lips.

28. If the drops of water touch on the feet when one performs the *Ācamana* rite, they are not defiled. They should be known as Bhūmikas (v.l. Bhūmiga - existent in the earth).

29. Manu says that there is no defect (of *Ucchiṣṭa*) when Madhuparka (mixture of honcy) or Soma is taken or when one chews the betel leaves. Nor is one defiled like this, when one eats fruits, roots or sugarcane.

30. If a Brāhmaṇa becomes defiled (while eating and drinking) food and water in plenty,* he should keep down on the ground the material (that he is carrying), perform *Ācamana* (after eating) and (then purify that material) by sprinkling water over it.

31. While taking with him a bright metallic thing (such as a Pot), if Brāhmaṇa becomes defiled by *Ucchiṣṭa*, he should place that article on the ground. He should then perform *Ācamana* and take up that again.

32. If he takes anything without chanting the Mantras and then becomes defiled by *Ucchiṣṭa,* he should become pure on performing *Ācamana* even without placing that article (on the ground).

33-34a. It is optional in the case of wearing apparel etc. where it is not touched (?).** At night, in the forest-path infested with thieves and tigers, if anyone discharges urine and faeces with some article in his hands, he is not defiled.

---

*v.l. *Pracaran*—while walking.

**v.l. *tat saṁspṛṣyācamed iha* should perform Ācamana after touching it (cloth, etc.)

34b-35a. During the day time, one should face the north and during the night he should face the south and discharge urine and faeces, after placing the sacred thread on the right ear.[1]

35b-36a. He should cover the ground with wooden pieces, leaves, grass or lumps of clay before passing urine and faeces. He should cover the head at that time.

36b-37. One should not evacuate the bowels or pass urine in shady place, near the wells or rivers, cowpens or monasteries, in the middle of the path, on ashes, in burning fire, within the house or in the cremation ground. He shall not do so in the path traversed by cows, in a ploughed field, in a place abounding in great trees, in a grassy meadow nor on the top of a mountain.

38-39. While answering the calls of nature one should not remain standing nor shall he be in the nude nor on a mountain peak. He shall never pass urine etc. in a dilapidated temple or an ant hill. He shall not do so in pits and ditches where there are animals. He shall not do so while passing through the the Royal road. He shall not discharge odour on husks, charcoal or broken pots.

40. One shall not do so in a holy centre nor in the sacred water nor in a quadrangle. He shall not discharge faeces in a garden or a nearby place; nor in a barren land nor in a very dirty place.

41-42. One shall not discharge faeces etc. with shoes on. While going in an aerial chariot (v.l. while holding an umbrella) or standing face to face with a woman, elders or Brāhmaṇas one shall not evacuate bowels. Neither in front of a shrine nor that of an idol shall one discharge urine or faeces. One shall not do so facing the luminaries or water nor in front of the sun, moon and the fire.

43. The purificatory rite shall be performed with clay brought from the banks. The stickiness and the odour shall be

1. Rules regarding answering calls of nature should be a part of hygiene. But Dharma Sūtras (e.g. Āpastamba 1.11.30, 15-30, Vasiṣṭha VI. 10-19) and Smṛtis like Manu (IV. 45-52, 56), Yāj. (I. 16-17) and Purāṇas like Vāyu (78.59-64) have dealt with this topic in details. KP. or rather *Auśanasa Smṛti.* has summarised them here concisely.

removed. He shall perform carefully the purifacatory rite with water taken out from it (before hand ?).

44. A Brāhmaṇa should not bring clay from a dusty place, or a marshy place. He shall not bring it from the high way nor from barren land. Nor from the soil defiled by *Ucchiṣṭa* of some one else performing *Śauca* (the purificatory rite.)

45. He should not bring the clay from a temple nor from a well nor from the open village nor from the waterbed. In accordance with the injunction mentioned before, he should always perform the *Ācamana* rite as well.

CHAPTER FOURTEEN[1]

Duties of Brahmacārins

Vyāsa said :

1. Thus (the Brahmacārin) equipped with the staff etc. and strictly adhering to *Śauca* (cleanliness) and *Ācāra* (good conduct) should start the study of the Vedas when called upon for it. He should look at his Guru's face and start his study.

2. He should continuously keep the hands lifted (in reverence) and should strictly abide by the rules of conduct at the time of dusk (?).* When peimitted (by the preceptor) saying, "be seated", he shall sit facing the preceptor.[2]

3-4. The disciple should not remain lying down when he listens to or converses (with the preceptor). While sitting or standing or getting up near the preceptor, the disciple should not keep his face averted from his *guru*. At no time should the

---

1. Most of the verses in this chapter are the same as those in Ch. III of Auśanasa Smṛti.

**Sandhyācāra* but a better v.l. is *Sādhvācāra*, 'good conduct'.

2. VV. 2-37 give the code of conduct to be followed by a pupil during his stay at Guru's hermitage. These are based on Dharma Sūtras (e.g. Gautama II. 13-25) & Smṛtis like Manu (II. 177-179.)

disciple be seated on a couch in the preceptor's presence. Within the range of the vision of the preceptor, the disciple should not sit as he pleases.

5. Even when not seen by him (i.e. in the absence of his *guru*), the preceptor's name should not be directly mentioned by the disciple. Nor should he mimic the preceptor's mode of walking or behaviour.

6. If, at any place, the preceptor is found to be censured or refuted in argument, the disciple should close his ears or walk out of that place to another place.

7. When standing far away, the disciple need not worship the preceptor. He shall not revere him angrily or (while he is) in the vicinity of a woman. The preceptor should not be answered gruffly. He should not be retorted. While the teacher is standing, the disciple should not remain seated.

8. For the sake of the teacher, the disciple should fetch potfulls of water, Kuśa grass, flowers and sacrificial twigs. He should anoint, wipe off or massage his limbs frequently.

9. He should neither tread over nor step across the garland previously worn by the teacher, his bedstead, his (wooden) sandals and (leather) shoes, seat, shadow and his oblong chair.

10. He should gather tooth-pick etc. for the sake of the preceptor. He should duly inform the preceptor about the duties carried out by himself. Without taking leave of the preceptor, he should not go anywhere. The disciple shall be engaged in activities pleasing and beneficial to the preceptor.

11-12. In his presence, the disciple should never stretch his legs. In the presence of the preceptor, the disciple should avoid yawning, loud laughter, covering of the neck etc. He should not speak words while cracking the joints of fingers. He shall study the Vedas at the proper time, as long as the preceptor is not dispirited.

13. At the preceptor's instance, he may sit on a plank with mental concentration. He should not by himself ever remain in the seat, bed or a vehicle (along with the preceptor ?).

14-16a. He should run after the preceptor, should he be running and follow him when he goes. He should not sit along with the preceptor in a bullock-cart, horse-carriage, camel-cart, top portions of mansions, mats, rock, planks and boats. He should always keep subdued the sense organs. He should not be angry, be pure, and should speak sweet and wholesome words.

16b-18. The religious student should avoid using fragrant garlands of white flowers and sweet beverages. He should refrain from injuring living beings. He should not take oil-bath or apply collyrium to the eyes, nor should he hold umbrellas. The following should be avoided very scrupulously by him : passion, covetousness, fear, slumber (during day time), songs musical instruments and dancing, gambling, spreading of false remours, glancing at or seizing women, attacking others and calumny.

19. He should collect and fetch the following things as much as necessary, viz., water pots, flowers, cowdung, clay and the Kuśa grass. Everyday, he should go begging for alms.

20. He should not witness dance-programmes. He should always be disinterested in songs etc. Artificial salt and all stale things shall be avoided. (All salted preparations, when stale, shall be avoided).

21. He shall not look at the sun (at the sunrise or sunset). He should not use tooth brush twigs. He should not go to a lonely spot in the company of unclean women nor should he have lengthy conversation with low castes and Śūdras.

22. He should do everything to please the preceptor and not out of passion or his sweet will. He should perform ablution somehow to remove impurities.

23. A Brāhmaṇa should not even think of abandoning his preceptor. If out of delusion or covetousness, he abandons (the preceptor), he shall be fallen.

24. He should never antagonise that person from whom he receives knowledge, whether secular, Vedic or spiritual.

25. Manu, however, has laid down that even a *Guru* (preceptor) can be abandoned, should he take to wrong paths, be arrogant or not know what should be done and what should not be done.

26. When the preceptor of the preceptor is nearby, the disciple should show as much devotion as towards the preceptor;

unless specifically allowed by his preceptor, he should not pay obeisance to his own elders.

27. This very behaviour should be constant in regard to the preceptors of other lores to one's kith and kin, to those who prevent one from *Adharmas* and who give instructions in beneficial things.

28. It is better that one should always behave towards the sons, wives and kinsmen of the preceptors as though towards the preceptors.

29. A young disciple should honour all persons worthy of honour (or shall help them) in the *Yajña* rite. The son of the preceptor deserves honour like him (the preceptor), if he also begins to teach.

30. The disciple should neither bathe the son of the preceptor nor apply cosmetics over his body. He should not partake of his leavings, nor should he clean his feet.

31. The wives of the preceptors should be honoured and respected like the preceptor, if they are of his own caste. But if they belong to lower castes, they are to be honoured only by greetings and standing up (when they come).

32. The disciple should not perform the following personal services to the wives of the preceptors, viz. : bathing them, anointing their bodies with oil, application of cosmetics over their bodies, and beautifying their tresses.

33. If the wife of the preceptor be a youthful maiden, she should not be bowed to by touching her feet. The disciple should touch the ground and make obeisance saying *asau aham* (This I am).

34. After return from a journey abroad, the disciple should pay respect by touching the feet of the wives of his preceptor (on the first day but afterwards) on every day, he should bow by touching the ground, remembering the duty (of good men).

35. Mother's sister, maternal uncle's wife, mother-in-law, father's sister and the wife of the preceptor—all these are to be respected equally like his preceptor's wife. They are equal to the wife of the preceptor.

36. Brother's wife of the same caste deserves greeting by touching the feet every day. The women folk of the

kinsmen and relatives are to be similarly worshipped by every Brāhmaṇa.

37. One should behave towards the sisters of one's father and mother and his own elder sister as though towards his mother. Of course the mother is greater than all of them.

38. The preceptor shall teach such a self-possessed, modest (non-arrogant) disciple, endowed with decency of conduct. He should continuously teach him the Vedas, the Dharmas (Dharma-Śāstra or smṛtis), the Purāṇas and the Aṅgas (Ancillary subjects like Śikṣā, grammar etc.)

39. If the disciple has lived a disciplined life (at his residence) for a full year but the preceptor fails to impart perfect knowledge to him, the preceptor incurs all the sins of the disciple.

40. As prescribed in the dharma-śāstra, a preceptor should teach the following ten persons : the preceptor's son, a person desirous of learning or one who serves the teacher, a person of the teaching profession, an abider by *dharma*, a (mentally and physically ?) pure person, the explainer of *sūktas* (*subhāṣitas* ?), one disinterested in erotics and a saintly person.

41. The following six should be duly instructed viz. : A grateful person, a non-malicious one, an intelligent one, a man who has rendered help, a trustworthy person and a beloved one.

42. The Brahman (Vedas) should be gifted to these and to others together what has already been mentioned (viz. Purāṇa etc. Facing the north, one should begin the Vedic study after performing *Ācamana* and remaining self-controlled.[1]

43. After touching his feet and glancing at the face of the preceptor, the disciple shall say *adhīṣva bho* (Recite, O sir). He shall indicate "cessation" by using the word *iti* and should stop there.

44. When the disciple is favourably seated, sanctified by Pavitras and rendered holy through three Prāṇāyāmas, he deserves the Oṁkāra.

45. A Brāhmaṇa should duly repeat the *Praṇava* at the end. A Brāhmaṇa should always perform the Vedic study with the palms joined in reverence.

1. VV. 42 ff. describe how the teaching work was done in those days.

46. The Vedas constitute the eternal 'Eye' of all living beings. (The Brāhmaṇa should recite the Vedas everyday. Otherwise he slips and falls off from Brahminhood.

47. He who recites the *ṛk* Mantras everyday, propitiates the deities as if by the offerings of milk *Āhutis*. The contented Devas delight him for ever by granting him his wishes.

48-49. He who regularly recites Yajus Mantras propitiates the deities as if by means of offering of curds. He who recites Sāman verses, everyday, propitiates (the deities as if) by means of the *Āhutis* of clarified butter. He who recites the Atharvāṅgiras verses, propitiates the deities everyday as if by means of oblations of honey. He who reads the Vedāṅgas and the Purāṇas, propitiates devas through meat.

50. A self-controlled person following the injunctions regarding daily religious duties should, after going to the forest and in the vicinity of water (a river, lake etc.), continuously, recite the Gāyatrī Mantra with concentration of mind.[1]

*51. Recitation of the Gāyatrī Mantra for one thousand times is the most excellent, for one hundred times is the medium and for ten times is the minimum. One should always mutter Gāyatrī. This is declared as the *Japa-Yajña* (sacrifice in the form of *Japa*).

52. The lord weighed once the Gāyatrī Mantra and the Vedas by means of a balance. On one side was the Gāyatrī Mantra and on the other side were the four Vedas.

---

1. VV. 50-58 contain instructions about the *Japa* of the Gāyatrī Mantra and its importance. Why this particular verse in ṚV (III. 62.10) came to be valued so much even before the Brāhmaṇa period, is anybody's guess. But even the Atharva Veda (XIX. 71-1) calls it mother of the Vedas (*Vedamātā*). Naturally Brāhmaṇa, Sūtra, Smṛti and Purāṇa works are as if competing with each other in eulogising it. The KP regards : *oṁ bhūḥ bhuvaḥ svaḥ* (*ṣuvaḥ*) *oṁ tat savitur vareṇyam* etc. as the Gāyatrī Mantra for Japa and not the other combinations of *vyāhṛtis* and *padas* given by Āpastamba and others.

*Due to oversight of the Printer, the Veṅkt. Text has omitted the No. 51 and has printed Verse No 51 as 52 and the mistake is carried on to the end.

53. He shall first recite Oṁkāra and thereafter the Vyāhṛtis. Thereafter, he shall recite the Gāyatrī Mantra with full faith and great concentration.

54. The three eternal great Vyāhṛtis, "Bhūḥ, Bhuvaḥ, Svaḥ" originated in the former Kalpa. They quell all inauspiciousness.

55. The three Vyāhṛtis in their order are regarded as follows :

(a) the Pradhāna, Puruṣa and Kāla.
(b) Viṣṇu, Brahmā and Maheśvara,
(c) Sattva, Rajas and Tamas Guṇas.

56. Oṁkāra is that great Brahman, Sāvitrī (i.e. Gāyatrī) is the imperishable one. This Mantra is of great potentiality. It is cited to be the essence of all essences.

57. Strictly observing the vow of celibacy, he who understanding the meaning of the Mantra, repeats Sāvitrī (the Gāyatrī Mantra) attains the greatest of goals.

58. Gāyatrī is the mother of the Vedas. Gāyatrī is the sanctifier of the worlds. There is no greater Japa (Mantra for the purpose of repetition) than the Gāyatrī. After realising this, one is liberated.

59. The rite of *Vedopākarman* (inaugural ceremony of the academic year) is to be performed on the full Moon day of the month of Śrāvaṇa. Excellent Brāhmaṇas, it may be performed on the full moon day in the month of Āṣāḍha or Bhādrapada as well.

60. A Brāhmaṇa should abandon the village and the city for a period of two and a half months. Observing celibacy he should study the Vedas, seated in a clean place, with full concentration and purity of the mind.

61-62. (?) O Brāhmaṇas, the external utsarjana (ritualistic conclusion) of the Chandas (Vedas and metres) should be performed in the month of Pauṣa. Or it may be performed on the first day of the bright half of the month of Māgha in the forenoon. O Brāhmaṇas, the Vedas and the metres are to be propitiated in their respective constellations. A man shall propitiate the Vedāṅgas and the Purāṇas in the dark half of the month.

63. Persons studying the Vedas as well as those who

teach them should avoid the *Anadhyāya*[1] day (holidays) (i.e. they shall not recite the Vedas on those days) as follows.

64-66a. Prajāpati has mentioned that the following occasions must be considered untimely for studies (till the next day) viz. at night if the wind blows with audible sound and during the day if columns of dust are raised : if there is lightning, thunder and rainfall, if there is subversion of great comets.

66b-67a. If there is the loud sound of hurricane, if there is an earthquake and when the luminaries are eclipsed, one should know that these occasions are for discontinuation (i.e. Vedic studies should be stopped) till the next day even in the rainy season.

67b-68a. If, after (sacrificial) fires have been kindled, there is the (roaring sound of) thunder and flashes of the lightning, there will be cessation of the Vedic studies till there is light (visibility). If this occurs out of season (*anṛtau*), there should be complete stoppage of studies that day (?).

68b-69a. For those who are desirous of religious merits and expertise (mastery over the subject), complete cessation of studies, both in the villages and towns, is advised when putrid smell prevails.

69b-70a. (The discontinuation of Vedic studies is prescribed) when a dead body lies in the village, in the vicinity of a Vṛṣala (an outcaste), during the (public) feasting (v.l. wailing) and in a crowd of people.

70b-71a. One should not even mentally think of (Vedic studies) in water, at dead of night, while discharging urine,

1. VV. 63-84 discuss the *anadhyāya* days i.e. the days on which new portion of the Veda should not be taught. This restriction does not apply to non-Vedic texts like Vedāṅgas, Itihāsa, Purāṇas and Dharma-śāstra (verse 82b-83a below)

The subject is discussed extensively in the Dharma (e.g. Āpastamba I.3.94 to 1.3.11), Gṛhya (e.g. Śāṅkhāyana IV. 7) Sūtras, Smṛtis e.g. Manu IV. 102-128) and Purāṇas (e.g. NP. I. 25.45-57). The list of holidays is pretty long. This cessation of Vedic studies was due to personal impurity (Āśauca) and impurity of the place (Tait. Ār. II. 15) and time like certain *tithis*, occasions like eclipse, natural disturbances like storms. But they did not affect much the progress of studies as the restrictions were not applicable to non-Vedic studies.

and faeces, one is defiled by remnants of food and one who has partaken of Śrāddha food.

71b-72a. A learned Brāhmaṇa should not repeat Vedic Mantras for these days. After accepting the invitation for the *Ekoddiṣṭaśrāddha* (funeral dinner), when the king has *Sūtaka* (i.e. impurity due to birth or death of relatives) and when there is Rāhu's *Sūtaka* (i.e. Eclipse), he shall not recite Vedic passages for three days.

72b-73a. As long as the viscidity and smell of the *Ekoddiṣṭa Śrāddha* (the funeral dinner for one forbear) in the big body of the (v.l. learned) Brāhmaṇa remains, he shall not recite Vedic mantras. A person lying down or keeping the legs lifted up or sitting down with a cloth girt round the knees shall not repeat the Vedas.

73b. A Brāhmaṇa should not study the Vedas in a supine position or sitting with feet raised or sitting with a cloth girt round the knees.

74-75a. One shall not study the Vedas after eating meat or the food offered by persons with impurity. When there is fog, when the arrows are discharged and during the two Sandhyās (dawn and dusk), on the new moon day, full moon day, Caturdaśī (fourteenth) and Aṣṭamī (eighth) days, Vedic Mantras are not repeated (for study purpose).

75b-76a. The cessation of Vedic studies for three days is prescribed at the time of *Upākarma* (beginning of the academic session) and *Utsarga,* and for one day on the *Aṣṭakā* days and last day (lit. night) of the seasons.

76b-77a. There are three *Aṣṭaka* days mentioned by learned men. They fall on the eighth day during the dark half of the months of Mārgaśīrṣa, Pauṣa and Māgha. (The Aṣṭakā days are *Anadhyāya* days).

77b-78a. One should not carry on Vedic study in the shade of the following trees viz. : Śleṣmātaka (*cordia Latifolia*), Śālmali (silk-cotton), Madhuka (*Baslia Latifolia*), Kovidāra (*Bauhinia Variegula*) and Kapittha (Feronia Elepthantum).

78b-79a. There is impurity for three days when a colleague or a fellow student or the preceptor dies. These days that are called *Anadhyāyas* are holes (vulnerable points) for Brāhmaṇas.

79b-81a. The Rākṣasas attack at those points. Hence, one shall avoid these (Anadhyāyas). In regard to Nitya rites and the worship of the Sandhyās, Upākarma (initial ceremony of Vedic studies after the monsoon), for completing a performance already commenced and *Homa* recitals, there is no *Anadhyāya*.

81b-82a. When the wind is very strongly blowing on the Aṣṭakā days, one may recite one Mantra out of the Ṛgveda or Yajurveda or Sāmaveda.

82b-83. There is no Anadhyāya in the case of the study of Vedāṅgas, Itihāsas, Purāṇas and other Dharma Śāstras. But Parvan days should be avoided. Thus the holy rites and duties of the religious students have been succinctly explained.

84a. Formerly, this had been recounted by god Brahmā to the sages of purified souls.

84b-85a. O Brāhmaṇa, a person who does not learn the Vedas but continues his efforts in other fields in foolish. He is out of the Vedic fold. He should not be talked to by the twice-born people.

85b-86a. An excellent Brāhmaṇa will not be contented merely by reading the Vedic texts. One who is devoid of practice (in accordance with the tenets of the Vedas) becomes dejected and dispirited like a cow stuck up in mud.

86b-87a. If the disciple wishes to remain with his teacher for ever, he should practise Yoga and serve him till the death, for he may go to the forest and perform Homa into the fire, as per prescribed method.[1]

87b-88. He who has duly learned the Vedic texts but does not ponder over the meanings of the passage, is blind. He is like a Śūdra. He does not understand the real meanings of the words.

89. With absolute faith in the Veda, he should always study Veda with concentration of mind. Strictly adhering to

1. VV. 86-89 refer to life-long celibates. Śabara on Jaimini I.3.3 remarks that such perpetual celibacy is not approved by Śruti. But Viṣṇu as (quoted by SMC I. P. 63) allows it to abnormal people who are not entitled to Vedic rites.

(the procedure of) *Bhasma-Snāna* (smearing of the holy ashes all over the body), he should be always self controlled and study especially *Sāvitrī* (the Gāyatrī Mantra) *Śatarudrīya* and the ancillaries of the Veda (like phonetics, prosody, grammar and others).

90. These injuctions are great and ancient ones. They have been well recounted in the Vedic treatises. This procedure is ancient and is in perfect accord with what is given in the Vedas. This is what lord Svāyambhuva Manu explained in days of old, when he was requested by great and excellent sages.

91. He who dedicates himself to Īśvara and performs all duties in accordance with the injunctions shall ward off all the shackles of delusion and attain immortality. He shall attain the auspicious region devoid of ailment.

CHAPTER FIFTEEN

The Duties of The Householder[1]

Vyāsa said :

I. O excellent Brāhmaṇas, a Brāhmaṇa should obtain (i.e. learn well), one, two or all the four Vedas. After studying them and comprehending the meanings, he should perform the ablution (signifying the conclusion of the period of religious studentship).

---

1. The stage of householder being the main stay of the subsistence of other *āśramas* (stages) in life, has been considered as the best Āśrama at least since the old Sūtra period (Gautama III. 3, Manu III. 77-78, Mbh. Śānti. 270.6-7). Hence the duties (*dharmas*) of householders are discussed in details in Smṛtis, Purāṇas and digests on Dharma-śāstra. For example vide Manu IV. 33 ff. Yājña-Valkya I.96-127, NP. I. 26.3-27, VP. III. 9.7-16, Pd. P. Svarga 54.2-42, SMC, Parāśara-Mādhava (ācārakāṇḍa) and others.

2. After giving the fees to the preceptor, he should perform the (concluding) ablution with his (*guru's*) permission.[1] One who is self-possessed and has performed all the rites (prescribed vows of Brahmacarya) becomes capable and hence deserves the the holy ablution.

3. He should hold the staff of bamboo. He should wear the undercloth and the upper garment. He should have two sacred threads, a water-pot (Kamaṇḍalu) with water.[2]

4. He should have an umbrella, an immaculately clean turban, sandals and shoes and golden earing and the Veda. He should be cleanly shaven, with nails clipped and thus shall be scrupulously clean.

5. He should continuously be engaged in the self-study of the Vedas. He should not wear garland outside. A Brāhmaṇa shall not wear a red garland except that of Kāñcana flowers.

6. He should wear white garments every day. He should use perfumes and appear neat and pleasing. If he has enough means, he should not wear old dirty clothes.

7. He should not wear red clothes or those of gaudy colours. Nor should he use the following things used by others : The cloth, the water-pot, leather shoes, garland sandals.

8. (He should not wear the following used by others, viz.: the sacred thread, ornaments as well as the skin of a black antelope. He should not wear the garment in the *apasavya* way (on the right shoulder and below the left arm) nor should he wear a loathsome garments.

9. He should duly marry a girl similar to him (in caste ?) of auspicious characteristics, beauty and features and suitable to him, she should not have any defect in her reproductory organs.

10. A Brāhmaṇa should accept as wife a girl who is not

The highest compliment paid to this Āśrama is by the ancient Sūtrakāras Gautama III.1 & 35 and Baudhāyana (Dh. S. II.6.29.42-43) who emphatically state that this is the only one real Āśrama (*aikāśramyaṁ tvācāryāḥ*)

1. Āśvalāyana Gr. S. III. 9.4.

2. VV. 3-8 deal with *Snātaka-dharmas* (duties of those who completed their studies and desire to be householders *vide* Manu IV 34 ff.

born in the *gotra* of his mother[1] and should be born in the *gotra* dissimilar to his sage (his gotra) and who is endowed with purity (cleanliness) and good character.

11. He should go unto his wife only on those nights (sanctioned by scripture) after the monthly menses till the conception of a son. He shall scrupulously avoid the forbidden days.

12. He shall observe the vow of celibacy and control over his senses on the sixth, eighth, twelfth, fourteenth and fifteenth days of the lunar fortnight.

13. He should maintain the *Āvasathya* fire (i.e. one of the five sacred fires to be kept in the house and used in sacrifices). He shall perform Homa in the sacrificial fire. A Snātaka (house-holder) should observe all holy vows.

14. He should actively perform everyday his duty as ordained by the Vedas. By not doing so, he immediately becomes fallen and goes to terrible hells.

15. Pure in body and mind, he should daily practise the recitation of the Vedas. He should perform the holy rites as mentioned in the *Gṛhyasūtras* as well as the *Sandhyā* worship.

16. He should cultivate friendship with persons of equal and superior status. He should always worship Īśvara. He shall attain the blessings of deities. He should bedeck his wife with ornaments.

17. He should not loudly proclaim his religious acts nor should he conceal his sinful activities; he should always do those things that increase his welfare and be sympathetic towards all living beings.[2]

18. He should always perform activities and speech suitable to and becoming in accordance with his age, duties, learning, nobility of birth, intellect and the Vedic injunctions.

19. He should resort to that way of life which has been invariably followed by good men, and ordained by the Śrutis and the Smṛtis. He should not wish for anything contrary to it.

20. That path through which one's fathers and grandfathers have gone should be followed by one. That is the path

---

1. This shows that the author is probably a north-Indian or a Mādhyandin.

2. In fact VV. 17 onward form a part of *Sadācāra*.

of the good. Going by that path, one shall cross the ocean of worldly existence.

21. He should regularly recite passages from (one's branch of) the Vedas. He should always wear the sacred thread. One who is truthful in speech and who has conquered anger, deserves to realise Brahman.

22. He who is interested in the performance of ablutions and Sandhyā-prayers everyday, who is devoted to Brahma-Yajña rite; the householder who is not malicious, who is soft and self-controlled, flourishes in heaven after death.

23. A householder devoid of passion, fear and fury, who is free from covetousness and delusion, who performs *Śrāddhas* and who is always engaged in the *Japa* of the Śāvitrī Mantra, is liberated.

24. He who is engaged in the welfare of his parents, is interested in the well-being of cows and Brāhmaṇas, has his senses subjected, performs Yajñas and is a devotee of Devas, is honoured in the Brahmaloka.

25. He should always be engaged in the realisation of the three aims of life (Virtue, love and wealth), should perform worship of the deities; he shall be pure in the mind and body and bow to the gods everyday.

26. One cannot be called a *Gṛhastha* (householder) merely because one has a house to live in. He who temperamentally always shares everything with others, is endowed with forgiveness and mercy, deserves to be called a householder.

27. These are the characteristic features of a Brāhmaṇa viz: forbearance, mercy, perfect knowledge, truthfulness, mental control and control over the sense-organs and interest in the spiritual knowledge.

28. An excellent Brāhmaṇa specially shall not err from all these. He should perform his duties in accordance with his capacity; and shall avoid all prohibited and censured activities.

29. No one need entertain any doubt for the fact that if a householder, eschewing the confused state of delusion, attains the excellent Yoga, he is liberated from the bondage of Saṁsāra.

30. Forbearance is the ability to endure the defects originating from others' anger, such as censure, transgression, defiance, violence, imprisonment and killing.

31. The sages say that kindness is that mercifulness due to friendship (gentleness of heart) in regard to miseries of others in the same way as (in the case of) one's own miseries. It is a direct means of Dharma (piety).

32. The actual retention in memory of the fourteen lores should be known as *Vijñāna* (perfect knowledge. It is thereby that Dharma flourishes.

33. If, after duly studing the Vedas and comprehending the meanings, one is averse to religious activities, that (which he has acquired) is not considered to be *Vijñāna* (perfect knowledge).

34. One conquers the worlds through *Satya* (Truth); Truth is the excellent region. Learned men explain that the narration in the same order in which something has happened is truthfulness.

35. *Dama* is the subjugation of the body. *Śama* originates from the clarity of intellect. *Adhyātma* (spirituality should be known as that imperishable attainment which one does not regret.

36. That learning whereby the supreme lord Mahādeva himself is known, is glorified as Jñāna (knowledge).

37. The learned person who is absolutcly devoted to him, wise, always free from anger and pure, is interested in (the five) "great sacrifices, becomes one with that supreme Deity.

38. One should maintain one's physical body with great effort as it is the abode of Dharma. Without one's physical body, Rudra, the greatest lord, cannot be known by men.

39. A Brāhmaṇa should invariably be engaged in Dharma (Virtue), Artha (Wealth) and Kāma (Love). He should never mentally conceive of that type of love or wealth which is devoid of Dharma.

40. Even if one perishes due to practice of Virtue, one should never take to Adharma. Dharma is the Lord himself. It is the goal of all creatures.

41. One shall always be pleasing to all living beings, he should never think of doing acts of injury against others. One

should never censure the Vedas nor the deities. One should not even associate with those people (who do so).

42. The pure Brāhmaṇa who invariably reads this chapter on Dharma, teaches it or narrates it (to others) is honoured in the Brahmaloka.

CHAPTER SIXTEEN

The Duties of the House Holder[1]
Rules of Good Conduct

Vyāsa said :

1. One should not injure any living being. On no occasion should he speak falsehood. One shall not speak unpalatable and unwholesome things. One should by no means be a thief.

2. The person who steals properties of others even if they be a blade of grass, a lump of clay, a plant or water, falls into the hell.

3. One should not accept monetary gifts from a fallen king, Śūdra or any other person. A learned man should avoid being a suppliant in front of a blameworthy person.

4. One should never be a beggar; (if one has to beg) one should not beg the same person twice. This evil-minded beggar will deprive him of his life there-by.

---

1. The 'duties' of householders are described in numerous works on Dharma-Śāstra—Dharma Sūtras (e.g. Āpastamba II. 1-11, Vasiṣṭha VIII. 1-17, XI. 1-48), Smṛtis (e.g. Manu IV, Yājñavalkya I.96-127), *Mbh-Anuśāsana* ch. 97, Purāṇas (e.g. Bh. P. VII. Ch. 11, XI. Ch. 17, NP. I. Ch. 43) and digests (e. g. SMC-I. pp. 88-282, Smṛtyarthasāra, pp. 18-48). A number of these verses prescribing 'Do's' and 'Don'ts' are actually *subhāṣitās* current among the ancient Indians as a number of these are common to Pāli and Prākrits. These verses shed light on the customs, manners, prejudices etc. of the people of those times.

The Daily duties (*Āhnika*) of a householder are described in Ch. XVIII.

5. O excellent Brāhmaṇas, he should not be one who misappropriates especially the properties of the deity. Even in emergency, he should never take away the wealth of a Brāhmaṇa.

6. They say that poison is not dangerous but the property of a Brāhmaṇa or that of the deity is the real poison. Hence one should scrupulously avoid these assets.

7. Manu, the Prajāpati, has said that the taking of any of these things, though not handed over to one (by the owner), is not stealing viz. flowers, greens, water, firewood, roots, fruits and grass.

8-9. Flowers can be taken by Brāhmaṇas at the time of the worship of the Lord. If they are taken without permission, they should not be taken from one single person. A sensible man should take away grass, firewood, fruits and flowers openly. They must be taken only for the purpose of a religious rite. Otherwise he will face downfall.

10. O Brāhmaṇas, if deeply afflicted by hunger on the way while travelling, a handful of gingelly seeds, green gram, barley and other articles may be taken (even without the permission of the owner) by persons knowing Dharma. They should not do so otherwise. This is the established conventional practice.

11-12. Under the pretext of a holy vow, one should not commit sins and perform holy rites. A Brāhmaṇa who conceals his sins by means of holy rites and depends on womenfolk and Śūdras, is despised here and hereafter by the expounders of the Brahman. A Vrata (holy rite) performed under a false pretext goes to the Rākṣasas.

13. If a non-liṅgin (a person who is not a Sannyāsin or Brahmacārin) maintains himself in the guise of a liṅgin (ascetic) he shall incur the sins of those persons and shall be born as a lower animal.

14. The religious hypocrites and impostors are the worst sinners in the world. They are the destroyers of Dharma. The fruit of their action is that they sink into sins immediately.

15. One should not even verbally revere and honour the heretics, those who indulge in wrong actions, those who perform black magic, the Pañcarātras and the Pāśupatas.

16. One should not even mentally think of those people who censure the Vedas, Devas and the Brāhmaṇas.

17. The creature (person) who officiates in their sacrifice, has matrimonial alliance with them, who talks to them and who stays along with them faces downfall. Hence, he should avoid it scrupulously.

18. Incurring the displeasure of the preceptor is a crore of times worse than incurring the displeasure of Devas. Censuring of perfect knowledge and atheism is a crore of times worse than that.

19. Those families which become devoid of Dharma through (sale-purchase of) cows, (paid service of) deities, and priesthood, agriculture, king's service sink to a lower status.

20. Families decline in prosperity through these evil activities viz.—contracting despicable marriages, non-performance of holy rites, non-study of the Vedas as well as by slighting the Brāhmaṇas.

21. A family perishes immediately due to uttering falsehoods, committing adultery, eating forbidden foodstuffs and by not performing the holy rites enjoined by the Śrutis.

22. Indeed, a family perishes quickly by making charitable gifts to those who are not well-read (in the Vedas) as well as to Vṛṣalas (Śūdras), who do not strictly follow the regulations of the conduct of life.

23. One shall never stay in a village surrounded by unrighteous persons or afflicted by many pestilences. One shall never stay in the kingdom of a Śūdra, or in a place inhabited by heretics.

24. A Brāhmaṇa should not stay in any other place except in the land between the mountains Himavān and the Vindhya and between the Eastern and Western oceans.

25. A Brāhmaṇa may reside in a land naturally frequented by black-antelope or inundated by holy and well-known rivers.

26. An excellent Brāhmaṇa shall not stay anywhere else except within half a *Krośa* of the holy river (1 Krośa = 3 Km). He shall not stay near the village of the Śūdras.

27. He should not live in the same place with that of fallen castes, Cāṇḍālas, Pukkasas, foolish fellows, arrogant

persons, Śūdras and the people of the lowliest castes called *Antyāvasāyins*.

28-29. The following eleven defects caused by mingling of the castes are called sins of intermixture (*Sāṁkarya Doṣas*) viz.—sharing the same bed, sharing a common seat, sitting in the same row, sharing of the same vessel, partaking of the cooked food together, presiding over the sacrifices, teaching, marriage alliance, taking of food together, studying together, and jointly presiding over the sacrifices.

30. Even by staying near-by the sin is transmitted from one man to another. Hence a sensible man shall scrupulously avoid intermingling of the castes.

31. If the people sitting in the same row do not touch one another and if ashes mark their boundary, there is no Saṁkara defect.

32. The row can be separated by means of these six :— fire, ashes, water, door, pillar and a pathway.

33. One should not pursue enmity that ends in sorrow, nor indulge in argument, nor in back-biting. Nor should one communicate to others if a cow is grazing in another man's field (!)

34. One shall not have social intercourse with a person having the impurity due to birth. One shall not touch the vulnerable points of others. One shall not indicate and mention to others the eclipse of the sun nor the rainbow nor the fire (consuming) the dead body.

35. A learned man shall never indicate and mention the moon. No man should ever incur the antagonism of the majority at the same time.

36. One should not do unto others what is unfavourable (or displeasing) to himself. He should not mention the Tithi (the serial number of that day in a lunar fortnight) of the fortnight nor should he point out the constellations (?)

37. An excellent Brāhmaṇa should not speak to a woman in her monthly course or to an unclean person. No one should prevent anything from being given to Devas, preceptors or Brāhmaṇas.

38. No one should praise himself. One should avoid censuring others. One should scrupulously avoid blaspheming Devas and the Vedas.

39. O great sages, no atonement is seen ordained in the scriptures in the case of a Brāhmaṇa who censures Devas, sages, Brāhmaṇas or the Vedas.

40. If a man loudly decries or censures the preceptors, Devas or the Vedas, he shall be cooked in the hell Raurava for hundreds of crores of Kalpas and even more.

41. If anyone rebukes or censures, it is better that one keeps quiet without saying anything by way of reply (and still better) he should close his ears and go away. He should not stop even to glance at them.

42. A sensible man should guard the secrets of others and refrain from divulging them. He should never enter into argument with his own kinsmen.

43. O excellent Brāhmaṇas, no one should call a sinner either a sinner or a sinless person. (In either case) he will be equally guilty of sins such as that of uttering falsehood.

44. The tears shed by those (innocent) persons who are falsely accused and so cry, destroy the sons and animals of those false accusers.

45. A way of expiation is mentioned by good men in the cases of Brāhmaṇa slaughter, addiction to wine, stealing and committing adultery with the preceptor's wife. But there is no atonement for false accusation.

46. One should not see the rising sun or the moon without cause. He should not see them setting, reflected in the water, stationed in the middle of the sky or under eclipse.

47. He should not see (the sun or the moon) covered with a cloth (i.e. screened by a cloth), nor reflected in a mirror. No one should even see a naked woman or a man.

48. No one should see anyone passing urine or discharging faeces or a couple in the act of copulation. No sensible man shall glance at the planets, the sun, the moon etc. while he is unclean.

49. One should not glance at a fallen person (outcaste) a maimed person, a Cāṇḍāla or a Person defiled by *ucchiṣṭa*. If

one is defiled by *Ucchiṣṭa* (or veiled) one should not glance at others arrogantly.*

50. One should not touch a person who has touched a dead body. One should not look at the face of the angry preceptor. One should not see one's reflection in oil or water; one should not touch one's wife during dinner or while her limbs are exposed due to untying of knot; one should not look at a mad and elated person.

51. One should not take food along with one's wife. Nor should one look at one's own wife urinating, sneezing or yawning, nor shall one see her cosily seated at ease.

52. One should not look out one's own reflection in water; one should not jump from one bank to another; one should not jump across a deep pit; one should never tread over urine or stand on it.

53. One should not impart intellect (i.e. topics of lore) to a Śūdra. Nor shall these things be given to him viz.—The *Kṛśara* (rice cooked with gingelly seeds), the milk-pudding, curds; nor the leavings *Ucchiṣṭa*), ghee, honey, black-antelope hide or *Havis* (sacrificial offerings).

54. Instructions regarding observance of holy vows should not be given to a Śūdra: a learned man should not expound Dharma unto him. No one should submit to anger and avoid hatred and passion.

55. Covetousness and arrogance should be avoided. One should avoid ridiculing religious travels and scorning perfect knowledge. One should desist from haughtiness and delusion, fury and hatred.

56. One should not inflict pain on anyone : one may however beat his son and disciple. One should never serve the mean and the base nor should he serve sharp-witted persons.

57. One should not dishonour oneself (the *Ātman*) ; one should scrupulously avoid dejectedness, (or should try to conceal one's miserable condition), one should not fail to honour one who is not one's disciple (?), a learned man should not praise himself.

---

*v.l. *avaguṇṭhitaḥ* 'veiled'.

58. One should not scribble on the ground with the nails; one shall not cohabit (or lie) with a cow (?) ; one should not speak of (another river while bathing in one) river nor should he speak (in praise of) other mountains while resting on one mountain (?)

59. One should not abandon a fellow traveller whether one stays with him overnight or not; one should not enter water in the nude state; nor should he walk over fire.

60. One should not anoint the limbs with the oil left over after applying it over the head; one should not play with weapons or serpents; one should not touch (i.e. scrape) the private parts of one's body (with a weapon).

61-62. (One shall not touch) the hairs on the private parts; one should not travel in the company of an uncultured fellow; one should not (warm) hands and feet in the fire, one should not indulge in unsteady act of the penis, belly and ears. One should not scratch oneself with nails. One should not drink water with palms joined together.

63. One should not keep water (in tanks or rivers) with the leg or strike it with the hand; one should not fell down fruits by hurling bricks or other fruits at them.

64-65. One should not learn the language (mode of speech) of the alien tribe; one should not drag a seat by means of the leg; one should not create dissension (among friends). One should not crack the finger joints or snap the fingers; one should not cut or scrape aimlessly. The sensible man should not thrash suddenly or aimlessly. One should not keep food on the lap while eating; one should not indulge in purposeless movements of the limbs.

66. One should neither dance, nor sing, nor play on musical instruments. One should not scratch one's head with all the fingers joined together.

67. One should not try to propitiate the deities with worldly hymns or medicine; one should not play with dice; one should not rush against others for assaulting them (?) ; one should not urinate or discharge faeces into water.

68. One should not cohabit when defiled by *Ucchiṣṭa*; one should not bathe in the nude: one should not read or touch one's head, while walking.

69. One should not cut the hairs or nails by means of the teeth; one should not waken the sleeper. One should not bask in the early morning sun; one should avoid smoke arising from the dead body.

70. One should not sleep alone in an empty abode; one should not bring shoes by oneself (with the hands ?). One should not spit without reason; one should not cross the river by means of the arms.

71. A learned man should not wash legs with the legs; one should not warm legs in the fire; one should not wash (his feet) in a bellmetal vessel.

72. One should not extend his feet towards the idols of gods, the Brāhmaṇas or the cow, the wind, the fire, the preceptor, the Brahmins, the sun or the moon.

73. By no means should an unclean person go to bed, travel, study the Vedas, take food without bathing or set out from the house.

74. One should avoid the following during the two *Sandhyās* (dawn and dusk) as well as at midday :—sleeping, study of the Vedas, travelling, excrement, taking food and walking.

75. A Brāhmaṇa defiled by *Ucchiṣṭa* shall not touch cows, Brāhmaṇas and the fire, with the hand, nor should he touch cooked rice or the divine idol with the foot.

76. No unclean person should circumambulate the fire: nor should he glorify the gods or the sages; one should not enter deep waters; one shall not hold fire on one side (?)

77. One should not drink water by lifting it up with the left hand and nor shall he drink with the mouth directly; one shall not reply (when impure) without performing the *Ācamana* rite; nor should one discharge semen virile into the water.

78. One should not cast into water any other thing smeared with *Amedhya* (filth, rubbish), blood or poisons. One should not cross a river; one should not indulge in sexual intercourse in water.

79. One should not chop off the trees in a monastery; one should not spit into water; one should not tread on bone, ashes, skulls, hair, thorn, burning charcoal or dry balls of cowdung.

80. No sensible man should cross the burning fire, nor should he keep it anywhere beneath; No sensible man should kick it with the leg nor blow it with the mouth.

81. One should not descend into the well; an unclean person should never look into a well; one should not throw fire into fire, nor extinguish it with water.

82. No one should himself tell others about the distress or death of a friend; one should not utilise for sale any article or merchandise which is unsaleable (due to its quality).

83. No sensible man, if unclean, should kindle fire by means of wind blown from the mouth; He should plough (i.e. transgress*) a land in a holy centre, near water or on the border (of a village ?).

84. One shall not break an earlier agreement accompanied by a promise; no one should rouse up animals, serpents or birds (?)

85. One should not inconvenience others through watersheds etc., one should not cause the artisans etc. to do great jobs and then forsake them. One should keep the doors of the house shut in the morning and in the evening to prevent the beggars.

86. One should avoid outside (over his dress) garland, alien scents, dining in the company of one's wife, argument with quarrels and entry by the bad way ?

87. A Brāhmaṇa should not stand up while eating. A sensible man should not spend much time prattling and laughing. One should not touch the fire with the hand; one should not stay too long under water.

88. One should not kindle the fire by generating the wind with a wing, a winnowing basket or the hand. He should blow the air with his mouth and kindle the fire. (It is said in the Vedas) that Agni was born of his mouth.

89. One shall not speak to another man's wife. No Brāhmaṇa should perform the Yajña on behalf of one not worthy of it. One should not enter an assembly singly. One should avoid a crowd of Brāhmaṇas; one should never go to the shrine of a deity in an anti-clockwise direction.

*Ft. note 7 in the Venk. Text.

90. One should not fan with the cloth, one should not sleep in a temple; one should not undertake a journey alone; nor should he travel with unrighteous people.

91. One should not undertake a journey in the company of persons defiled by sickness, or of Śūdras or of fallen men (out-caste). One should never travel without shoes or without taking water and other requisites.

92. At night one should not travel in the company of one's enemy. One should not travel without a waterpot. One should not go between fires, Brāhmaṇas, cows etc.

93. O excellent Brāhmaṇas, one should not transgress a woman longing for sexual intercourse. One should not censure Siddhas, Yogins and ascetics of good qualities.

94. In the temple and in the presence of *devas*, one should not wantonly tread on the shadow of the Brāhmaṇas and the cows.

95. One should not let one's own shadow to be tread on by sick persons, fallen people or others. One should never stand on burning coal or ashes or hair or similar things.

96. O Brāhmaṇas, one should avoid the dust particles rising from the broom and the water that remains in a pot after washing clothes or taking bath. Forbidden foodstuffs should not be eaten nor should one drink impotable water.

CHAPTER SEVENTEEN

Decision about Acceptable and Prohibited Food[1]

Vyāsa said :

1. A Brāhmaṇa should not eat food offered by a Śūdra whether out of delusion or otherwise. He who eats it, except in an emergency, is born as a Śūdra.

1. Great importance has been attached to purity of food since ancient times. Chāndogya Up. (vii. 26.2) emphasizes the purity of food as it is conducive to the remembrance or meditation of the Ātman. The Smṛtis deal extensively with this topic. So do Mbh. *Anuśāsana* chs. 135 and 136 and Purāṇas like Bm. P. 221-109-112 Bv. P. I. 27. 3-45 and others.

2. The Brāhmaṇa who partakes of the condemned food of a Śūdra for six months becomes a Śūdra even while he is alive, and after death he becomes a dog (*v.l.* as a Śūdra).

3. O leading sages, a person is reborn as a Brāhmaṇa, a Kṣatriya, a Vaiśya or a Śūdra according as the food offered by these is still in his belly when he dies, (e.g. he dies with the food of a Brāhmaṇa in his stomach, he is reborn as a Brāhmaṇa, so on).

4. One should avoid the cooked food of six groups of people viz. : the actor, the dancer, the carpenter, the smith, a gang of rogues and the prostitute.[1]

5. One should avoid food offered by an oil-monger, washerman, thief and the vendor of spirituous liquors. He should avoid the food of a minstrel, a blacksmith or an impure person.

6. He should avoid the food offered by a potter, a painter, a usurer, a fallen man, a goldsmith, a dancer, a hunter, an imprisoned fellow or an ailing person.

Vṛddha-Hārita XI. 122-123 and Bs. P. as quoted by Aparārka (P. 241) give the following classification of "pollutions" and hence prohibition of food articles:

1. *Jāti-duṣṭa* 'inherently or by nature polluted' e.g. onions, garlic.
2. *Kriyā-duṣṭa* 'polluted by action' e.g. served with bare hands, seen by a dog or an out-caste.
3. *Kāla-duṣṭa*—'polluted by passage of or inappropriateness of time." e.g. stale food, eating during solar or lunar eclipse.
4. *Saṁsarga-duṣṭa* 'polluted by contact' e.g. contacted with a dog, insects or wine.
5. *Sahṛllekha* 'disgusting to the mind' e.g. faeces.
6. *Parigraha-duṣṭa* 'polluted due to its belonging to an undesirable person' e.g. an out-caste.

The intake of 'polluted' food being a sin, the topic is treated in details by Dharma-Śāstra-writers of old. (vide KP. 17-15b and 16a below).

The KP does not deal exhaustively with this topic.

1. VV. 4-15 give the list of persons food from whom is not acceptable. That food is *Parigraha-duṣṭa* as explained above. The belief was that the eater of that food eats up the sins also of the giver (vide v. 16a below).

We find this belief and the list of such polluters in the Dharma Sūtras of Āpastamba (I. 6. 18. 16-33), Vasiṣṭha 14. 2-11 and in old Smṛtis like Manu IV 205-220 Yāj. I. 160-165.

7. He should avoid the food offered by a physician, an unchaste woman, a staff-bearer (a police-man ?), a thief, an atheist or a person who blasphemes gods.

8. One should avoid the food offered by a person who sells Soma juice and especially of Cāṇḍāla. He should avoid food offered by one who is hen-pecked or one who allows the paramour of his wife to remain in his house.

9. One should avoid taking these cooked-stuff, viz.; that of one who is defiled by *Ucchiṣṭa*, that of miser, that of one who partakes of the leaving of others' food-stuffs, the cooked food of a person who is inferior—not worth allowing to sit in row for dinner, the cooked food meant for a multitude and that of one who maintains himself by means of weapons.

10. One should avoid food offered by an ascetic, by a eunuch, the food of an insane or a drunkard fellow, of a frightened one or a crying person, the food that is of inferior quality and that offered as charitable gift.

11. One should avoid food offered in *Śrāddha* or, offered by an hater of Brāhmaṇas, one who is interested in sins and a man who is defiled by the impurity of birth (sūtaka, the food of one who cooks in vain (?) the food of a rogue and that of the shrewd fellow, (v.l. father-in-law).

12. One should avoid the cooked food of all these:—viz: women without children, a servant, a mason and one who sells weapons.

13. The cooked food served by these should be avoided-one who is addicted to drinking wine, a murderer, the physician, one whose organ of generation is mutilated and person who, though a younger brother, married earlier than the elder brother.

14. One should particularly avoid the food served by a widowed woman who has remarried, nor should he partake of the food served by one who carnally enjoys the wife of his dead brother. Similarly, he should avoid partaking of the food served with contempt or anger, spurning, dislike or arrogance or astonishment.

15. Even the cooked food served by the preceptor should not be eaten if it is devoid of due consecration. All the evil deeds of man are stabilised in his food.

16-17. If a person partakes of the food of anyone he shares his sins too. The following persons viz. : A farm-labourer, a friend of the family, cowherd, barber, musician, potter, ploughman of the fields. After eating food among these Śūdras, some money is given to them by the wise. The following things can be taken on payment, from a Śūdra[1] viz.:—Milk pudding, articles fried in oil, Milk products, Saktu (Powdered fried grain), oilcake and oil.

18-23. One should avoid these plants:[2] *Vṛntāka* (a kind of Brinjal), *Jālikāśāka* (a kind of green), the Safflower, the *Aśmantaka* (the plant) the fibres of which are used to make the girdle (*Mekhalā*) of a Brāhmaṇa. He should avoid onion, garlic, sour articles and thick exudations from trees. He should avoid *Chatraka* (Mushroom), Viḍvarāha (a plant growing in filth), śaila (Śleṣmāntaka fruit ?), beestings, *Vilaya* (a milk product ? *Simukha* and *Kavaka* (Mushrooms). A Brāhmaṇa eating Gṛñjana (the meat of an animal killed by a poisoned arrow), a fowl, the gourds, the Kiṃśuka, the Udumbara etc. undergoes downfall. One must scrupulously avoid (purposelessly prepared i.e. not for offering to deity), the *Kṛśara* (rice cooked with gingelly seeds), the wheatcake, Milk pudding, pie, cooked meat but not consecrated, food offerings to gods, *Yavāgu* (rice gruel), *Mātuliṅga* (Citrons), non-consecrated fish, the Kadamba tree, wood-apple and Plakṣa (Indian fig tree). During daytime* he should avoid

---

**divadhana* is probably a mistake for *deva-dhānya* 'God's grain', recorded as v.l.

1. VV. 16-17 give the list of Śūdras whose food was acceptable to Brāhmaṇas, cf.

su (*sva-*) *dāso nāpito gopaḥ kumbhakāraḥ kṛṣīvalaḥ* /
Brāhmaṇairapi bhojyānnāḥ pañcaite śūdra-yonayaḥ //
—Devala Smṛ.

also Cf. Parāśara Smṛ. XI. 20-24

In fact realities of life forced the Dharma-śāstra to accept these exceptions.

2. VV. 18-23 contains the list of articles of food, vegetables, herbs etc. which were by their nature regarded as 'polluted' and are known as *Jāti-duṣṭa*.

The list of 'polluted' herbs, vegetables etc. is found in old works like the Dh. s. of Āpastamba (I. 5. 17. 25-27) Vasiṣṭha 14.33. KP. assimilated the following verses from Manu V. 5-7, 12, 14, 19.

the oilcake from which oil has been extracted as well as fried barley.

24. During night, he should scrupulously avoid everything connected with gingelly seeds as well as curds. One should not take in milk and butter milk together.

25. One should avoid food polluted by action, served indifferently (bhāva-duṣṭa) and polluted by bad contact (as with dogs) and by falling therein of hair, insects and disrespectfully given.[1]

26. One shall avoid an article once smelt by a dog and cooked again. So also the article seen by a Cāṇḍāla, or a woman in her menses, or smelt by a cow, or seen by fallen men, shall be avoided.

27-28a. He should avoid these articles as well—that with which no worship has been performed, that which is stale, that which has been touched by crows and fowls, that which is infested by germs, that which is smelt by men or touched by a leper.

28b-30a. One should not make use of any article given by a women in her menses, or by an unchaste woman, or by a woman angrily. Manu has said that the milk of a cow whose calf has died should not be drunk. Similarly, the milk of a camel, within ten days of her calving, shall not be drunk. So also the milk of a ewe and that of a cow milked unseasonably.[2]

30b-33. The following birds and animals shall not be eaten viz.[3] the crane, the swan, the watercrow, the sparrow, the parrot, the osprey, the tusk of a hog, the webfooted birds, the cuckoo, the *Cāṣa* (blue jay), the Khañjarīṭa (the wag-tail), the falcon, the vulture, the owl, the ruddy goose, the cock, the dove, the pigeons, the Tiṭṭibha (lapwing), the village fowl, the

---

1. VV. 25 ff give the list of *Kriyā-duṣṭa* foods.

2. *Sandhinī*—Mitākṣarā on Yāj. I. 17—explains it as (i) a cow in heat (2) a cow that gives milk once a day (3) a cow which yields milk on account of another calf brought to it, its own being dead.

3. Dharma Sūtras give a number of rules about the flesh of beasts, birds and fish, *vide.* Gautama 17. 27-31, 34-35 Viṣṇu 51.6, 29-31. Smṛtis like Manu v. 12-14 Yāj. I. 172-175 give long lists of such birds etc. fit to be eaten. KP based its list on the Smṛtis.

lion, the tiger, the cat, the dog, the hound, the jackal, the monkey and the donkey.

34a. All types of deer should not be eaten nor should wild birds be eaten whether the living beings move about in the water or on the land. This is the established convention.

34b-35a- Manu the Prajāpati has said that these five-clawed animals[1] may be eaten viz. Godhā (alligator), *Kūrma* (tortoise), Śaśa (hare), Śvaviț and Sallaki (the small and the big porcupine).

35b-36a. O excellent men, one may eat those fish with thorny scales (?) and the flash of the deer Ruru. They can be eaten after offering them to the deities and the Brāhmaṇas and not otherwise.

36b-37a. The Prajāpati has said that the peacock, the francoline partridge, the Kapiñjala (a variety of the ruddy goose), the rhenocero and the panther can be eaten.

37b-38. O leading sages, among fishes, these are mentioned as worthy of being eaten, viz. : the Rājīvas (lotus-like ones) the Siṁhatuṇḍas (lion-snouted), the Pāṭhīnas and the Rohitas.[2] The flesh of these must be sprinkled with holy water and consecrated before eating if the Brāhmaṇa so desires.

39. One shall eat meat in accordance with the injunctions or as enjoined at a time when life is in danger. One who eats the remainder (i.e. what is left after worship) or as a medicine or when one is powerless or is deputed, he is not affected by sin.

40. If a person invited for the Śrāddha or the worship of a deity eschews meat he may have to be in the hell as many years as there are hairs on the body of the animal.[3]

41. The established rule is that, wine should not be drunk, should not be touched and should never be thought of by the twice-born.

---

1. This injunction about the eatability of five-clawed animals appears in VR, Kiṣkindhā 17.39, cf. MK. P. 35. 2-4 which shows a common source of KP. and MK.

2. Cf. Manu V. 16

3. Although KP insists on acceptance of non-vegetarian food when served in a Śrāddha, it staunchly prohibits wine under all circumstances. Dh. S. of Āpastamba 1.7.21.8, Viṣṇu 35.1 and Manu XI. 54 and Yāj. III. 227 hold that wine-drinking is a very grave sin.

42. Hence, one shall scrupulously avoid wine which is despicable. By drinking it, one incurs downfall and loses his merits (good acts) nor should he be talked to by Brahmin.

43-44. (Partly defective) By eating foodstuffs that should not be eaten and drinking that should not be drunk, a Brāhmaṇa loses his rights. He then faces downfall.

45. Hence, one should scrupulously avoid forbidden foodstuffs. He goes alone after elevation* (?). And after death goes to the hell Raurava.

CHAPTER NINETEEN

Daily Duties of a Householder

The Sages said :

1. O Great sage, please describe all the duties of a Brāhmaṇa, which have to be performed every day and whereby one is liberated from bondage of Saṁsāra.

Vyāsa said :

2. Listen attentively all of you, while I recount the daily duties of Brāhmaṇas and the order of their performance.

3. Getting up in the Brāhma Muhūrta (the closing part of the night just before dawn), one should think about one's duties and monetary affairs wherefore he has to exert his body. He should then meditate on Īśvara in his mind.

4. When the dawn sets in, the learned man should perform all requisite activities (answer the call of nature) and then carry out the purificatory rites duly. He should then take his bath in the pure (holy) rivers.[1]

---

*Veṅk. Text, *āropya yāti caiveko* is not satisfactory as the text reads : Āpeyāni ca vipro . . . the Brāhmaṇa avoids forbidden drinks.

1. VV. 4-16 describe the importance of morning-bath in cold water. The six types of baths described in vv. 12-16 and its emphasis of *Yaugika* bath in *Ātma-tīrtha* is significant.

5. Even those people who commit sins are purified, thanks to the morning ablution. Hence, one should assiduously perform the morning ablution.

6. They praise the early morning ablution which brings forth visible and invisible benefits; there is no doubt in this that the sagehood of the sages is due to their daily ablution in the early morning.

7. When a man is asleep, the saliva drips constantly from his mouth. Hence, no one should perform any holy rite without taking bath at the outset.

8. There is no doubt about it that poverty (*alakṣmī*), a misfortune (*Kālakarṇī*),* an inauspicious dream and evil thoughts—all these and sins are purified by means of a morning bath.

9. Hence, without the morning ablution, no morning duty is prescribed, especially in Homa and Japa activities. So one shall take morning bath regularly.

10. In case of inability, a bath keeping the head dry is enjoined. Wiping off with a wet cloth is remembered as sanctifying.** This is called *Kāpila* bath.

11. When Āyatya*** (Dependence ?) is generated, one should perform ablution like this :- Learned men have mentioned these ablutions (viz.) Brāhma etc. in case of inability (to bathe).

12. Ablution can be briefly divided into six types viz. : 1) Brāhma, 2) Āgneya, 3) Vāyavya, 4) Divya, 5) Vāruṇa and 6) Yaugika.

13. Sprinkling with the Kuśa grass dripping with water while repeating the Mantras, is called the Brāhma ablution. Dusting of the whole body from foot to head with Bhasma is called Āgneya ablution.

**alakṣmako jalaṁ kiñcit* in Veṅk. text, is confusing. Hence the v.l. *alakṣmi Kālakarṇi ca* is accepted.

**v. l. *Pāvanam* 'No other act is regarded (lit. remembered) as sanctifying than the morning bath.'

***v. l. *asāmarthye* 'in case of inability'.

14. The excellent bath by means of the dust particles raised by the kine is called Vāyavya ablution. The bath in the rain accompanied by sunshine is called Divya ablution.

15. Plunging into the water is the "Vāruṇa" ablution. The dedication of the mind by the Yogins is called Yaugika ablution, as the Yogins think about Viśva ·(the universe, God in the Cosmic form) etc. in the course of the practice of Yoga.

16. That is called *Ātma-tīrtha* and it is resorted to by the expounders of the Veda (or knowers of Brahman). It is purifier of the minds of men. One should always perform his ablution (there-in).

17-18a. If he is competent, the learned man should perform Vāruṇa ablution, and the act of atonement also. He should wash the tooth brush twig and then chew it duly. Thereafter he should perform the *Ācamana* rite, and perform the early morning ablution every day.

18b-19a. The toothbrush twig shall be as thick as the middle finger. It shall be twelve *Aṅgulas* long. The tooth brush twig shall have its bark in tact. One should clean (the teeth) with its tip.[1]

19b. It must be cut out from a tree of milky exudation. The twigs of the Mālatī tree are auspicious. Apāmārga,* Bilva and Karavīra are particularly good.

20. He should avoid the forbidden (trees). He should avoid the sinful (forbidden) days also. In the manner mentioned, he should chew the twig. The knower of the procedure of (washing the teeth) should do this.

21. One should not split the toothbrush twig, nor should clean the teeth with the tips of the fingers. After cleaning (the teeth), he should break it and cast it carefully in a clean place.

---

1. There seems no regular arrangement of duties in KP. Hence the topic of 'brushing the teeth' in vv. 18-21 comes after bath. Smṛtis have laid down detailed rules about the names of trees the twig of which it so be selected, the length of the twig etc. But the view of KP is generally accepted.

*Apāmārga (the plant Achyranthes Aspera), Bilva Aegle marmelos and Karvīra (Oleander, Nerium odorum).

22-24. After taking bath, he should perform Tarpaṇa[1] rites to Devas, sages and the groups of the Pitṛs. The knower of the Mantra should perform *Ācamana* twice silently. He should repeat the Mantras and sprinkle his body with Kuśa grass dripping with water. He should repeat the auspicious Mantras of Lord Varuṇa beginning with *Āpo hi ṣṭhā* and the Sāvitrī Mantra along with the Vyāhṛtis. He should perform the Japa of Gāyatrī, the mother of the Vedas. The Sāvitrī Mantra should be prefixed with the Oṁkāra, Vyāhṛti. With the mind fixed on the sun he should offer a handful of water to the sun.

25. *Smṛti* has prescribed that he should then be seated on the Darbha grass with the concentration of mind and he should then perform three Prāṇāyāmas and meditate on the Sandhyā.

26. What is termed Sandhyā is the source of origin of the universe. It is beyond Māyā, entire and absolute power of God, originating from the three Tattvas (principles).

27. The learned devotee should meditate on Sāvitrī stationed in the solar sphere and repeat the Mantra of Sāvitrī. A Brāhmaṇa should always perform the worship of Sandhyā, facing the East.

28. A Brāhmaṇa devoid of (the worship of) Sandhyā is impure. He does not deserve performance of any of the rites. Even if he does anything else, he shall not derive the benefit thereof.

29 Quiescent Brāhmaṇas of yore who were masters of ten Vedas and who did not think of anything else, duly worshipped the Sandhyā and attained the greatest goal.

30. If an excellent Brāhmaṇa eschews the worship of the Sandhyās and puts in his effort in other religious activities, attains Naraka (Hell) and remains there for ten thousand years.

31. Hence, one should assiduously perform the worship of Sandhyā. The greatest Deity, the Yoga incarnate, would be worshipped by him in that case.

---

1. *Tarpaṇa* (satiation by offering water) of gods, sages and ancestors (Pitṛs) is obligatory to all. For more instructions vide vv. 85-88 below. So is the *sandhyā-prayer* (both in the morning and evening). VV. 22-32 emphasize the supreme importance of the sandhyā-prayer the *sine qua non* of Brahminhood, the most essential part of it is the Japa of Sāvitrī.

32. The learned man should with perfect purity, be seated facing the east and perform the Japa of Sāvitrī of which the repetition for one thousand times are regarded as the maximum and best, one hundred times as average and ten times as the minimum.

33. He should then, with concentration and mental purity worship the sun, repeating the various kinds of Mantras pertaining to the sun and taken from the Ṛgveda, Yajurveda and the Sāmaveda.[1]

34. After respectfully approaching the sun, the lord of Devas of great Yoga, one shall make a great bow touching the ground with the head repeating those Mantras.

Sūrya-hṛdaya Hymn :

35. Om obeisance unto you Khakholka (the sky-meteor), the quiescent, the source of the three causes. I dedicate myself unto you; the embodiment of the universe I bow to you.

36. Obeisance unto you, the compassionate one; salute to you the Sun the manifest form of Brahman. You alone are the greatest Brahman, the waters, the Brilliance, the essence, the nectar or immortal; you are the Vyāhṛtis Bhūḥ, Bhuvaḥ, Svaḥ. You are Oṁkāra, Śarva, Rudra, the eternal great god.

37. You are *Puruṣa* of glory and brilliance. I bow unto Kapardin (god of matted hair), the immanent soul. You alone are the universe, that had originated in many ways and that is yet originating. Obeisance, to you, Rudra, the sun. I seek refuge in you.

38. Obeisance to you Pracetas; salutation to the most bountilful god. Obeisance, obeisance to you, Rudra. I seek refuge in you. Obeisance to you Hiraṇyabāhu (of golden arms); obeisance to Hiraṇyapati (the lord of gold).

---

1. The worship of the Sun is to be immediately done after Sandhyā. It appears that the cult of solar-worship has become popular, or was being popularised at the time of KP. Hence this special hymn called *Sūrya-hṛdaya*. In this hymn the identification of the sun mainly with god Śiva is significant.

In the compulsory six duties of a Brāhmaṇa as given by Parāśara I. 39, this worship is not mentioned specifically unless we extend the meaning of *devatātithi-pūjanam* to cover this worship.

39. Bow to you the lord of Ambikā; obeisance to the consort of Umā; salutation to the blue-necked. Obeisance to you, the holder of the Pināka Bow.

40. Hail to you *Vilohita* (very ruddy), *Bharga* (Brilliant) obeisance to you the thousand-eyed one. Obeisance to you for ever, to the dispeller of darkness, obeisance be to you Āditya.

41. Obeisance to you Vajrahasta (one with the thunderbolt in the hand). Obeisance, again and again to Tryambaka (the three-eyed god). I resort unto you, Virūpākṣa, the great supreme Lord.

42. I bow to the Ātman well-preserved in the golden abode. I bow down to the supreme brilliance, to you, Brahmā, the great and the immortal one.

43. I bow to Paśupati (the master of individual souls), the universe, the terrible one, having (simulaneously) the male and female forms. Obeisance to the sun, to Rudra, the shining one, to Parameṣṭhin (the highest deity).

44-46. Obeisance to Ugra, the destroyer of all. I resort to you for ever. After performing the Japa (the repetition) of this excellent *Sūrya-Hṛdaya* hymn, one should bow down to the sun both in the morning and at Midday. This hymn to *Sūrya-Hṛdaya*, (as) pointed out by Brahmā, should be imparted to one's own son, disciple and to a virtuous twice-born. It subdues all sins; it has originated as the essence of the Vedas. It is meritorious and beneficial unto the Brāhmaṇas, and is resorted to by the multitudes of great men.

47. Thereafter, the Brāhmaṇa should return home, perform the *Ācamana* rite in accordance with the injunctions, kindle the fire duly and perform the *Homa* in the fire.[1]

But this worship of the sun is to be performed at the place of bath which is presumed to be out of the house. Hence the words "after returning home" (*athāgamya gṛham*) in v. 47 vide also vv. 56-57 below.

1. *Homa* or Fire-worship and offering oblations into the fire was essential to pay off the debt of gods. Dakṣa (II. 28) prescribes that Home is to be performed after completing the Sandhyā-worship (*Sandhyā-karmāvasāne*), but KP advises it after the worship of the sun. VV. 47-50 give general instruction about the worship of deities, recitation of Vedic passages and Japa. This is the order presribed in KP.

48. The Homa can be performed by the Ṛtvik's son, wife, disciple or brother after obtaining the permission. It can particularly be performed by the Adhvaryu in accordance with the injunction.

49. (Whoever performs it) he should wear Pavitra (Kuśa grass made in the form of a ring with a tail) in his hand, wear white cloth, be pure in mind and body and have full control over the sense-organs. He should perform the Homa with full concentration of the mind (which does not wander elsewhere).

50. The rite that is performed without the Darbha grass or without the *Sūtra* (sacred thread) shall be demonic. It does not yield any benefit either here or hereafter.

51. He should make obeisance to all deities, should offer presents; flowers etc. should be given. He should then prostrate before elders.

52. He should then honour and revere his preceptor; he should do what is beneficent unto him; O Brāhmaṇas, he should then recite the Vedic passages as much as he can, with assiduity.

53. He should perform the Japa; he should teach his disciples; retain everything in memory and ponder over everything; O excellent Brāhmaṇas, he should view Dharma etc. in the light of the scriptures.

54. He should go through the Vedic Nigamas and all Vedāṅgas (Ancillary subjects of the Vedas). For the achievement of *Yogakṣema* (*Yoga*—attaining what has not been attained; *Kṣema*—preserving what has been attained) he should resort to Īśvara.

55. Thereafter, the Brāhmaṇa should gather together the various articles for his household. Then at midday, he should fetch clay for the bath.

56. He should also fetch flowers, raw rice grains, Kuśa grass, gingelly seeds as well as pure cowdung. He should always perform his ablution in rivers, in tanks, dug up by gods (i.e. natural), in lakes, in puddles or in fountains.

57. One should never take bath in a water reservoir

belonging to others. In emergency, he should take out at least five lumps of mud from it, before bath.

58. (He should divide the clay into many small lumps). With one of the lumps of the clay, the head is to be cleaned, with two (such lumps) he should clean the portion above the umbilical region and with three lumps he should clean the lower region. The legs and the feet shall be cleaned with six lumps of clay.

59. It is enjoined that the clay should be wet and of the size of a big myrobalan. The size of the cowdung is also that much. One should smear it over one's limps.

60. While standing on the bank, he should first smear the body chanting the relevant Mantras. After washing his hand and performing *Ācamana*, he should then carefully take his bath.

61. Sanctifying the water with auspicious Mantras pertaining to Varuṇa and symbolic of water, he should meditate upon the unmanifest eternal Viṣṇu and get purified at heart while bathing.

62. The waters have been originated from Nārāyaṇa. Waters alone constitute his *Ayana* (receptacle). Hence a learned man should remember lord Nārāyaṇa at the time of ablution.

63. After glancing at the sun with the repetitions of the Oṁkāra, he should dip himself in the water three times.

64. After performing the *Ācamana* rite twice, the knower of the Mantras should repeat the following Mantra.

65. "You move about within the living beings, in the cavity of the heart, you have faces all round. You are Yajña; you are Vaṣaṭkāra; O waters, you are the brilliance, the nectarine juice".

66. He should then repeat the *Drupadā* Mantra three times, or he shall repeat the Vyāhṛtis along with the Praṇava. The learned man should repeat the Sāvitrī Mantra or the *Aghamarṣaṇa mantra.*

67. Then he should perform the Sammārjana rite (wiping off) by repeating the Mantra, *Āpo hi ṣṭhā mayo bhuvaḥ*

(RV. X.9.1) or the Mantra, *Idam āpaḥ Pravahato*" (RV.I.23. 22), or by means of the Vyāhṛtis.

68. With the three Mantras beginning with "Āpo hi ṣṭhā" RV.X. 9.1) etc. he should sanctify the water and then dip himself under. He should then repeat the *Aghamarṣaṇa* Mantra (RV. X. 190-3) three times.

69. He should also repeat the *Drupadā* (Vāj. Saṁ. 20. 20) or the Sāvitri Mantra. That is the greatest world of Viṣṇu. Or he should repeat the Praṇava or remember Lord Hari.

70. (Defective) After repeating three times the Mantra established in the Yajurveda like *Drupadāiva* (Vāj. Saṁ-20.20) under the water, one is liberated from all sins.

71. He should take water in the palm, perform Japa and the *Mārjana*[1] rite and place that water (sprinkle it over the head. He is liberated from all sins.

72. Just as the horse-sacrifice is the king of all sacrifices and dispels all sins, so also the Mantra *Aghamarṣaṇa* is said to be destructive of all sins.

73. He should then pray unto the sun[2]. He should throw up flowers along with the Akṣatas (raw rice grains) and glance at the lord who is above and beyond darkness.

74-75. Any of these Mantras pertaining to the sun and destructive of sins can be repeated[3] :—Mantras beginning with *Udu tyam* (RV. I. 150.1) and *Citram* (RV.I.115.1.) *Taccakṣuḥ* (RV. VII.66.16) the Mantra ending with *Haṁsaḥ Śuciṣat*, (RV. IV. 40. 5) particularly the Sāvitrī Mantra and other Vedic Mantras addressed to the Sun. Afterwards, he should repeat the Sāvitrī Mantra. This is remembered as *Japayajña* (The sacrifice called *Japa*).

76-77. He should repeat various other holy Mantras as well, such as the esoteric Vidyās, Śatarudrīya, Atharvaśiras and all solar Mantras. He should be seated on the Darbha grass with their tips towards the east. He should be pure and he should face

---

1. *mārjana*—sprinkling of water with Kuśa grass and repeating the three RV verses *āpo hi ṣṭhā* (Rv. X. 9. 1-3).

2. The second (mid-day) bath is also followed by the sun-worship.

3. VV. 74-83 give instruction about the performance of Japa which is mentioned by the glorificatory term *Japa-yajña*.

the east himself. He should repeat the Japya with great concentration and glance at the sun.

78. He should make the rosary with crystal beads, Indrākṣas, Rudrākṣas or Putrajīvas (Putrañjīva : *Rox burghii*). The later ones are better than the earlier ones.

79. (Defective) while repeating Japa, the sensible man should not speak, not look at any external thing, not shake the head or the neck, nor show the teeth outside.

80. Since the Guhyakas, Rākṣasas and the Siddhas remove the benefit, one should perform the Japa-rite in an isolated, pure place.

81. On seeing a Cāṇḍāla or a fallen man or one with Āśauca (impurity), one shall perform the Japa once again. If he talks to them, he should bathe again and perform the Japa once again.

82. If one sees anything impure, one should immediately perform the Ācamana rite and perform the Japa with purity. He should repeat Mantras pertaining to the sun in accordance to his capacity and the "Pāvamānī" hymns as he likes.

83. If he happens to wear wet cloth, he can perform the Japa in the middle of water. Otherwise he should sit in a pure, clean place on the Darbha grass with great concentration.

84. He should circumambulate, prostrate on the ground, perform the *Ācamana* rite in accordance with the scripture and then begin his self-study of the Vedas with devotion.

85-86. Thereafter, he should perform *Tarpaṇa* rite for Devas, sages and the groups of the pitṛs. He should utter Oṁkāra at the outset and then the name. At the end he should say *Tārayām vaḥ*." (I propitiate you). The *Tarpaṇa* rite for Devas and the Brahminical sages shall be performed with raw rice grains and water. The *Tarpaṇa* rite for the Pitṛs shall be performed with gingelly seeds and water. The *Tarpaṇa* rites should be performed with great devotion in accordance with his Gṛhyasūtra.

87. While performing the rite of *Tarpaṇa* to Devas and the sages, he should do so with his right hand supported by the left hand (below). The intelligent man should perform *Tarpaṇa* rite of the Pitṛs with handfuls of water. While performing *Deva-Tarpaṇa* the sacred thread is worn (*savya*) as usual;

during the *Ṛṣi-Tarpaṇa* (to the sages), he should wear the sacred thread like a garland.

88. During the *Pitṛtarpaṇa*, he should wear the sacred thread on the right shoulder and under the left arm. After squeezing out the water from the cloth with which he takes bath, he should perform *Ācamana* silently. He should worship Devas with their own Mantras by means of flowers, leaves and water.

89. An excellent man with good conduct and devotion should worship Brahmā, Śaṅkara, Viṣṇu (the slayer of Madhu) and the sun. He should worship other deities also according to his desire.

90. He should offer them flowers with the *Puruṣa Sūkta*. All the deities are well worshipped with water, as waters are all deities.

91. One should meditate on the deities along with the Praṇava, with great concentration : Repeating the word *Namaḥ* (obeisance), he should offer the flowers one by one.

92. The holiness of all Vedic rites is due to the propitiation of Viṣṇu. Hence, one should propitiate for ever Hari, the deity without beginning, middle, or end.

93. (One should propitiate Hari) with the Mantra beginning with the words *Tad Viṣṇoḥ* (RV.I.22.20 or with the *Puruṣa Sūkta*). He should do so with great concentration of mind, There is no other mantra mentioned in the four Vedas, which can be equal to these two. His soul and mind should be dedicated unto the lord. He will be calm (in mind) by (the power of) the Mantra *Tad Viṣṇoḥ*.

94. Or he should propitiate the eternal Lord Īśāna, Mahādeva, Maheśvara. He shall be sanctified by means of good feelings and thoughts.

95. With great concentration he should propitiate Maheśvara by means of the Praṇava Mantra, Rudragāyatrī, Īśāna Mantra, Tryambaka Mantra or Rudra Mantras.

96. He should worship Maheśvara with flowers, leaves, water or sandal-paste and other articles. Or he should perform Japa by means of this Mantra *Namaḥ Śivāya* (Obeisance to Śiva).

97. One should make obeisance unto Mahādeva, Īśvara, the conqueror of Death. He should dedicate his own self unto Īśvara with the Mantra *Yo Brahmāṇam.* (AV. 5.18.49).

98. ABrāhmaṇa should circumambulate for five years (?)* He should meditate on god Īśāna, Śiva who is in the middle of the firmament.

99. Afterwards, he should repeat the RK *Haṁsaḥ, Śuciṣat* (RV.IV.40.5) and look at the sun, etc., After going home, he should perform the five great Yajña with great attention.

100. They are Deva yajña, Pitṛ yajña, Bhūta yajña, Mānuṣya-yajña (human beings i.e. guests) and Brahma yajña (study of the Vedas).

101. If, after the tarpaṇa rite Brahma yajña rite is not performed, he should begin self-study of Vedas after performing Mānuṣya yajña (hospitality to guests).

102. At the end of Bhūta Yajña, he should sit on a heap of Kuśa grass in a spot to the west of the fire. He should be pure in mind and body and hold Kuśa grass in his hand.

103. The Vaiśvadeva rite must be performed in the sacrificial or secular fire or in water or on the ground. This is remembered as Deva Yajña.

104. If the rice to be offered as oblation is cooked on secular fire, it (the oblations) be offered to that fire. If one were to cook that on sacrificial fire, that food is oblated to that sacrificial fire. This is the eternal procedure.

105. With the cooked food that remains after the offering unto Devas, one should offer Bhūta Bali. This should be known as Bhūta Yajña. It is the bestower of prosperity unto all embodied beings.

106. O excellent Brāhmaṇas, the cooked food should be given to dogs, cookers of dogs (i.e. Cāṇḍālas), fallen persons (i.e. outcastes) and birds, on the ground outside.

107. In the evening, his wife shall offer cooked food as Bali (offering to all beings) without uttering any Mantras. This is the Bhūta-Yajña to be performed both in the morning and in the evening.

---

*v.l. *Pañca-brahmāṇi vai japan* 'muttering five Brahmans (Vedic Mantras)'.

108. With the Pitṛs in view, one should feed one Brāhmaṇa daily. This *Nitya Śrāddha* (with respect to manes) is called Pitṛ yajña. It is the bestower of good goals.

109. One should take up some cooked rice according to his capacity and offer it to a Brāhmaṇa scholar who knows the meanings of Vedic passages.

110. One should honour one's guest verbally, mentally and physically. The lord (guest) should be bowed to and worshipped. He should be calm and should welcome the guest who has come to his house.

111. A Brāhmaṇa should offer the alms of any of the three types.[1] *Hantakāra*, *Agra* or *Bhikṣā* by means of his right hand supported by the left (below), in accordance with his capacity.

112-113. He should give this unto the guest every day. He should consider him (the guest) as the great god. If one mouthful is given as alms it is called *Bhikṣā.* Four times that quantity is called *Agra.* Four times that which is a considerable quantity, is called *Hantakāra.* The guest should be awaited up to the time of milking a cow.

114. One should always honour and worship the guests coming to his house, in accordance with his capacity. One should give Bhikṣā unto the mandicant and the Brahmacārin duly. One should be devoid of covetousness and give as much food as he can, unto the suppliants.

115. If no guest is available, he should offer food unto the cows. One should be silent, while taking food. One should not find fault with the food served. One should take food along with many persons (v.l. with relatives).

116. O excellent Brāhmaṇas, if a Brāhmaṇa takes food without performing the five great Yajñas, the foolish soul shall be reborn among the animals.

117. Daily study of the Vedas, the performance of Mahā-Yajñas (the above-mentioned five great sacrifices)—an imperishable act—and the worship of gods quickly dispel all sins.

---

1. The three types of alms are described below in (vv. 112-113). The importance of feeding the hungry before one takes one's meals—one of the great sacrifices 'Mahā-yajña'—was a commendable feature of the old tradition.

118. There is no doubt in this that a person who, out of delusion or ignorance takes food without performing the worship of the deities, attains the hell called *Sūkara* (Boar).

119. Hence, O Brāhmaṇa, one should assiduously perform all rites and take food along with his own kinsmen and he attains the greatest goal.

CHAPTER NINETEEN

Daily Duties of a Householder : Mode of taking meals[1]

Vyāsa said :

1. Facing the east or the sun, one should be seated on a good clean seat with his feet resting on the ground and take food.

2. One who takes food facing the east, enjoys longevity; facing the south, one enjoys good fame; facing the west, one enjoys glory and prosperity and facing the north, one enjoys truth and orderliness.[2]

3. One should take food with five things wet. The plate should be placed on the ground. Manu, the Prajāpati, says that it (such manner of eating) is on a par with the observance of fasts.

4. One should take food with five things wet as follows : the place should be well smeared (with cowdung) and clean; the hands and the feet should be washed; he should perform *Ācamana* and keep the face wet, and he should not be furious.[3]

---

1. As purity of mind depends on the purity of food consumed (Chāndogya Up. VII. 26. 2), *Bhojana* or meals has been one of the most important subject in Dharma Śāstra.

2. Mbh. Anuśāsana 104.57 and Manu II. 52.

3. *Pañcārdra*—One whose five limbs (viz. hands, feet and mouth) are wet. This instruction is found in Mbh. *Śānti* 193-6, Vyāsa quoted in SMC. I. p. 221.

5. He should sprinkle food with water repeating the great *Vyāhṛtis*. He should sip water[1] ritualistically repeating the Mantra *Amṛtopastaraṇamasi* (you are the seat of Amṛta)

6-7. He should then take in particle by particle as oblations repeating (therewith) the Oṁkara Svāhā (as *Oṁ Prāṇāya Svāhā*). This is the *Āhuti* of Prāṇa etc. He should then say *Apānāya Svāhā, Vyānāya Svāhā, Udānāya Svāha* and finally *Samānāya Svāhā* as the fifth one.[2] The Brāhmaṇa should know the reality of these and perform *Homa* offering oblations to the *Ātman*.

8. He should eat the remaining food as he pleases, mixing it with side dishes, pickles etc. After meditating on the Devas with full concentration. he should meditate on Ātman, the Prajāpati.

9. He should then sip water ritualistically repeating the Mantra *Amṛtāpidhānam asi*. You are the cover of the Nectar). After performing *Ācamana* rite, he should perform the rite once again, repeating the Mantra *Ayaṁ gauḥ* etc.

10. Or he should repeat the Drupadā Mantra three times. It is destructive of all sins. He should then stroke his belly repeating the Mantra *Prāṇānāṁ granthirasi* (you are the knot of vital airs).

11. (Defective verse). After performing the *Ācamana* rite, he should let go some water on the toe of the right foot from the thumb of the right hand held up. (He should do this) with concentration.

*12. With the Mantra *Śandhyāyām* he should perform the the *Kṛtānumantraṇa* rite. He should then unite his self with the imperishable Brahman with the Mantra *Brahmāṇa*.

---

1. This sipping of water is called *āpoṣaṇa* (Yāj. Smṛ. I. 106) and its purpose is to make food beneficial as nectar and this sipping is taken at the beginning and the end of the dinner.

2. These five morsels taken in for different vital airs (like *prāṇa, Apāna* etc.) are called Prāṇāhutis 'oblations to Prāṇas' KP. does not mention that the 6th morsel is taken for Brahman (*Brahmaṇe svāhā*).

*The Veṅkt. Text is corrupt. The verse in the Crt. Text reads : *ḥutānumantraṇaṁ kuryāt Śraddhāyām iti mantrataḥ|*

'With the mantra 'Śraddhāyām' one should perform the post sacrificial recitation.'

13. Among all Yogas, Ātmayoga is the greatest. He who shall perform everything in accordance with these injunctions is himself a wise sage.*

14. One shall take food with the sacred thread on (his left shoulder—*Upavīta* fashion) and embellished with scented garlands. He should not take food in the twilights of the morning and evening especially at dusk.

15. One should not take food immediately before the Solar eclipse.[1] If there is a lunar eclipse, he should not take food in that evening. In the course of the duration of the eclipse also, one should not take food. After the liberation (i.e. close of the eclipse), he should (first) take bath and take food.

16. When the moon is liberated, one may take food unless it happens in the second or the third watch of the night. If the sun or the moon sets before liberation (i.e. if the eclipse is not over when they set), he should take food only the next day after seeing (the liberated sun or the moon as the case may be).

17. One should not be wicked-minded enough to take foodwithout giving anything to the lookers-on. He should partake of the remainder after the Yajña. One should not take food while one is angry or when the mind is elsewhere.

18. Indeed, one's life is in vain, if the food is solely taken only by oneself, if the intercourse is solely for sexual pleasure, if the sole purpose of learning is to take up an avocation.

19. If one takes food with the head covered with a cloth, or facing the north or with the shoes on, it is an Āsuraic (demonic) practice.

20. One should not take food at midnight or midday or when the food taken before is not digested. One should not eat food wearing a wet cloth, or sitting in a moving vehicle

21. One shall not take food from a broken vessel or from the ground or in the hands (keeping the foodstuffs in the hands).

---

*v.l. *sa yāti Brahmaṇaḥ kṣayam* 'He goes to the abode of Brahmā.'

1. VV. 15-23 give a number of rules about taking food. We find similar rules in Smṛtis like Manu VI. 207-223, Yājñavalkya I. 167-181.

If one is defiled by Ucchiṣṭa one should not take in ghee, nor should he touch his own head then.

22. (If one is defiled by Ucchiṣṭa) one should not glorify (repeat) the Vedic passages. One should not take food without leaving something behind. One should not take food along with one's wife. One should not take food in darkness, or in the twilight periods or in temples (and similar places).

23. One should not take food with a single garment on; one should not take food in a moving vehicle or lying down in the couch; one should not take food without slipping off the sandals nor one should take food while laughing or crying.

24. After taking food, one should rest comfortable so that the food is well digested. One should elaborately ascertain further the meanings of the Vedic passages through (or with the help of) Itihāsas (Epics) and Purāṇas.

25. Then he should perform the worship of the Sandhyā in accordance with the procedure mentioned before. He should be pure. Seated and facing the west, one should perform Japa of the goddess Gāyatrī.

26. He who does not worship either the morning Sandhyā or the evening Sandhyā is on a par with a Śūdra in this world. He is devoid of all holy rites.

27. After performing the *Homa* duly, repeating the requisite Mantras after partaking of the remainder of the Yajña, one shall retire to sleep along with the attendents and kinsman. At that time his feet should be dry.

28. One should not sleep facing (i.e. with the head in that direction) the north or the west.[1] Nor should he lie under the open sky. One should not sleep in the nude, nor unclean (in body), nor should one sleep on a seat.

29. One should not sleep in a tottering cot nor in a deserted house; one should never lie down on a bed of Palāśa (wood) or of bamboos.

30. Thus the various daily activities and duties of the Brāhmaṇas have been wholly described by me. They bestow the benefit of Apavarga (salvation).

1. Viṣṇu Dh. S. ch. 70; Manu IV, 175-176; VP. III. 11. 107-109.

31. If any Brāhmaṇa does not practise his duty either due to atheism or due to lethargy, he falls into the terrible hells and is reborn as a crow.

32. There is no other way for liberation excepting performance of the duties of one's own Āśrama (stage of life). Hence one should perform the holy rites for the satisfaction of Parameṣṭhin (god Brahmā).

CHAPTER TWENTY[1]

Procedure of Performance of Śrāddha[1]

Vyāsa said :

1. When it is the New Moon day, the Śrāddha called *Piṇḍānvāharyaka*[2] should be devotedly performed by excellent Brāhmaṇas. This bestows worldly pleasures and salvation (as its fruit).

---

1. Chapters 20-22 constitute the *Śrāddha Kalpa* or the procedure of performing a Śrāddha. It is based on the belief of after-death survival of deceased forefathers and the existence of a separate world of manes (*Pitṛ-loka*) This belief is current since the Indo-Iranian period and hence pre-Vedic (vide S. B. E. IV-p. 262 for the Iranian belief). Ṛgvedic people believed in and performed ancestor-worship for prosperity and continuity of one's race. As this topic forms an integral part of Hindu Dharma-Śāstra, we find it discussed in a number of Purāṇas also e. g. Āp. 163. 2-42, GP. I. 210, NP. I. 28, Pd. p (Sṛṣṭi-Khaṇḍa) 9. 140-186, V. P. III. 15. 13-49.

Most of these prescribe the same procedure as prescribed in Gṛhya Sūtras and old Smṛtis like Manu, Yājñavalkya and others; thus there is a repetition of common verses in variovs Smṛtis and Purāṇas.

But in the case of KP., *the author has borrowed en mass practically the whole of Śrāddha Kalpa from the Auśanasa Smṛti* (ch. III. 110 to the end of the Chapter and chs. IV and V.

2. *Piṇḍānvāhāryaka*:

Anvāhārya or Piṇḍānvāhāryaka (=that which is performed after Piṇḍa-offerings) Medhātithi.

2. The *Śrāddha* called *Piṇḍānvāhāryaka* is recommended when it is the dark half of the month (lit. the moon is on the wane). To the twice-born it is better if it is performed in the afternoon with meat.

3. All other *tithis* in the dark half of the month beginning from the first, except the fourteenth day, are excellent but the later Tithi is more commendable than the former.

4. The three new-moon days and the eighth day in the dark half of the three months beginning with Pauṣa are good days. The three Aṣṭakās are holy as well as the fifteenth day (the new moon day) in the month of Māgha.

5. Particularly in the rainy season, the Trayodaśī (thirteenth day) united with the Maghā constellation is good when the corn is ripe. These are prescribed as suitable for obligatory (*Nitya*) *Śrāddha*.

6. During the eclipse of the moon and the sun, the *Naimittika* (occasional) *Śrāddha* must be performed extensively among relatives. Otherwise, one is likely to be consigned to hell.

7. The *Kāmya* (urged by a desire for benefit) *Śrāddhas* are recommended during eclipse etc. and during the Vernal and equinotical transit of the sun and during Vyatīpāta the last giving infinite merit.

8. The *Śrāddha* at the time of Saṁkrānti (tropical transit of the sun) as well as on birthdays is of everlasting benefit. It is so particularly in all the Nakṣatras (constellations) and must be performed at the proper time.[1]

It was to be performed after *Pitṛ-yajña* by an *Agni-hotrin* on the Amāvāsyā day (Manu III. 122-123). This funeral sacrifice is not now in vogue among the Agnihotris in the Deccan.

1. After describing the three varieties of Śrāddha—*Nitya* (daily), *Naimittika* (occasional) and *Kāmya* (for attaining a desired object), for such Śrāddhas vv. 9-15 enumerate the fruit one derives by performing a Śrāddha on a particular constellation (*Nakṣatra*).

It is Viṣṇu Dh. S. 78. 8-15 first, which mentions what rewards follow from the performance of Śrāddha on 28 Nakṣattras from Kṛttikā to Bharaṇī. KP follows the same order though not always with the same rewards. Cf. Bd. P. *upodghāta-pāda* 18. 1 ff, Bm. P. 220.33-42.

9. By performing the Śrāddha in the constellation Kṛttikā the excellent Brāhmaṇa attains heaven; by performing it in Rohiṇī, he obtains progeny; by performing it in Mṛgaśiras constellation, he obtains Brahminical splendour.

10. By performing the *Śrāddha* in the Ārdrā constellation, one attains the benefits of the holy rites pertaining to Rudra as well as heroism; by performing it in the Punarvasu star, he attains lands, and by performing it in Puṣya he obtains glory and prosperity.

11-12. By performing the *Śrāddha* in the Āśleṣā constellation, one attains all desires; in the constellation pertaining to the Pitṛs (i.e. Maghā), one attains good fortune. In the constellation to Aryaman (Uttarā Phālgunī) one attains wealth; in the (Pūrvā) Phālgunī star, the sins are quelled; if the *Śrāddha* is performed in Hasta, one attains excellence among Kinsmen; by performing Śrāddha in the Citrā constellation, one attains many sons. If *Śrāddha* is performed in Svātī constellation one attains the greatest achievement in trading transactions; by performing *Śrāddha* in the Viśākhā star one obtains gold.

13. By performing *Śrāddha* in the constellation Anurādhā, one attains many friends; in the constellation Jyeṣṭhā, one attains kingdom; by performing *Śrāddha* in Mūla, one attains (flourishing) cultivation; by performing Śrāddha in Pūrvāṣāḍhā, one attains perfect knowledge and achievement.

14. By performing *Śrāddha*, in Vaiśvadeva (Uttarāṣāḍhā) constellation one attains all desires; in the Śravaṇa constellation, one attains excellence; by performing *Śrāddha* in Dhaniṣṭhā one attains all desires; and in Śatabhiṣak star, one attains the greatest strength.

15. By performing *Śrāddha* in the Pūrvābhādrapadā constellation, one shall obtain the base metals; in the constellation of Uttarā Bhādrapadā, one attains excellent house; by performing Śrāddha in the Revatī constellation, one attains many cows; and in the constellation *Aśvinī* one attains horses. If one offers Śrāddha in the Bharaṇī constellation, one's life becomes perfect.

16-18. By performing *Śrāddha* on Sunday, one attains health; on Monday, good fortune; on Tuesday, success everywhere and by performing *Śrāddha* on Wednesday, one attains all desires; by performing *Śrāddha* on Friday, one attains wealth and by performing *Śrāddha* on Saturday, one attains longevity.[1] By performing *Śrāddha* on the Pratipat[2] (i.e. first day in the lunar fortnight), one attains auspicious sons. On the second day, one begets daughters; and on the third day, one gets animals, on the fourth day, he attains small animals or things and by performing *Śrāddha* on the fifth day, one attains splendid sons.

19. A person performing *Śrāddha* on the sixth day, attains lustre as well as good cultivation; the man who gives *Śrāddha* on the seventh day, attains wealth; he who offers *Śrāddha* on the eighth day, obtains good trading transactions.

20. He who performs *Śrāddha* on the ninth day, obtains single-hoofed animals; he who performs *Śrāddha* on the tenth day, obtains double-hoofed animals in plenty. One who performs *Śrāddha* on the eleventh day, obtains silver and sons of Brahmanical splendour.

21. One who performs *Śrāddha* on the twelfth day, obtains gold, silver and base metals. One who performs *Śrāddha* on the thirteenth day, obtains excellent kinsmen and one who performs *Śrāddha* on the fourteenth day, obtains ignoble progeny. One who performs *Śrāddha* on the fifteenth day (i.e. on the new moon day), always obtains all desires.

22. Hence *Śrāddha* should not be performed by the twice-borns on the fourteenth day. The *Śrāddha* pertaining to those killed by means of weapons should be assigned to that day.

23. There is no restriction as to the time, if Brāhmaṇas and the materials are available. Hence, the twice-borns should perform *Śrāddha* for the purpose of worldly enjoyment as well as salvation.

1. VV. 16-17 mention the reward for performing Śrāddha on several week-days. Cf. Viṣṇu Dh. s. 71. 1. 7.

2. VV. 18-21 state the fruit of performing Śrāddha on each day from the 1st to the 15th day of the dark half. Āpastamba Dh. S. II. 7. 16. 8-22. Mbh. Anuśāsana 87, Vāyu P. 81. 10-19, Bd. P. III. 17. 10-22, Bm. P. 220. 15-21 deal with same topic, though with some difference about the rewards.

24. The *Śrāddha* should be performed at the beginning of all noble enterprises. It should again be performed on the achievement of prosperity, or when a son is born and in similar instances. The *Pārvaṇa Śrāddha* is to be performed in *Parvans* (particular holy days).

25-26. *Śrāddha* that is to be performed every day is the *Nitya Śrāddha*; that which is performed for achieving a desirable object is occasional (*Naimittika*). There is *Ekoddiṣṭa-Śrāddha* (intended for one forebear) and others Bahūddiṣṭa (?) (v.l. *Vṛddhi-śrāddha*) *Śrāddha* and *Pārvaṇa-Śrāddha*. These five kinds of *Śrāddha* are glorified by Manu. In the course of journey, the sixth kind is prescribed and it should be performed assiduously (or regularly).

27. A seventh *Śrāddha* has been enunciated by Brahmā for the achievement of purity. The eighth *Śrāddha* is *Daivika* (divine) by the performance of which, one is liberated from fear.

28. A *Śrāddha* is not to be performed either in the evening or at night except at the time of eclipse.

The merit of performing *Śrāddha* at particular (holy) place is infinite.[1]

29. The *Śrāddha* on the Gaṅgā, at Prayāga and at Amarakaṇṭaka is of everlasting benefit. The Pitṛs sing the religious verse and the learned men dance.

30. "Many sons of good conduct endowed with attributes should be sought by one. Perhaps (at least) one among all those may go to Gayā.

31. After reaching Gayā if one performs *Śrāddha* incidentally, the Pitṛs are redeemed by him. He attains the greatest goal".

32-36. In the following holy centres, the Pitṛs are perpetually delighted, viz.:—Varāha mountain, Gayā in particular, in Vārāṇasī where lord Hara himself is present, at the source

1. As KP. (infra II. 22. 17) states, holy places are no one's private property. Hence, vv. 28-36 recommend a list of holy places (rivers, forests, mountains, etc) where performance of śrāddha is more efficacious. *Vide* also Viṣṇu Dh. S. ch. 85, Śaṅkha Smṛ. 14. 27-29, Vāyu P. Ch. 77 and Ma. P. ch. 22 for the lists of such holy places for Śrāddha.

of Gaṅgā, Prabhāsa, Bilvaka, on the Nīla mountain, Kurukṣetra, Kubjāmra, Bhṛgutuṅga, Mahālaya, Kedāra, Phalgu tīrtha, in the Naimiṣa forest, particularly in Sarasvatī and Puṣkara, in the Narmadā, at Kuśāvarta, Śrīśaila, Bhadrakarṇaka in the Vetravatī, (the Betwa in M.P.) the Visākhā (v.l. Vipāśā i.e. the Beas), particularly in the Godāvarī and on the banks of the other holy rivers.

37. One propitiates the Pitṛs for a month, if the *Śrāddha* is offered with grains, barleys, pulses, water, fruits and roots, Śyāmāka grains, Kāśas, Nīvāras, Priyaṅgus, wheat, gingelly seeds and green gram.[1]

38. At the time of the *Śrāddha*, one should offer the juice of mango, sugarcane, bunches of grapes and pomegranates. He shall also give *Viḍaśvas* and *Kuraṇḍas** (different kinds of grass).

39. He should give fried grains with honey, powdered fried grains with sugar, assiduously at the time of the *Śrāddha*. He should give water caltrops and water chestunt (*Śṛṅgāṭaka kaśerukas* (?)).

40. Manes are satisfied with the meat of fish for two months; with Venison for three months; with the meat of the ram for four months; with the meat of birds for five months; with the meat of goats for six months and with the meat of the spotted antelope for seven months.

41. The Pitṛs are propitiated for eight months, if *Śrāddha* is offered with the meat of *Eṇa* (deer) and for nine months with the meat of Ruru deer. With the meat of the boar and the buffalo they are propitiated for ten months.

42. With the flesh of rabbit and tortoise, he should propitiate them for eleven months. With the cow's milk and

1. VV. 37-39 show that Pitṛs are satisfied for a month by articles of vegetarian food and fruit but vv. 40-45 state the periods of time for which Pitṛs are gratified when the flesh of certain animals is served to Brāhmaṇas at the time of Srāddha. We have similar list of this type in Manu III. 267-272, Yāj. 258-260, Vāyu P. 83. 3-9, Mt. P. 17. 31-35, Bm. P. 220. 23-29 though there is some divergence in some details. Refusal to eat flesh would punish the refuser by birth as a beast in the next birth, stay in the hell for as many years as the killed animal had hair on its body (*supra* I. 18-40)—A relic of an old non-vegetarian age.

*v.l. *vidārīñca bharandām* (?)

milk pudding he shall propitiate them for a year. The satisfaction due to the *Śrāddha* with the meat of Vārdhrīṇasa (rhinoceros or old white goat) extends to twelve years.

43. The Kālaśāka, (?) the Mahāśalka (sea-crab), the meat of rhinoceros and the red goat and the honey, —the food-stuffs of the sages are capable of being beneficent endlessly.

44. Whether by buying or securing oneself or bringing the dead body (of the animal), the Brāhmaṇa should assiduously offer it in the *Śrāddha.* It is called everlasting for him.

45-47. The following articles are used in the *Śrāddha,* viz. :—(long pepper) Pippalī, Rucaka, Musūraka (lentil), Kūṣmāṇḍa (pumpkin) Alābu (gourd), Vārtāka, Bhūtṛṇa (a fragrant grass), the juicy root of Kusumbha Piṇḍa and Tandulīyaka. At the time of the Śrāddha, an excellent Brāhmaṇa should avoid seven articles assiduously, viz. :— Rājamāṣa pulse, buffalo's milk, goat's milk, Āḍhakīs, Kovidāras, Pālakīs and Maricas (chillis).

CHAPTER TWENTYONE

Rules governing Śrāddha (contd.)

Vyāsa said :

1. On the new moon day, a Brāhmaṇa should take his bath and propitiate the Pitṛs as mentiond before. With purity and gentlemanliness, he should perform the Śrāddha called *Piṇḍānvāhāryaka.*

2. At the very outset, he should look up for a Brāhmaṇa who is a master of the Vedas.[1] He is the holy centre (deserves

1. These verses describe the qualifications of the Brāhmaṇa to be invited for the Śrāddha. Heredity, personality, learning, character are some of the main considerations of such an invitee. Cf Mt. P. 16. 8-10, NP. I. 28-6-10; also Smr. C. (*Smṛti Candrikā*) III (*Śrāddha Kāṇḍa*) pp. 389-394. Ancient Smṛtis insist on purity of Character. Says Manu (II. 118). "Better a Brāhmaṇa who knows only the Gāyatrī Mantra but is self-controlled, than a knower of three Vedas but lacking in self-control, eats everything and sells anything (despite the prohibition of *dharma*").

to be the recepient of offerings meant for gods and Pitṛs).

3. The Brāhmaṇas to be invited must be Soma-imbibers, (in Yajñas), free from passion (*Rajas* quality), knowers of Dharma, of calm mind, performing holy rites, observers of rules restraining the mind, those who approach unto their wives only on the prescribed days after menstruation.

4. The Brāhmaṇa must be one who maintains the five (sacrificial) fires. He must be a student of the Vedas, a knower of Yajurveda, conversant with many Ṛk mantras *Trisauparṇa*[1] and *Trimadhus*.[2]

5. He must know the mantras of *Triṇāciketas*,[3] be a chanter of the Sāma-veda and must know the *Jyeṣṭha Sāmans*[4] He must have studied Atharvaśiras[5] especially the section called Rudra Adhyāya mantras.

6. He must be devoted to the performance of Agnihotra. He must be a scholar knowing Nyāyas and the six Aṅgas

---

1. *Trisuparṇa*—The three *Anuvākas* beginning from *Brahmametu mām* (tait. Ār. X. 41-50)

2. *Tri-madhu*—Three Vedic verses (RV. I. 90. 6-9, Vāj. S. 13. 27-29. Tait. S. IV. 2. 9. 3.) in which the word *Madhu* occurs thrice.

3. *Tri-ṇāciketas*—variously explained as:

   1. A person who knows the Nāciketa fire
   2. A person who has thrice kindled the Nāciketa fire.
   3. One who has studied the *Anuvāka* called *Virajas*, Tait. Br. III. 11. 7-8 which describes the Nāciketa fire and the story of Naciketas.

4. *Jyeṣṭha-sāman*—Two interpretations according to the branches of the Sāma-veda.

   i. *Talavakāra śākhā*: *Sāman* sung on *Udu tvam* (Rv. I. 50. 1) *Citraṁ devānām* (Rv. I. 115. 1)

   ii. *Chāndoga Śākhā*: Three *sāmans* sung on *mūrdhānaṁ divo* (Rv. VI. 7. 1, Sām. V. Pūrvārcika 67, *ibid* uttarārcika 1140). vv. 4 and 5 of KP repeat Āpa. Dh. S. (*Āpastamba-Dharma Sūtra*) II. 7. 17-22 where it is regarded as a qualification of a '*Paṅkti-pāvana*' (purifier of a row of 'fallen' persons by sitting in their row for meals).

5. N. of an Upaniṣad.

(auxiliary studies of the Veda). He must be a knower of the Mantra Brāhmaṇas and a reciter of Dharma Śāstra.

7. He must be observing vows of sages and a (lit. a minor sage) prospective sage of calm mind who has subdued sense-organs. He must belong to family of hereditary Vedic Teachers. He must be pure ever since the conception. He must be a bestower of a thousand cows.

8. He must regularly perform the Cāndrāyaṇa rite. He must be truthful in speech, a knower of the Purāṇas, devoted to the worship of the preceptor, Devas and the fire-god. He must be devoted to the perfect knowledge.

9. One liberated from all sides, of firm mind, an excellent Brāhmaṇa who has realised the Brahman, and who is self-possessed, a devotee of Viṣṇu, engaged in the worship of Mahādeva and one called Paṅktipāvana[1] (one who sanctifies the row in which he sits for meals.)

10. A person who is as follows, should be known as a Paṅktipāvana; one who is engaged in non-violence, one who never accepts monetary gifts; one who performs *Satra* (sacrificial sessions) and one who is engaged in charitable gifts.

Additional Verses in Brackets

A. Brāhmaṇas who are young and healthy and well versed in Śrutis or Vedas, devoted to the performance of great Yajñas and those Brāhmaṇas who are engaged in the Japa of the Sāvitrī Mantra are Paṅkti-Pāvanas.

B. Those who belong to good families, are endowed with Vedic learning, those who are of good conduct, performers of Penance, a Brāhmaṇa householder who maintains (sacrifical) fires—these should be known as Paṅktipāvanas.

11. A Brāhmaṇa who is engaged in what is beneficial to his parents, who regularly takes his bath early in the morning, a sage knowing spiritual topics and a person of self control should be known as Paṅkti-Pāvana.

---

1. *Paṅkti-pāvana*: Persons who sanctify others by their presence in the row of diners (even at funeral repast). This belief is pretty old, *vide Baudh. Dh. S.* (*Baudhāyana Dharma Sūtra*) II. 8. 2. Manu III 185-186. The list of such Brāhmaṇas given here (vv. 1-14) is found in the Mbh. Anu. 90-25-31, also cf. Mt. P. 16. 7-13, Vāyu p. 79. 56-59.

12. A great Yogin, well-stabilised in perfect knowledge, one who ponders over the meanings of Vedāntas; one who has faith, one who is engaged in Śrāddha—such a Brāhmaṇa is Paṅkti-Pāvana.

13. A Brāhmaṇa who is engaged in the Vedic lore, one always devoted to celibacy, who is well versed in the Atharvaveda and who desires liberation is a Paṅkti-Pāvana.

14. A Brāhmaṇa who has no common *Pravaras* (with the performer of the Śrāddha) and who belongs to a different *Gotra*[1] and who is thus unrelated, should be regarded as Paṅktipāvana.

15. One shall feed a quiescent Yogin[2] engaged in the perfect knowledge of the reality. In his absence, he may feed a Naiṣṭhika (perpetual) celibate sage or a religious student who has completed his religious studentship and who takes to the life of a householder.

16. In his absence, he shall feed a householder who is desirous of salvation and who has no attachment. If all these are not available, one shall feed a householder who is an aspirant.

17. If an ascetic who knows the Guṇas of the Prakṛti and all the principles (tattvas) partakes of one's *Havis*, the merit that one attains exceeds feeding even a thousand knowers of Vedānta.

18. Hence, with great effort, one should feed a leading Yogin engaged in the pursuit of perfect knowledge of Īśvara (in rites pertaining to gods and Pitṛs) by means of *Havyas* and *Kavyas*. In case he be not available, he should feed other Brāhmaṇas.

19. This is the best alternative in the matter of giving *Havya* and *Kavya*. The *Anukalpa*[3] (next alternative) which is always practised by pious men should be known as follows :

1. Cf. Baudh Dh. S. II. 2. 7.

2. VV. 15-18 cf. Viṣṇu Dh. S. 83. 19-20. It specially recommends Yogins as invitees to Śrāddha and quotes a Gāthā in which Pitṛs express their yearning for a Brāhmaṇa Yogin fed at their Śrāddha. Purāṇas vie with each other in describing the quantitative and qualitative efficacy in feeding a Yogin at a Śrāddha than other Brāhmaṇas in different *āśramas* (stages of life). Cf. Bd. P. III. 9. 70 Mk. P. 29. 29.

3. Medhātithi on Manu III 147 explains this as the second best course: *mukhyābhāve yo 'nuṣṭīyate pratinidhi-nyāyena*

20. One should (then) feed (one's) maternal grandfather,[1] maternal uncle, sisters' son, father-in-law, preceptor, daughter's son, a king, a kinsman, as well as a Ṛtvik and a Yājya (one on whose behalf a Yajña can be performed)

21. One should not feed a friend[2] in the Śrāddha. He should be pleased with wealth(?). Desire for Dakṣiṇās is demonic and is not conducive to any benefit either here or hereafter.

22. In case of non-availability of a suitable Brāhmaṇa one may very well feed and honour a friend but not an enemy, even though he may be learned and enlightened. The *Havis* partaken of by an enemy becomes futile after death.

23. A Brāhmaṇa who has not learned the Vedas becomes extinct like the fire of (dry) grass. *Havya* shall not be given unto him, for *Homa* is not performed in the ashes indeed.

24. Just as by sowing seeds in a barren land, the sower does not reap any fruit thereof, similarly, by offering Havis to one without Ṛk *mantras* (i.e. one who has not learned Ṛk *mantras*) one does not reap the fruit of that offer.

25. If a non-knower of Mantras partakes of food-oblations in *Havya* and *Kavya* (offered to gods and Pitṛs), the performer of that Srāddha is compelled to swallow after death as many burning thick balls of iron (in number) as the rice-balls swallowed by that non-knower[3] (of *mantras*).

26. O Brāhmaṇa, that abode (place of sacrifice) becomes Asura (unholy and demonaic) where these base men of evil conduct partake of the *Havya*, though they may be endowed with the knowledge and birth in noble family.

27.* If the Vedas and Vedis (sacrificial platforms) are in disuse upto three generations, that person becomes an evil Brāhmaṇa; He never deserves invitation to feeding in Śrāddhas[4] etc.

1. Yāj. Smṛ. I. 220, Mt. P. 16. 10-11.

2. VV. 21-22. Cf. Manu III. 138-139 but he modifies his view and allows invitation to a friend in emergency but not an enemy however learned III. 144.

3. Manu III. 133.

*Auśanasa Smṛti.

4. VV. 27-47 describe the disqualifications for invitation to a Śrāddha. Most of these verses are common to Manu III. 151-166 Cf. Yāj. Smṛ. I. 222-

28. The person mentioned above, a servant of a Śūdra, a salaried attendant of the king, the sacrificial priest of Śūdras, a person who sustains himself by killing and a person whose livelihood is imprisoning others—these six are Brahmabandhus (not true Brāhmaṇas—nominal Brāhmaṇas).

29. (Defective verse) Manu says that they are fallen for the sake of wealth. These sellers of Vedas are not approved of for the Śrāddha.

30. Those who sell their sons, those who are born as sons of a remarried widow, those who perform the Yajñas of even ordinary persons—all these are spoken of as fallen ones.

31. Those teachers who are not cultured, those who read and teach Vedas for salary—are called fallen ones.

32-33. That Śrāddha wherein the wicked *Tāmasikas* such as old Śrāvakas (Buddhists), Jainas, knowers of Pañcarātra, followers of Kāpālika and Pāśupata sects, atheists, and others like them eat food offered to gods, does not bestow excellent benefit here and hereafter.[1]

34. A Brāhmaṇa not belonging to any Āśrama, or a non-performer of the prescribed duties of his own Āśrama (stage of life) and who falsely poses as belonging to a particular Aśrama—all these should be known as defilers of rows of people participating in a feast.

224, Bṛhad-Yama Smṛ. III. 34-38, Mbh. *Anuśāsana* 90. 6-11, Mt. P. 16. 14-17, Bm. P. 220. 127-135. Bd. P. Upodghāta 15. 39-43, 19. 39-41, NP. I. 30-41. The textual similarity between these verses from different works is significant. Out of these, Manu's list of disqualifications is the most comprehensive one. A reference to *Smṛ. Candrikā* III, pp. 394-403 shows how writers on Dharma Sūtras, Smṛtis and Purāṇas attached great importance to the selection of Brāhmaṇas for Śrāddha. As Manu III 149. puts it, one may not put Brāhmaṇas to test for work pertaining to gods, but in the case of *Pitṛs* (i. e. for Śrāddha) one must be scrupulously careful—a view endorsed by most other writers on Dharma Śāstra.

1. Here the followers of Pañca-rātra, Kāpālika and Pāśupata sects are disqualified as these sects were regarded to have been outside the vedic fold duc to their recognition of their sectarian Āgamas as against the Vedas. Pāśupatas of the vedic fold described so elaborately in this Purāṇa are different.

Cf. Bd. P. III. 14. 38-39, Vāyu 78. 30-31

35-42. The following persons are shunned in Śrāddha and similar rites : A person with a hideous skin; one with ill-formed rotten nails, a leper, one with white leprosy, one with black teeth, one whose penis is mutilated, a thief, an impotent person, an atheist, a drink-addict, a paramour of a Śūdra woman, a murderer of a hero, one who indulges in sexual intercourse with one's brother's widow,[1] one who commits arson, a pimp, the seller of Soma, the young brother who marries before the elder brother,[2] the violent man, the elder brother who remains unmarried when the younger brother has married, non-performer of Mahā-yajñas, an expelled one, a widow's son, a usurer, a stargazer) one indulging in songs and musical instruments, a sickly person, a one-eyed fellow, one deficient in any limb, an *Avakīrṇin* (a religious student who breaks his vow), one who has an additional limb, a person who defiles food, bastard, a person accused of a crime, a Devala (a person maintaining himself by worshipping idols) ; a person who injures his friend; a back-biter, a henpecked husband; a person who has abandoned his parents and the preceptor, a wife-forsaker, the creator of discord in one's clan, one who is impure, a worthless fellow; an issueless person, a perjuror, a beggar, a person living by means of dramas, a seafarer, an ungrateful person, a person committing breach of promise, and one who censures Vedas, Devas and the Brāhmaṇas. All these should be avoided in a Śrāddha.

43. The following are defilers of rows :—an ungrateful person, a back-biter, a ruthless person, an atheist, a person who censures the Vedas, a person injuring friends and a cheat.

44. All these should not be fed (in a Śrāddha). They cannot be given any gift in holy rites A murderer of a Brāhmaṇa and a person who is accused should be avoided scrupulously.

45. A Brāhmaṇa who has fattened himself on the food and drink offered py Śūdras and a person not performing Sandnyā

1. *didhiṣūpati*—one who lasciviously dallies with the widow of his deceased brother even though he be appointed to procreate a son from her as per law (*dharma*), Manu III. 173.

2. *Parivettā*—a younger brother who marries or kindles sacred fires before his elder brother—Manu III. 171.

prayers and five great *Yajñas*—are the defilers of the rows (in feasts).

46. A Brāhmaṇa who destroys what he has learned, one devoid of an ablution and charitable gifts and a Brāhmaṇa with predominance of Tamas and Rajas Guṇas—all of these are defilers of rows.[1]

47. Of what use is an expiation beyond limit. Those who do not perform the enjoined duties but perform those acts which are forbidden are to be scrupulously avoided in the Śrāddha.

CHAPTER TWENTY-TWO

Rules for performance of Śrāddha[2] (*contd.*)

Vyāsa said :

1-2. Having purified the ground with cowdung and water on the day previous to that of *Śrāddha*, the performer of *Śrāddha* should invite the Brāhmaṇas with the above-mentioned quilifications, through good persons with the invitation : "Tomorrow there will be *Śrāddha* at my place." If this is not possible, he may invite on the next day[3] (i.e, on the day of *Śrāddha*.

3. Hearing that the time of *Śrāddha* has arrived, his manes will mentally communicate with each other and with the speed of the mind, they gather near him.

1. Though KP. does not explicitly discuss it there is a distinction between one who should not be invited as a Brāhmaṇa for Śrāddha because being *Sagotra* and those who are *apāṅkteyas* or *Paṅkti-dūṣakas* i. e. whose presence defiles the row of diners. The list of such defilers (Paṅkti-dūṣakas) is given above in this chapter.

2. As this chapter is *verbatim* the same as *Auśanasa Smṛti* ch. V, parallels for comparison from this *Smṛti* are not cited.

3. Cf. Mt. P. 16. 17-20; Prajāpati Smṛ. 63.

4. The *Pitṛs* take food along with those Brāhmaṇas, though they (themselves) are in firmament.[1] They remain in their airy state. After taking food, they attain their greatest goal.

5. The Brāhmaṇas who have been invited shall invariably observe celibacy, be self-controlled when the time for the *Śrāddha* has arrived.[2]

6. The person who performs *Śrāddha* must certainly avoid anger, hurry, carelessness; should speak the truth and have concentration of the mind, refrain from carrying heavy weight, sexual intercourse and long journey.

7. If a Brāhmaṇa, invited by one accepts the invitation of another, he falls into the terrible hell and becomes a pig.

8. If the Brāhmaṇa (householder), after inviting one Brāhmaṇa for the Śrāddha invites another also out of delusion he is a greater sinner. He is reborn as a worm in the faeces.

9. If a Brāhmaṇa invited for partaking of the Śrāddha indulges in sexual intercourse, he incurs the sin of a Brāhmaṇa-slaughter. He is reborn as an animal.

10. If a Brāhmaṇa invited for a Śrāddha (accepts the invitation and) goes on a journey, the *Pitṛs* of the wicked Brāhmaṇa subsist on sinful food that month.

11. If a Brāhmaṇa, invited for a Śrāddha were to quarrel, the *Pitṛs* of that Brāhmaṇa become the eaters of filth that month.

12. Hence, the Brāhmaṇa invitee for a Śrāddha should control himself, be free from anger and devoted to cleanliness. The performer (of the *Śrāddha*) also shall be one who has conquered his sense-organs.

13. (Defective verse). On the morning of the next day (i.e. on the *Śrāddha* day) he should go in the southern direction and with great concentration bring the Kuśa grass alongwith their roots, and (he shall place them) with their tips to the South and water (?). They shall be clean.

---

1. The idea of ancestors hovering in the sky for participation of food on the Śrāddha day and entering the body of Brāhmaṇas invited for Śrāddha is found elsewhere also, vide Pd. P. Sṛṣṭi Khaṇḍa 9. 85-86, Vāyu P. 75. 13-15.

2. About the religious restrictions on the inviter and the invitee to Śrāddha cf. *Laghu Śaṅkha Smṛ.*

14. He shall select a clean isolated spot of all auspicious characteristics. It shall be smooth and sloping towards the south. He shall scrub it and smear cowdung over it.[1]

15. The *Pitṛs* are always delighted with the *Śrāddha* offered in holy centres, on the banks of the rivers, on his plot of land in isolated places but not in waters.

16. One shall never perform *Śrāddhas* in a plot of land belonging to others. What is done by men may be obstructed by the owner out of delusion.

17. Forests, mountains, sacred holy centres and shrines —they say that these are without owners. No one can claim these as theirs.

18. (Defective verse). He shall scatter gingelly seeds there all round, but see that they do not grow (i.e. germinate ?) A Śrāddha affected by the Asuras becomes purified through the gingelly seeds if they do not germinate.

19. He shall then prepare various kinds of cooked food with diverse pickles and side dishes. In accordance with his ability, he should prepare lambatives, beverages and cooked food.

20. (Defective verse). Then, after midday, he should approach the Brāhmaṇas who have shaved their hairs and pared their nails and give unto them the tooth-brush twig.

21. When requested "Ye be seated", they will sit separately. He should give them oil for anointing themselves with as well as water for bath, and various other necessary requisites. These shall be given in vessels made of Udumbara wood. Everything shall be given with *Vaiśvadaivatya* rites (i.e. uttering Vaiśvadeva hymns).

22. When they return after taking bath, he should greet them with palms joined in reverence. He should offer them *Pādya* and *Ācamanīya*, (water for washing the feet and the Ācamana) sipping water-rite in due order.

1. For the selection of a spot for Śrāddha, cf. Manu III 206-207, Yāj, I. 227.

23. The seats of those Brāhmaṇas who had been previously invited on behalf of Viśve-Devas, are covered with three blades(?) of Darbha grass with their tips towards the East.

24. The seats of the Brāhmaṇas on behalf of the *Pitṛs* are the Darbha grasses facing the South. They must be sprinkled with water and gingelly seeds.

25. He should make them sit on these. Touching the seat he should request : "Ye be seated", They shall seat separately.

26. Two (Brāhmaṇas) shall represent Viśvedevas (?) They shall face the east. Three Brāhmaṇas represent the *Pitṛs* They face the north. One shall represent *Pitāmaha* (grandfather) and one shall represent Mātāmaha (maternal grandfather) Or one Brāhmaṇa represents gods and one paternal and maternal grandfather.

27. Five things are spoiled if performed elaborately in a crowd, viz.-hospitality, purity of the place (of respect), the time of respect, cleanliness, and the selection of a Brāhmaṇa. Hence one shall not wish for elaborateness and a big gathering.

28. Or one shall feed only one Brāhmaṇa who is a master of the Vedas, endowed with learning, good conduct etc. and devoid of evil characteristics.

29. Out of all articles of food thereof, he should take a portion (in a vessel and offer it to the Brāhmaṇa representing gods, in the shrine, and then pass it to others.

30. He shall consign that cooked food to the fire. He should give that to a Brahmacārin. Hence, one shall feed only one Brāhmaṇa but he should be an excellent scholar.

31. If a mendicant or a Brahmacārin be present for the purpose of food and he seats himself in the *Śrāddha*, one should feed him also.

32. Śrāddha wherein the guest does not partake of the food, is not praised. Hence, guests should be worshipped in the *Śrāddhas* by the Brāhmaṇas.

33. Those twice-born ones who partake of the food in a *Śrāddha* devoid of hospitality (to a guest), are reborn as crows. There is no doubt about this. The performer of the *Śrāddha* too (is reborn as a crow).

34. The following shall be shunned and kept at a great distance from *Śrāddhas* viz. one who is deficient in any limb, a fallen one, a leper, one with running sores, an atheist, a cock, a pig and a dog.

35. One shall avoid a loathsome fellow, an unclean fellow, the naked one, the intoxicated one, the rogue, a women in her monthly course, the blue-garmented, the ochre-garmented and the heretic.

36. Whatever rite is performed in a *Śrāddha* towards the Brāhmaṇas shall be performed alongwith Vaiśvadeva rites or invoking Viśvedevas.

37. Even as they are seated, one should bedeck them in ornaments, garlands, coronets, fumigating incenses and unguents.

38. Then with the permission of the Brāhmaṇas, he should invoke Devas by means of the Ṛk *Viśvedevāsaḥ* (RV. II, 41. 13) etc. He shall duly recite it and face the north.

39-40. He shall wear two Pavitras (the Darbha grass made to resemble a ring with a tail). Repeating the mantra *Śanno devīḥ*, etc. he shall (RV.X. 9.4) pour water in the cleaned vessel. Repeating the mantra *Yavosi* (Vāja V. 26) etc. he should place Yavas (barley grains) there. Repeating the mantra "Yā Divyā" (Tait. Br. II. 7. 15. 4) he should pour the Arghya on to the hand. He should then offer scents and garlands, incense etc. according to his ability.

41. He shall then turn round anticlockwise and face the south, repeating the Ṛk. *Uśantas Tvā* (RV. X. 16. 12) etc. the learned man shall invoke the *Pitṛs*,

42-43. After invoking the *Pitṛs* and being permitted by the Brāhmaṇas he shall perform the Japa of the Mantra *Āyantu nah: Pitaraḥ* (Vāj. Saṁ 19. 58) etc. Repeating the Mantra *Śanno Devīḥ* etc. he should pour water in the vessel and place gingelly seed, repeating the mantra *Tilosi* etc. Pouring Arghya on the hands as before, he should, with concentration, put the *Saṁsravas* (mixing of waters from the Argha-vessel and vessel for Pitṛs).

44-45. At the seat of the Pitṛs, he should place the vessel face downwards. He should take the cooked rice soaked in ghee. Desirous of consigning it into the fire, he shall ask the Brāhmaṇas' permission for the same. On being permitted by them saying

"Do so", he should perform *Homa,* wearing the sacred thread in the usual manner.

45. *Homa* should be performed by one with the Kuśa grass in the hand, wearing the sacred thread in the normal manner. All the rites of the *Pitṛs* should be performed with the sacred thread worn over the right shoulder and under the left arm. The Vaiśvadeva rite is performed like *Homa.*

46. While rendering homage to Devas, one shall always kneel upon the right knee; and during the obeisance and service to the *Pitṛs* one shall kneel upon the other knee.

47. At the time he should repeat the Mantra *Somāya vai pitṛmate svadhā namaḥ* [svadhā and obeisance into Soma (the deity) with the Pitṛs]. Then he shall perform *Homa* by saying *Agnaye kavya-vāhāya svadhā* [svadhā unto Agni (fire-god) the bearer of *Kavyas*].

48. In case fire is not available one should make use of the right hand of the Brāhmaṇas. Or he shall perform it near god Mahādeva or in a cowshed with due concentration.

49-51. Thereafter, on being permitted by them he should go to the southern direction. After cleaning and smearing the place with cowdung, he should cover it with sand. It shall be inclined towards the South and be auspicious. With a Darbha grass he shall scratch and scrape its middle thrice. On that spot he should strew Darbha grass, the tips of which are turned to the south. With the remainder of the *Havis* he shall make three Piṇḍas there and offer them with great concentration.

52. After placing the Piṇḍas he shall wipe off the hand on the Darbha grass to remove the greasiness to *Pitṛs* who partake of the *Lepa.*[1] He should then perform the *Ācamana* rite thrice. He shall smell the cooked rice thrice slowly. The knower of the Mantras then shall make obeisance unto the *Pitṛs.*

53. The remainder of the holy water, he should pour round and near the Piṇḍas. After offering the Piṇḍas he shall smell the Piṇḍas with great concentration.

---

1. Manu III 216 Mt. P. 18. 29 state that ancestors from the fourth are entitled to this *lepa* (food stuck to the hand of the performer of Śrāddha).

54. He shall then feed the Brāhmaṇas duly with the rice other than that of the Piṇḍas. He should also offer them meat, pies, etc. of various kinds, auspiciously prepared in accordance with the Śrāddha Kalpa.

55-56. After they have started taking food, he should strew the cooked rice of the Piṇḍas in front of them on the ground. He should ask them "What shall I do with this rice ? (?) When they are satisfied, he should make them perform the *Ācamana* rite. After they have performed the *Ācamana*, he should urge them saying "Be diverted all round". The Brāhmaṇas will say then *Svadhā be to you.*

57. Then when they have finished taking food, he should inquire of them about the remainder of the food. On being permitted by those Brāhmaṇas he shall do so as they say.

58. In the *Pitṛ* rite one shall say *Svaditam* (May it be well tasted). In the cow-sheds it shall be mentioned thus—*Suśṛtam* (well-cooked). In prosperity it shall be mentioned thus : *Sampannam*—well endowed. In regard to a Deva *Sevitam* (served) should be mentioned.

59. After bidding farewell to the Brāhmaṇas he should stand before the Pitṛs silently facing the southern direction. He shall then beg of the Pitṛs the following boons :

60. "May the liberal person flourish. May the Vedas and our progeny flourish. May not our faith slip off. May there be much with us for giving."

61. The Piṇḍas may be given to cows, goats, or Brāhmaṇas or cast into fire or water. The wife, desirous of a son, may eat the middle Piṇḍa.[1]

62-64. He shall wash his hands and perform *Ācamana*. With the remainder of the foodstuff, he should propitiate kinsmen. He shall give unto the Brāhmaṇas whatever is liked by them viz: cereals, vegetables, fruits, sugarcane, milk, curds, ghee, honey, cooked rice as much as they want and various kinds of edibles and beverages. He should give them various kinds of grains and gingelly seeds of all kinds and different kinds of sugar. Except in the case of fruits, roots and *Pānakas* (sweetened

1. Manu III. 260-261, Yāj. I. 257, Mt. P, 16. 52-53.

cold water), hot food should be given to the twice-born by one who wishes for welfare.

65. One shall not rest the knee on the ground nor shall be furious. He shall not utter a falsehood. He shall not touch food with the foot. Nor shall he shun and reject it.

66. The demons take away the benefit of what is partaken of in fury or against the conventional procedure or when served by one who prattles.

67. O excellent Brāhmaṇas one should not stand near if one perspires profusely, he should not see* the crows and other birds going contrary to the natural order. The *Pitṛs* desirous of eating, come there assuming those forms.

68. He should not directly give salt into the hand. Nor should the food be served in an iron vessel. It should never be served with carelessness.

69. What is offered in the following types of vessels yields everlasting benefit viz.—golden, silvery, made of Udumbara wood or made of horn of rhenoceros.

70. He who feeds Brāhmaṇas in mud pots at the time of of the *Śrāddha* falls into the terrible hell. He who partakes of the offerings too falls into the hell.

71. One should not discriminate between persons sitting in the same row and serve irregularly. One shall not beg nor force anyone to give (?). He who begs, who forces anyone to give and who serves with partiality falls into the terrible hells.

72. They should eat the most excellent things prior to others. (v. l. *vāgyataḥ* 'observing silence'). But they should not speak out their material good qualities (?). The Pitṛs partake of food only as long as the qualities of the Havis are not mentioned.

73. The Brāhmaṇa occupying the seat of priority should not eat it at the very outset. If he eats while many look on, he will incur the sin of all sitting in the row.

---

*'paśyet' in this instruction is unsuitable as it stands. The v.l. *na pratiṣedhayet*, one should not drive away crows etc. is better."

74. An excellent Brāhmaṇa engaged in the *Śrāddha* should not avoid anything served. He should not refuse even the meat offered. One should not look at the food served to another person.

75. If the Brāhmaṇa who engaged in the *Pitṛ* rite, does not partake of the meat served, he is reborn as an animal for twenty-one births.

76. One shall read or narrate unto these Vedic passages of self-study, the Dharmaśāstras, Itihāsas, Purāṇas and the auspicious Śrāddhakalpas.

77. Then the partaker of the food should strew the cooked food in front on the ground. He shall ask them *Svaditam* ? "Well tasted ?". If they are satisfied, he should make them perform the *Ācamana* rite.

78. If they have performed the *Ācamana* rite, he should permit them saying 'Be diverted'. Thereafter, the Brāhmaṇas shall say to him—"May Svadhā be unto you."

79. When they have partaken of the food he should inform them about remaining cooked food. On being permitted by those Brāhmaṇas, he should do as they mention.

80. In the Pitṛ rite, the word*Svaditam* is to be mentioned, in the *goṣṭha-Śrāddha* word, it shall be mentioned thus *Śuśṛtam.* In *Ābhyudayika Śrāddha,*[1] *Sampannam* is mentioned and in regard to Deva, *Sevitam* shall be mentioned.

81. After eulogising and bidding farewell to the Brāmaṇas, he should stand silently before the Pitṛs facing the southern direction and beg of the Pitṛs these boons.

82. "May those charitable donors around flourish. May the Vedas and progeny flourish. May not our faith decrease. May there be much with us to be given."

83. He shall give the Piṇḍas to the cows, goats or Brāhmaṇas. Or he should consign them to the fire or to the water. The wife who is desirous of a son shall partake of the middle Piṇḍa.

---

1. *Ābhyudayika* or *Vṛddhi Śrāddha* is performed in recognition of prosperity or good luck e.g. birth of a son, marriage of a son or daughter. The Pitṛs are called here Nāndīmukhas. It is also called Nāndī-Śrāddha.

84. He should then wash his hands and perform the *Ācamana* rite. With the food that remains, he shall feed his own servants.

85. Afterwards he himself should take the remaining food alongwith the womenfolk. One should not remove their leavings before sunset.

86-87. The husband and wife should observe celibacy on the night. After performing the *Śrāddha* or partaking of it, he who indulges in sexual intercourse falls into the hell Mahāraurava and then attains the birth of a worm.

88. He should be pure and clean; quiescent and truthful. He should not be furious. He shall have good concentration. The performer and the partaker should avoid self-study and travel.

89. The Brāhmaṇas, who partake of another *Śrāddha* (immediately) after partaking of a *Śrāddha*, are on a par with the great sinners. They fall into many hells.

90. Thus the *Śrāddhakalpa* has been explained briefly but clearly to you. A Brāhmaṇa in difficulties shall prosper by performing it.

91. When he performs *Amāśrāddha* (i.e. śrāddha without cooked food) the knower of the procedure endowed with faith should perform the *Agnaukaraṇa*[1] rite (consigning offerings into the fire) as well as the offerings of Piṇḍas with that alone (i.e. the material used).

92. He whose mind is quiet, who is devoid of sins, and who performs *Śrāddha* in accordance with this procedure shall attain the region of ascetics.

93. Hence, an excellent Brāhmaṇa should assiduously perform the *Śrāddha* rite. Thereby the eternal Īśvara would be well-propitiated by him.

---

1. *Agnaukaraṇa* literally means offering unto the fire. Mitākṣarā on Yāj. I. 236 quotes Mārkaṇḍeya's decision that if the performer of Śrāddha is an Agnihotrī, he should oblate the offerings in Dakṣiṇāgni; if he does not keep Śrauta fire but only Aupāsana fire (*gṛhyāgni*) he should oblate in that fire; if the performer keeps neither (as in the case with most of us), the offering is to be made in the right hand of the Brāhmaṇa (invited for Śrāddha).

—Visnudharmottara I. 140. 18

94. An indigent Brāhmaṇa may perform *Śrāddha* even with fruits and roots after taking the ablution, with great concentration and performing the *Pitṛ-Tarpaṇa* rites with water and gingelly seeds.

95. A person whose father is alive should not perform *Śrāddha*. Some say that he can perform Śrāddha to those Pitṛs to whom his father offers *Śrāddha*. Or he can perform those rites upto the Homa.

96. One can offer *Śrāddha* unto one's father, grandfather and great grandfather. He should offer Śrāddha unto him who is his beloved* and not to anyone else.

97. One must feed him with devotion who is alive and to his satisfaction. One who is pure and self-controlled does not give unto the dead by transgressing the living one.

98. *Dvyāmuṣyāyaṇika*[1] son of two fathers i.e. natural as well as father by adoption) shall offer *Śrāddha* to both. Similarly a son born of the Niyoga rite should perform *Śrāddha* to his progenitor as well as the dead husband of his mother. Then he shall be the true heir.

99. If a son is born out of the semen virile without the sanction of Niyoga, the son should offer Piṇḍas to the progenitor. However, he may perform *Śrāddha* to the *Kṣetrin* (mother's husband).

100. He should prepare two separate Piṇḍas to the *Kṣetrin* (mother's husband) and to the *Bījin* (progenitor). He should proclaim the *Kṣetrin* and the *Bījin* in the course of the rite.[1] The *Ekoddiṣṭa* type of *Śrāddha* is to be performed on the (anniversary) day of the death in accordance with the procedure. When the *Āśauca* (impurity) period is over, he can perform any Kāmya rite as he pleases.

---

*v.l. *mṛyate* 'is dead', is better as *Śrāddha* is to be offered to the dead.

1. VV. 98-100 refer to sons having two fathers: Though *Niyoga* is now an obsolete custom, the injunction regarding *Piṇḍa-dāna* giving priority to the procreator (*bījin*) first and to the *Kṣetrin* (mother's husband) next is supported by Hārīta:

teṣām utpādayituḥ prathamaḥ pravaraḥ bhavati|

quoted in Madana-Pārijāta, pp. 607-608.

101-103a. The *Ābhyudayīka Śrāddha* should be performed in the forenoon by one who seeks prosperity. All the rites should be performed as though towards Devas. No rites should be performed with gingelly seeds. The Darbhas shall be made straight. He should feed the Brāhmaṇas in even number. As an auspicious beginning, he should recite – "May the Pitṛs be pleased."

103b. The *Śrāddha* to the mothers should be performed at the outset. That to the Pitṛs should be performed thereafter.

104. Thereafter, the *Śrāddha* to the maternal grandfather shall be performed. These three *Śrāddhas* are to be performed when there is a prosperous occasion in the family, such as a birth of a son. This shall be offered along with Vaiśvadeva rites. The anti-clockwise circumambulation is not performed.

105-107. The scholar should sit facing the east and wear the sacred thread in the normal manner with good concentration and then perform *Śrāddha.* The mothers alongwith the Gaṇeśvaras should be worshipped at the outset, with devotion, either on the ground coloured in diverse ways or in idols or in Brāhmaṇas. One should worship with incense, food offerings and ornaments. A Brāhmaṇa should perform the three *Śrāddhas* after worshipping the groups of Mātṛs (mothers). If anyone performs *Śrāddhas* without the worship of the Mātṛs, they become infuriated and cause injuries.

CHAPTER TWENTY-THREE

Rules regarding Impurities caused by
Birth or Death[1]

Vyāsa said :

1. O excellent Brāhmaṇas ! They (the authorities) enjoined that if *Sapiṇḍas* (to whom Piṇḍas are to be offerd—six

1. *Āśauca* or the impurity caused by birth (*Sūtaka*) or death of a close relative. It is a sort of untouchability entailing a temporary loss of privilege

generations) are born or die, Brāhmaṇas have to observe impurity for ten days.

2. Neither the *Nitya* (daily) rites nor the *Kāmya* rites (for attaining desired ends) shall be performed, nor shall any other prescribed duty be done. As to *Svādhyāya* (Vedic recitation), it should not be even mentally attempted during this period.[1]

3. One shall appoint pure, unragable (quiescent) Brāhmaṇas of the earth (local area), for offering oblations in the fire in the sacrificial hall, (or) he should perform Homa in the sacrificial fire by means of dry rice-grains or dry fruits.

4. During the days of impurity others should not touch these. Nor should they take their food along with them. Since the fourth or fifth day, touching them is permitted by learned men.

5. In the case of *Sūtaka* (impurity due to birth) excepting the woman who has given birth and her child (?), there is no harm in touching each other among the *Sapiṇḍa* members.

6. If the father be teaching the Vedas and be the knower of the Vedas, all these may be touched after they have performed a bath. The mother (who has delivered the child) however, becomes so after bathing after the period of ten days.

7. The *Āśauca* is said to be for ten days in the case of *Nirguṇa* (devoid of qualities) and *Atinirguṇa* (extremly devoid of qualities). One who is endowed with one, two or three *guṇas* becomes pure in four, two or one days respectively.

---

to perform religious acts, to prosecute Vedic study and to participate freely in social functions like dinners etc.

There is a distinction about the periods of *Āśauca* and the persons affected by them. *Āśauca* on death has many distinctions e.g. after abortion before the 4th month and after that, death of a child before and after cutting the teeth, before or after performance of Upanayana or marriage. The duration of *āśauca* depended upon the nearness of blood relation, place of death and the time-limit of being informed about it.

KP deals with these topics in a loose Purāṇic way.

1. VV. 2-5 describe the loss of privileges during the *Āśauca* period.

8. After ten days, one can very well pursue the study of the Vedas and perform Homas. Manu the Prajāpati says that he can be touched on the fourth day.

9. In the case of the following, the impurity ends with the death of the person concerned :—one who is devoid of holy rites, a fool, a person attacked by a grave ailment (foul disease), and one who does as he pleases.

10. *Āśauca,* in the case of Brāhmaṇas is for three days or ten days. If the dead one is less than a year in age, the impurity is for three days. If the age is beyond one year, the impurity is for ten days.[1]

Extra verse in brackets :

A. When the dead one is less that two years old, the *Āśauca* is (for ten days) to the parents. Others become clean in three days, if the dead one is extremely devoid of qualities. If the child dies before cutting the teeth, the parents have *Āśauca* for one day.

11. If the child has cut teeth, the *Āśauca* is for three days, if both of the parents are Nirguṇas (?).

12. As for the Sapiṇḍakas (kinsmen), the impurity is only for that nonce, if the dead child has not cut teeth; the impurity is for one day, if the tonsure ceremony has not been performed. It is for three days, if the *Upanayana* (sacred thread investiture) rite has not been performed.

13. If the child dies immediately after the birth, the impurity is limited only for the father and the mother. But the father may be touched.

14. In the case of a brother, the Sapiṇḍas (near kinsmen) should always observe *Āśauca* (for the prescribed period). If the brother is (not qualified) (?), the impurity is for one more day after ten days.

15. After the cutting of teeth, the impurity of the Sapiṇḍas is for one day if they are *Nirguṇa*s. After the tonsure ceremony, the impurity is for three days.

---

1. VV. 10-17 deal mainly with the *Āśauca* after abortion, death of an infant, etc.

16. O excellent ones, if the death of the child before the cutting of teeth takes place, the impurity for the Sapiṇḍas is for one day, if they are extremely *Nirguṇas* (?)

Verses in Brackets :

B. If there is abortion in the first four months (*srāva*) or miscarriage in the 5th or 6th month (*pāta*), Vrata is enjoined on the Sapiṇḍas. In the case of all Guṇins, the contrariness is beyond that. (?)

C. If the miscarriage is before six months of pregnancy, the *Āśauca* is for as many days as the number of months that have gone by.

D. If the miscarriage is after that (i.e. after six months) the *Āśauca* for women is for twelve days. In the case of (*Srāva*-abortion upto the fourth month) the Sapiṇḍas get purity instantaneously.

17. If the Sapiṇḍa is extremely *Nirguṇa*, the impurity is for one day and one night as a result of miscarriage. If the kinsman is one who does as he pleases, the impurity is for three days. This is the conclusion.

18. In the case of *Āśauca-sannipāta*—that is if there is another impurity due to birth when already one is current or if there is another death when already one impurity due to death is current, the purity is after the remaining impurity is over. If the remainder is only a day, the impurity continues for three days.

19. When death and birth overlap, the conclusion (of that period) is with the end of the death impurity. If the first *Āśauca* is with *Vṛddhi* (birth of a son), it becomes clean by means of the previous one (?)[1]

Verse in the Bracket :

E. Then the impurity may go beyond the fifth day.

20. A man is impure after hearing the birth or death occurring in another land as long as the remainder of that period is to be concluded.

1. Regarding *Āśauca-sannipāta* or *Sampāta* cf. Gautama Dh. S. 14. 5-6, Manu V. 79 also Laghu-Hārita verse 80.

Verse in Bracket (4 *verses*)

F. to I. If the period of *Sūtaka* (birth impurity) is over it is said that the Sapiṇḍakas must observe it for three days.

If the death is of one above one year in age only a bath is needed.

One shall be immediately pure if one is a knower of the meanings of the Vedas, or is a student of the Vedas, or maintains fires (sacrificial fires) or is emaciated due to livelihood. It shall be so in all states and for ever.

If the daughters are not married, the Āśauca for the Sapiṇḍakas is for three days; if they are married, the impurity is for the husband alone. It is also said that the impurity due to the death of girls not given in marriage is for a day. On the death of a girl less than two years, the purity is instantaneous after bath. Upto the cutting of teeth, no impurity even to the brother, upto the tonsure ceremony the impurity is for a day.

21. Upto the marriage, the impurity is for three days and beyond that it is for ten days.

22. On the death of maternal grandfather, the Āśauca is for three days. In the case of *Sūtaka* (birth) impurity to the same is the case.

23. In the case of relatives through marriage, the preceptor and a classmate (i.e. disciple of the same preceptor), the impurity is said to be for one Pakṣiṇī i.e. two days with a night between or *vice versa* .

24. When the king dies, everyone in the kingdom observes impurity till the coming of the day or night next to that on which the king dies.[1] If the daughters die in his house, the father observes impurity for three days.

25-26. If the wife who had previously married another, dies or if an adopted son dies, the impurity is for three days. If the wife of the preceptor, whether of the same caste or of another caste dies, if the son of the preceptor dies, the impurity

1. Vide Manu V. 82. Yāj. III. 25, Mitākṣarā explains *sa-jyotiḥ* as follows: If the king's death takes place at day, then the *āśauca* is till the next sunrise; if at night, till the stars appear next night (*ahni ced yāvat sūrya-darśanam, rātrau ced yāvan nakṣatra-darśanam*).

is for a day and a night. If a priest, or a learned Paṇḍita dies in one's own village, the impurity is for one day.

27. If the Asapiṇḍas die in one's own house, the impurity to be observed is for three days only.

28. On the death of the mother-in-law or the father-in-law, the impurity is for three days. If any one belonging to one's own Gotra dies, the impurity is only for the moment (after bath).

29. A Brāhmaṇa becomes free from impurity within ten days, a king within twelve days, a Vaiśya within fifteen days and a Śūdra becomes free from impurity within a month.[1]

30. If a Brāhmaṇa were to have a Kṣatriya, a Vaiśya or a Śūdra as his kinsman and if he were to die, the Brāhmaṇa becomes free from impurity in ten days.[2]

31. A Kṣatriya as well as a Vaiśya should observe impurity in the case of the death of kinsmen of the lower castes and should certainly perform the rites prescribed (for their respective caste) for purification.

32. All people should observe impurity for the death of a higher caste man with respect, in accordance with the rules governing that caste. In regard to people of his own caste, he should observe his own purity according to rules of their caste.

33. The impurity to be observed in the case of (birth or death) of a Sapiṇḍa (?) Śūdra kinsman, for Vaiśyas, Kṣatriyas and Brāhmaṇas is for six nights, three nights, and one night respectively.

34. The impurity to be observed in the case of a Sapiṇḍa Vaiśya, O excellent leading Brāhmaṇas, by Śūdras, Kṣatriyas and Brāhmaṇas is for half a month, six nights and three nights respectively.

35. O leading Brāhmaṇas, the impurity to be observed in the case of (birth or death of) Brāhmaṇa kinsman by Kṣattriyas and Vaiśya is six nights (i.e. days) and ten days respectively.

---

1. Manu V. 83, Yāj. III. 23, Mt. P. 18. 2-3.

2. VV. 30-36 record the period of *āśauca* to be observed in the case of Anuloma and Pratiloma marriages. Cf. Dakṣa Smṛ. VI. 12, Viṣṇu Dh. S. 22. 22-24.

36. The consort of Kamalā (i.e. Viṣṇu) ordains that a Brāhmaṇa becomes pure within ten days from the impurity of a Śūdra, a Vaiśya and a Kṣatriya.*

37.[1] If a Brāhmaṇa carries the dead body of a Brāhmaṇa who is not his Sapiṇḍa, to the burning ghat like one of his kinsmen, and takes food as well as stays with them (the kinsmen of the dead man), he shall become pure within ten days.

38. If he takes their food, he becomes pure in three nights. If he does not take food (he becomes purified in one day but) he should not stay in that house.

39. The same thing shall be in the case of the *samānodakas* and the kinsmen of the mother and other close relatives. The person—a sapiṇḍa—who touches the dead body becomes pure within ten days.

40-41. If one (belonging to Brāhmaṇa, Kṣattriya, Vaiśya or Śūdra caste) carries the dead body out of covetousness, the Brāhmaṇa becomes pure within ten days and the king or Kṣattriya within twelve days. The Vaiśya becomes free within half a month and the Śūdra within a month. Or all of them become pure in six days, or they shall be pure in three days.

42. If Brāhmaṇas and others carry the dead body of an orphan or a helpless Brāhmaṇa devoid of wealth, they become pure by taking bath and drinking ghee.

43. If a man of the lower caste touches one of the upper caste or if a man of the upper caste touches one of the lower caste during impurity, and if he does so out of friendship, he becomes pure by ordinary purificatory procedure (bath, etc.)

44. If a Brāhmaṇa were to follow the dead body of a Brāhmaṇa out of his own will, he becomes pure by taking bath alongwith the clothes he wears at the time, touching the fire and taking in ghee.

45. (If one follows the dead body) the purity in following the corpse of a Kṣattriya is within a day; that in the case

*but the v.l. *brāhmaṇe saṁsthite sati* changes the whole verse : It means, 'In the case of (the birth or death of) a Brāhmaṇa (Sapiṇḍa kinsman), the impurity to be observed by Śūdra, Vaiśya and Kṣattriya is for ten nights (days).

1. VV. 37-42 deal with *āśauca* by carrying a dead body. Cf. Manu V. 101-102.

of a Vaiśya shall be within two days; it is said that three days impurity should be observed if the dead body of a Śūdra is followed. But one must perform a hundred *prāṇāyāmas* (breath-control exercises) (in addition to all these cases).

46. When the bones of the dead Śūdra have not been collected and if the Brāhmaṇa cries along with his own people over the death of the Śūdra, the impurity shall be for three nights. Otherwise, it is only a single day.

47. (Under the same circumstances) if he laments the death of a Kṣattriya or a Vaiśya before the bones are collected, the impurity is observed for one day; otherwise it is till the rise of the sun or of stars (as the case may be). In the case of (lamentation on) the death of a Brāhmaṇa (before bone-collection), the impurity lasts till the performance of bath.

48. If a Brāhmaṇa cries over the death of a Brāhmaṇa before his bones are collected, he becomes pure by means of an ablution alongwith the clothes worn. There is no doubt about this.

49. He who takes food alongwith them and associates closely with them by sharing their bed, seat etc., he becomes pure in ten days irrespective of his being a kinsman.

50. He who takes food alongwith them even once, out of his own free will, becomes free from impurity by taking bath when the period of impurity ceases.

51. If a man overwhelmed by famine, takes their food, he should observe impurity for as many days as he had taken their food. Thereafter, he should observe religious atonement.

52. In the case of the Brāhmaṇa who maintained *Agni-Hotra* (a sacred fire), the impurity is to be observed from the time of his cremation. In the case of Sapiṇḍas the impurity begins at death and in cases other than death (i.e. birth).

53. Sapiṇḍa relationship ceases from the seventh generation. The *Samānodakabhāva* (state of offering water oblation) ceases if the birth and the names are not known.

54. The father, the grandfather and the great-grand father—these three should be known as *Lepabhāks* (enjoyers of the portion of Piṇḍas sticking to the hand of the performer of *Śrāddha*). (Actually the ancestors of fourth, fifth and sixth

generations are the *Lepabhāks*. The Sapiṇḍa relationship lasts till the seventh generation.

55. The Sapiṇḍa relationship of women not given in marriage extends to seven generations of the family of their birth. Lord Pitāmaha says that the Sapiṇḍa relationship of those (married) women is the same* as that of their husbands.

56. Among the many descendants of the same man but of different castes (through mothers of different castes), the Sapiṇḍa relationship extends upto the third generation in descent.

57. In the case of artisans, craftsmen, physicians, servant-maids and attendants, regular donors, the knowers of the Brahman, the Brahmacārins (celibates), the *Sattrins* (performers of Yajñas) of long-durations) and the *Vratins* (those who have regular observance of holy rites), the purity is instantaneous.[1]

58. In the case of a crowned king, and the performers of *Annasatras* (?) at the time of Yajñas and marriage as well as during divine intercession (?) during famine and chaotic upheavals, the purity is instantaneous.

59-60. In the case of those who are killed in *Dimbāhava* (petty warfare and skirmishes), in the case of the death of *Jñātis* (near cousins) due to serpent bite etc., the purity is instantaneous. (Defective verse) If any one dies in fire or whirlwind, if any one dies in an unforgettable (lit. imperishable) heroic path; if one dies for the sake of cows or Brāhmaṇas or if one dies after renunciation, the purity is instantaneous.

61. In the case of *Naiṣṭhikas* (life-long celibates), forest dwellers, ascetics and religious students, no impurity is enjoined by good men. When a fallen man dies, there is no impurity.

62. In the case of fallen men there is no cremation, no obsequies, no collection of bones; no tear is shed, no Piṇḍa is offered and no Śrāddha or similar rite is performed.

63. If a man kills himself by means of fire, poison etc., no impurity is to be observed, no cremation is performed, no water libation is offered to him.

---

*vide Mt. P. 13-29 : *Lepa-bhājas caturthādyāḥ pitrādyāḥ piṇḍa-bhāginaḥ*/

1. VV. 57-62 enumerate the cases of *Sadyaḥ-śauca* i.e. those after whose death purification is on the same day after bath.

64. If one dies through fire, poison etc. due to oversight, impurity should be observed and water libation should be offered to him.

65-66. (?) When a son is born, one may very well accept the following as gifts viz. gold, cereals, cow, cloth, gingelly seeds alongwith jaggery and ghee, fruits, flowers, vegetables, salt, firewood, buttermilk, curds, ghee, oil, medicine and milk. One may take raw grains every day from the house of one who has impurity.

67. A person who maintains the three sacrificial fires duly, should be cremated by means of the three fires. A person who has not maintained the three fires shall be cremated by the *Gṛhya* (household) fire and the other people shall be cremated by means of the secular fire.

68. If the dead body is not available, a representative figure should be made by means of Palāśa leaves and twigs and the cremation shall be duly performed by Sapiṇḍa relations endowed with faith.

69. He should sprinkle the figure with water uttering the name and Gotra (of the dead man). He shall not speak unnecessarily. All the kinsmen should exercise self-control and should perform *Śrāddha* for ten days.

70. Everyday, they should offer the Piṇḍa both in the morning as well as in the evening to the dead man at the entrance to the house. On the fourth day, they shall feed the Brāhmaṇas.

71. On the second day, the shaving rite should be performed alongwith the kinsmen. On the fourth day, the bones should be collected, (?) by all the kinsmen. With great faith, they should employ pure Brāhmaṇas (as priests) in even numbers (v.l. feed Brāhmaṇas).

72. Brāhmaṇas should be fed in even (?) numbers on the fifth, ninth and eleventh days. O Brāhmaṇas, this is called *Navaśrāddha*.

73. This rite shall be performed on behalf of the dead one, on the eleventh, twelfth or the ninth day. The rite shall be performed with great faith. One *Pavitra* (Kuśa-grass ring), one *Argha* (vessel of offerings), and one vessel for the Piṇḍas should be used.

74. This rite shall be performed every month for a year on the day of death, at the end of which should be performed the rite called *Sapiṇḍīkaraṇa*.[1]

75. O excellent Brāhmaṇas, four vessels should be assigned to the four ancestors from the dead person. On behalf of the dead one, water shall be poured in the vessels of the Pitṛs.

76. While the Piṇḍas are joined together, the *mantras* recited are the two stanzas beginning with *Ye samānā* (Vāj. Saṁ. 19.45) etc. The *Śrāddha* of *Sapiṇḍīkaraṇa* is performed after the *Śrāddha* meant for gods.

77. He should invoke the Pitṛs there. Then he should point out the dead man (?) There are no separate rites (*Śrāddha*) in the case of those dead whose *Sapiṇḍīkaraṇa* rite has been performed. He who separates the Piṇḍas (i.e. offers separate ones) becomes the slayer of the Pitṛs.

78. When the father dies, the son should offer the Piṇḍaṣ for a year. He should offer food and the pot with water every day, in accordance with the rites of the dead.

79. Every year this should be performed in accordance with the injunctions governing *Pārvaṇa Śrāddhas*. This is the eternal traditional rite.

80. The offering of Piṇḍas and other rites to parents should be performed by the son. If there is no son, the wife should perform these rites. If there is no wife, the co-uterine brother should perform it.

81. One should with great faith and concentration perform the rites of Dāna etc. and perform the *Śrāddha* in accordance with this procedure.

82. Thus, the procedure for the rites of householders has been clearly explained to you. As for women, their holy rite is rendering of service to their husbands. No other holy rite is prescribed for them.

---

1. VV.74-77 *Sapiṇḍīkaraṇa* is a symbolic process of uniting the deceased person with his *Pitṛs*. Four Piṇḍas are prepared, one for the *Preta* (deceased person) and three for his deceased paternal ancestors. Then the performer of *Śrāddha* divides the *preta-piṇḍa* in three parts and puts each third into each of the three Piṇḍas with the two mantras *ye samānā* (Yāj. sam. 19. 45).

83. They should be devoted to their duties for ever. They should dedicate their minds unto God. Thus they attain the greatest abode that has been described by the expounders of the Vedas.

CHAPTER TWENTYFOUR

The Duties of Agnihotrin

Vyāsa said :

1. One should perform the *Agnihotra* rite both in the morning and the evening. On *Darśa* (the new moon) days after the conclusion of a beneficial rite and on reaping the harvest afresh this rite shall be performed.*

2. At the close of a season, the Brāhmaṇa should duly perform sacrifices. At the close of an *Ayana*, he should perform an animal sacrifice. At the end of a year he should perform the sacrifices in the fires (?) (v.l. the Soma sacrifice).

3. A Brāhmaṇa maintaining sacred fires and desirous of living for a long time should not eat cooked food or meat without performing the Yajña of fresh harvest and the animal sacrifice.

4. Without performing the sacrifice with fresh grains or with animals as *Havyas* (oblations), those people who are desirous of fresh grains and meat, actually desire to eat their own vital airs.

5. He should always perform the Śāntihomas (propitiatory *Homas*) for peace pertaining to Savitṛ (the sun-god) during the Parvans. During the Aṣṭakā and Anvaṣṭakā days, he should worship the pitṛs.

*A better v.l. *darśena caiva pakṣānte paurṇamāsena caiva hi*/'He should perform the Agnihotra rite on the new moon and full moon day at the end of a fortnight.'

6. This is the greatest Dharma of three higher castes, in the stage of householders. All other rites are called *Āpaddharmas*, (non-righteous).

7. Either due to atheistic feelings or due to lethargy, if anyone does not wish to maintain sacrificial fires, nor does he perform Yajñas, he falls into many hells.

Verses in Brackets :

A-B). The evil-minded person falls into the following hells viz. :—Tāmisra, Andhatāmisra, Raurava, Mahāraurava, Kumbhīpāka Vaitaraṇī, Asipatravana and many other terrible hells as well. O Brāhmaṇas, he is reborn in the families of outcastes or as a Śūdra.

8. Hence, a Brāhmaṇa should particularly maintain the sacrificial fire very assiduously. With his soul sanctified, he should worship Parameśvara.

9. There is no greater Dharma than *Agnihotra* in the case of Brāhmaṇas. Hence, one should always worship by means of *Agnihotra*.

10. He who is one who maintains sacrificial fires but does not wish to perform sacrifice to the lord by means of meditation, is a confused person. He should not be conversed with. What more (need be said) that man is an atheist.

11. He who possesses enough foodstuff to maintain his servants for three years or more, deserves to drink Soma juice.

12. The Soma sacrifice is considered first among all Yajñas. One should propitiate lord Maheśvara of the Region of Soma, through Soma.

13. There is no sacrifice equal to or greater than the Soma sacrifice that propitiates Maheśa. Hence, one should propitiate the greatest one through Soma* (sacrifice).

14. The sacrificial animal has been taken and enjoined on the Brāhmaṇas by Pitāmaha (god Brahmā). There are two types of Dharma conducive to salvation—the Śrauta and the Smārta.

---

*Due to oversight the Veṅkt. Text has given one and the same number to two verses. Hence verse No. 14 is included under 13 there. The mistake is rectified here.

15. Śrauta is that rite which is connected with the three fires. Smārta has been mentioned by me before. The Śrauta is more beneficial. Hence, one should perform the Śrauta rite.

16. Both of them are beneficial. They are holy rites prescribed in the Vedas. *Śiṣṭācāra* (the conduct of good men) shall be the third source of religion[1] when Śruti and Smṛti are not available.

17. They by whom the Vedas have been acquired along with their supplementary works, are *Śiṣṭas* (good men). They are so called because they are always endowed with the qualities of the *Ātman*.

18. What is approved by them for ever is called Dharma by good men. And not the behaviour of anyone else. This is what should be retained in the mind.

19. The Purāṇas and the Dharmaśāstras augment the Vedas (as amplification). From one the Brahman is realised. From the other Dharma (rituals of religion) is realised.

20-21.* They have been mentioned as the greatest authority by those who wish to know more of Dharma. They are the Dharmaśāstras and the Purāṇas. The knowledge of Brahman is from the other. Dharma is not born of anything else. The knowledge of Brahman is from the Vedas. Hence, the Dharma and Purāṇa should be believed (as divine revelation) by the learned men.

---

1. VV. 16-19 Cf. Manu XII. 108-109 where in matters not decided in Dharma-Śāstra texts the opinion of Śiṣṭas is regarded as Dharma.

*vide ft. note on verse 13. The total No. of verses is 21 though the Veṅk. Text. gives No. 20 to the last verse.

CHAPTER TWENTYFIVE[1]

The Means of Livelihood of a Brāhmaṇa Householder

Vyāsa said :

1. Thus the entire great Dharma of a Brāhmaṇa householder has been described to you. (Now listen and) understand the means of livelihood (of a Brāhmaṇa householder).

2. The householder is of two types. One is to be known as *Sādhaka* (one who works and achieves) and the other as *Asādhaka* (non-worker). They say that the means of livelihood of the former is teaching, presiding over Yajña or acceptance of monetary gifts. He can practise usury and look after agriculture or trading activities himself or through agents.

3. If agriculture is not possible, trading activity be undertaken. In its absence usury may be pursued. This is the arrangement in time of emergeney. What has been mentioned before (viz. teaching, priesthood and acceptance of *dāna*) is desired to be the main occupation.

4. He should himself pursue cultivation, business, activities or usury. Usury (of course) is a sinful activity involving pain and strain. One should (if possible) avoid it.

5. Some say that martial activity as the greatest (occupation) and cultivation of the field by the Brāhmaṇas themselves should be avoided. A Brāhmaṇa can pursue martial activity even when there is no emergency (?)

6. If the Brāhmaṇa does not maintain himself by that (i.e. martial activity), he should pursue the means of livelihood of a Vaiśya. But a Brāhmaṇa should by no means plough or till himself.

7. Acquiring profit in these activities, he should worship and propitiate the Pitṛs, Devas and the Brāhmaṇas.

---

1. This chapter describes the means of livelihood of both types of Brāhmaṇas—*Sādhakas* and *Asādhakas* which correspond to the classification into *Śālīna* and *Yāyāvara* given in Baudhāyana Dh. S. III. 1. 1. 3-5.

The verses in this chapter are quoted in SMC. pp. 454-56, and Parāśara Mādhava—*Ācāra Kāṇḍa*, p. 309.

There is no doubt in this that if they are satisfied they will quell his defects.

8. A Brāhmaṇa who pursues agricultural occupation should offer one-twentieth of the produce to Devas and the Pitṛs and one thirtieth to the Brāhmaṇas. He shall then incur no sin.

9. If he is engaged in trading activities, he should offer twice the previous offerings and one who practises usury should offer three times of what an agriculturist offers. He shall then be not involved in sin. There is no doubt about this.

10. A *Sādhaka* householder may also live on gleanings of corns or by irregular occupations. There are many other means of livelihood like learning, craftsmanship, etc.

11. Two means of livelihood have been prescribed by the great sages in regard to that type of householder who is mentioned as *Asādhaka*. They are gleaning of corns and irregular occupations.

12. Or he should maintain himself by *Amṛta* or *Mṛta*. What he gets without begging is called *Amṛta* and the alms received by begging is *Mṛta*.

13-14. There are four types of *Asādhaka* Brāhmaṇas[1] who gather grain thus :

1. *Kusūladhānyaka* (i.e. one who has hoarded grain enough for three years (Medhātithi) in his granary.
2. *Kumbhidhānyaka* (i.e. one who has hoarded grain sufficient for six days—for one year (according to the Medhātithi).
3. *Tryāhnika* (i.e. one who has food-grains for three days, and
4. *Aśvastanika* (i.e. one who has the grain sufficient for the day but not for the morrow).

The later ones are better than the earlier ones among these Brāhmaṇa householders. By means of piety he conquers the worlds (i.e. the last one).

15. The first one shall be Ṣaṭkarman (i.e. one who performs all the six duties viz. study of Vedas, teachings of the

1. The same as Manu IV. 7. The explanation of the terms herein are based on Medhātithi's com. of Manu.

Vedas, performance of the Yajñas, presiding over the Yajñas of others, gifts and acceptance of gifts). The second one shall perform three of them, the third, two of them and the fourth, one. He should maintain himself by *Brahmasatra* (study of the Vedas).

16. He who maintains himself by gleaning corn (and such other irregular professions) and is devoted to *Agnihotra* should perform ordinary sacrifices ending with these on the New Moon and Full Moon day.

17. A Brāhmaṇa should not pursue ordinary worldly professions. He should not pursue agriculture for livelihood. He should maintain himself with non-cooked, non-roguish (straightforward, honest) pure Brāhmaṇa-like profession.

18. After begging of moneyed good persons for alms, he should propitiate the Pitṛs and Devas. Or he should beg of pure person with self-control. He should be himself satisfied thereby.

19. He who after earning sufficient wealth does not duly propitiate Devas and the Pitṛs, is reborn as a lower animal such as a dog etc.

20-21. The four things—virtue, wealth, love and salvation-are beneficial. In the case of Brāhmaṇa, the love shall not be against Dharma and not the other. That wealth which is for the propagation of Dharma is real wealth and not one which is used for the self. Hence after attaining wealth a Brāhmaṇa should offer it to others and perform sacrifices to gods.

CHAPTER TWENTYSIX

Rules of offering religious gifts

Vyāsa said :

1. Now I shall recount the excellent *dharma* of charitable gifts,[1] formerly narrated by Brahmā to the sages, expounders of *Brahman*.

1. Apart from the *Dāna-stutis* in ṚV (I. 125, V. 61, VII 18 etc) *Dāna-dharma* (offering of religious gifts) is regarded as the principal aspect o

2. The handing over of riches with faith to the deserving persons is pointed out as *Dāna* (charitable gift). It yields worldly pleasures and salvation.[1]

3. I consider that as a wonderful (gift)[2] which is given with great faith to good men of distinction. What he keeps without giving is protected (saved) for others.

4. There are three types of charitable gifts the *Nitya*, the *Naimittika* and the *Kāmya*. A fourth type of charitable gift is also mentioned viz. *Vimala*[3] (the pure one) which is the most excellent of all the charitable gifts.

5. The *Nitya* charitable gift is as follows : Everday something is given to a Brāhmaṇa who does not give anything in return. Nor does the donor expect any fruit thereof.

6. The *Naimittika* (occasional) charitable gift is that which is given to scholars for the purpose of wiping off one's sins. This is *Dāna* (charitable gift) practised by good men.

7. What is given for the purpose of obtaining childern, success, prosperity and heaven is called a *Kāmyadāna* (charitable gift for the achievement of the desired object) by sages who have pondered over topics of piety.

8. What is handed over to the knowers of the *Brahman* for the propitiation of Īśvara, with a righteous mind, is called the auspicious *Vimala* (pure) *Dāna*.

9. One should resort to the *dharma* of charitable gifts in accordance with one's capacity, after getting the deserving persons. Indeed, a deserving person will be available and he will enable one to cross the entire ocean of Existence.

---

religious life in the Kali age (Manu I. 96, Mbh. *Sānti*. 232. 28, Vāyu P. 8. 65-66). Naturally, this topic is discussed in details in Smṛtis and Purāṇas, such as *Yājñavalkya* I. 198-216, *Vyāsa* IV 17-23, *Āp*. chs. 209-213, *NP*. I. Ch. 12, 31.

1. Cf. Devala quoted by Aparārka, p. 287.

2. Cf (*Veda*) *Vyāsa-smṛ*. IV. 16. The reading *tac ca vittam aham manye* 'that is what I regard is his real wealth or property' is better than *tad vicitram* in Veṅk. text.

3. VV. 4-8 give the classification of *Dānas* as *Nitya* (daily), *naimittika* (occasional), *Kāmya* (*dāna* for obtaining a dcsirable object) and *Vimala* (pure) the last is a special class specified in the KP.

10. What remains after providing food, clothing etc. to the family should be given as charitable gift. If it is given otherwise, that charitable gift does not yield any fruit.

11. *Dāna* should be given to a noble-born Brāhmaṇa well-versed in the Vedas. He should be humble and performer of penance. He shall be indigent and one who maintains holy rites. Everything given shall be offered with due devotion.

12. He who gives with great devotion a plot of land[1] to a Brāhmaṇa who maintains the sacrificial fires, attains that great abode after reaching which one has no cause for sorrow.

13. He who gives to a great scholar of Vedas a very fertile land producing barley and wheat and overgrown with sugar cane plants, is not born again.

14. He who gives at least a plot of land extending to a *Gocarman** (cow's hide) to an indigent Brāhmaṇa is liberated from all sins.

15. There is no other gift greater than the gift of lands here. The gift of cooked food is on a par with it. The gift of learning excels it.

16. He who duly imparts learning to a Brāhmaṇa of pure, pious conduct and excellent character, is honoured in Brahmaloka.

17. If one gives cooked food with due faith everyday to a Brahmacārin (religious student), one shall be freed from all sins and shall attain the abode of *Brahmā*.

18. A man obtains great benefit by giving cooked food to a householder. It must be given unto him (immediately) on arrival. After giving thus one attains the greatest goal.

19-20. One should observe fast on the full moon day in the month of Vaiśākha[2]. He should then duly worship seven or five Brāhmaṇas of clean habits, quiet temper and pure minds. He

1. VV. 12-15 describe the greatness of land-grant though Brāhmaṇas like *Aitareya* (39-7), *Śatapatha* (XIII. 7. 1. 15) prohibit kings from such grants, *Vasiṣṭha* smṛti. (29. 20) and Mbh. *Anuśāsana* (62. 2) eulogise it as *atidāna* (superior gift).

*According to Vasiṣṭha Gocarman is that plot of land which extends to hundred and fifty *Hastas* (hands) all round.

2. VV. 19-34 describe the reward from *dāna* on particular days.

should propitiate them with black gingelly seeds and honey in particular. He shall honour them with the application of sweet scents and unguent and make them spell out (blessings) or shall say oneself.

21. "O Dharmarāja be pleased." Whatever is in one's mind (shall be realised). Every sin committed in the course of whole life shall perish at that very moment.

22. He who places gold, honey and ghee, gingelly seeds on the hide of a black antelope and gives it to a Brāhmaṇa, surmounts all evils.

23. Particularly on the full moon day in the month of Vaiśākha, one should ritualistically offer cooked food and water pot to Dharmarāja and hand it over to Brāhmaṇas. He shall be relieved of fear.

24. One shall propitiate seven or five Brāhmaṇas with water-pots accompanied by gold and gingelly seeds. One can thereby expell the sin of even Brāhmaṇa slaughter.

25. On the Dvādaśī (twelfth) day in the month of Māgha a Brāhmaṇa should observe fast. He should wear white garments. He should perform Homa with black gingelly seeds in the holy fire. With great concentration he should offer gifts to the Brāhmaṇas well-versed in the Vedas. Whatever sin he might have committed ever since his birth, the Brāhmaṇa shall surmount it.

26-27. On the New Moon Day, one should offer anything unto a saintly Brāhmaṇa after dedicating the same to Śaṅkara, lord of Devas and their chiefs, by saying—"May the eternal Mahādeva, the lord accompanied by Umā, be pleased." The sin accumulated in the course of seven births perishes at the same moment.

28. He who takes his holy dip on the fourteenth day in the dark half of the month and propitiates the Pināka bearing lord Śiva through Brāhmaṇas is not reborn again in the world.

29-30. Particularly on the eighth day in the dark half of the month, one should take ablution and honour a righteous Brāhmaṇa duly by means of washing the feet etc. He should then say "May Mahādeva be pleased with me." He should then hand over his own wealth to him. He shall be relieved of all sins.

31. The three-eyed deity is to be particularly worshipped by Brāhmaṇa devotees on the fourteenth and eighth of the dark half and on the new moon day.

32. One should observe fast on the eleventh day and worship Puruṣottama on the twelfth day through a Brāhmaṇa. He shall attain the greatest region.

33. The twelfth day in the bright half is a Tithi belonging to Viṣṇu. One should assiduously propitiate lord Janārdana on that day.

34. Whatever is offered to a pure Brāhmaṇa after dedicating the same to lord Īśāna or Viṣṇu yields endless (i.e. eternal) benefits.

35. A man may wish to propitiate any deity. If he is a wise scholar he should worship Brāhmaṇas in order to satisfy that deity.

36. All deities assume the forms of the Brāhmaṇas; they always exist. If Brāhmaṇas are not available, they are worshipped in idols etc. in some places.

37. Hence, the deities must be particularly worshipped in the Brāhmaṇas always and very assiduously by those who wish to attain the different kinds of benefits.

38. A person desirous of prosperity should always worship Purandara (god Indra). A person desirous of attaining *Brahman* and Brahmanical splendour should worship Brahmā.

39. A person desirous of good health shall worship the sun god; one who is desirous of cows shall worship fire and one who is desirous of the fruition of holy rites shall worship Vināyaka.

40. One who is desirous of worldly pleasures should worship the moon; a person desirous of power and strength should worship the wind-god and a person desirous of being liberated from the entire worldly existence shall worship Hari.

41. He who wishes for Yoga, salvation and that perfect knowledge of Īśvara shall assiduously worship Virūpākṣa Maheśvara.

42. He who wishes for perfect knowledge through the the great Yoga should worship Maheśvara. They shall become enjoyers of pleasures, they who worship Bhūteśa and Keśava.

43. A person who freely gives water attains satisfaction,[1] a person who gives cooked food attains inexhaustible happiness; a person who gives gingelly seeds obtains desirable progeny and a person who gives lamps attains excellent vision.

44. A person who gifts away lands obtains everything, a giver of gold attains longevity; a giver of a house attains excellent abodes and a person who gives silver attains excellent comeliness.

45. A person who gives clothes, attains the same world as the Moon; a person who gives horses, attains the same world as that of the Aśvins; a person who gives oxen, attains well nourished glory and riches and a giver of cows attains the world of Bradhna (the sun).

46. A person who gives vehicles and coaches attains a good wife; a person who offers relief from fear, attains prosperity; a person who offers food grains, obtains perpetual happiness and a person who gives Brahman (Vedas), attains identity with Brahman.

47. One should give food-grains to the Brāhmaṇas in accordance with one's capacity and especially to excellent ones knowing the Vedas. After death, he shall attain heaven.

48. By giving away cows one is relieved of all sins ; by the gift of fuel, a man becomes like a blazing fire.

49. One should give fruits, roots, vegetables and foodstuffs of various kinds to the Brāhmṇas, he shall himself be happy and rejoicing.

50. A person who gives medicine, diets, oil, ghee etc. to a sick person in order to cure him of it, shall himself be free from ailments. He shall enjoy longevity and be happy.

51. A man who makes gifts of umbrellas and shoes escapes the path to hell called Asipatravana (full of edges as sharp as the edge of a razor) and surmounts severe scorching pain.

1. VV. 43-51. Fruits accruing from particular *dānas*.

52. Whatever is most pleasing to him in the world and whatever is excessively cherished by one in the house, should be given to a meritorious person by one who wishes the same for himself to be inexhaustible.

53. Whatever is given during the equinotical or tropical transit of the sun or during the eclipse of the sun or the moon or during the time of the transit of the sun from one zodiac to another, shall become everlasting.

54. By making gifts in the holy centres such as Prayāga etc. in the sacred shrines and near the holy rivers and forests, one obtains everlasting benefits.

55. There is no greater or meritorious act than that of making gifts in the case of any living being. Hence gifts should be made over to a Brāhmaṇa well-versed in the Vedas, by the twice-born.

56. Gifts should be made by one who wishes for heaven, longevity and prosperity and for subduing sins. Everday charitable gifts should be made unto Brāhmaṇas by one who wishes for salvation.

57. If out of delusion, any sinful soul prevents the gift from being given to the Brāhmaṇas, fire-god or the Devas, shall be reborn as an animal.

58. If after earning much wealth, anyone does not worship Brāhmaṇas and Devas, he must be banished from the kingdom after confiscating his property.

59. A Brāhmaṇa who does not give cooked food etc. during famines when animals die, is a despicable person.

60. No one should accept monetary gifts from him nor should anything be given unto him. The king should stamp his seal on him and banish him from his kingdom.

61. The man who does not give wealth to good persons nor means of piety, is a greater sinner and he is cooked in the hell.

62. O excellent Brāhmaṇas, gifts must be made to those Brāhmaṇas who regularly study the Vedas, who are endowed with learning, who have conquered their sense-organs and who are endowed with full self-control.

63. One shall feed a learned and righteous Brāhmaṇa again even if he has already taken a hearty meal; one should not

feed a fool who has no good conduct even if he is starving for ten days.

64. If any one makes any gift overlooking the learned Brāhmaṇa of the locality, he becomes a sinner by means of that action. He burns his family upto the seventh generation.

65. If the Brāhmaṇa outsider were to be superior in conduct, learning etc., gifts must be made over to him even by overlooking the man at hand.

66. The person who accepts what is offered with due respect and the person who offers with due respect—both of them go to heaven. If it is the contrary, both of them go to hell.

67. A person who knows Dharma should not offer even water to an atheist or a heretic or to a sceptic or to a person who does not know the Vedas.

68. If a person who is not learned accepts the gifts of sweet pies, gold, cow, horse, land or gingelly seeds, he is reduced to ashes like a log of wood.[1]

69. An excellent Brāhmaṇa shall wish to receive wealth only from high class praise-worthy Brāhmaṇas or from all twice born persons but by no means from a Śūdra.

70. A Brahmaṇa should try dimunition of his expenditure for livelihood but should not wish for the expansion of wealth. One who is in the clutches of covetousness for wealth falls off from Brahmanahood.

71. Even after studying the Vedas and after performing 11 Yajñas, one does not attain that goal which one attains by means of diminution of avocation (i.e. curtailment of expenses).

72. No Brāhmaṇa shall be excessively interested in monetary gifts; one may accept the amount required for a religious journey. A Brāhmaṇa accepting more than what is required for sustenance faces downfall.

73. One who perpetually begs cannot attain heaven. Just as a thief annoys all living beings, so also the perpetual beggar.

74. A person desirous of uplifting preceptors, elders or servants, a person desirous of worshipping deities and guests, can

1. Manu IV. 188.

accept gifts from everywhere. He should not be satiated in this respect by himself.

75. A householder with his soul absorbed in meditation, who worships deities and guests and who remains endowed with self-control, attains the greatest region.

76. Or he should entrust everything to his son and go to the forest. As a knower of reality, he should wander alone. He should be indifferent to worldly affairs and endowed with great concentration (in spiritual activities).

77. O excellent Brāhmaṇas, the duty of the householders has been expounded to you thus. One should abide by these after knowing them and shall make other Brāhmaṇas follow the same.

78. Thus, one should always worship the only primordial lord by following the duties of the householder. He shall surmount the *Prakṛti*, the source of origin of all living beings and he does not take another birth.

CHAPTER TWENTYSEVEN

Duties in Vānaprastha (Hermit's) Stage[1]

Vyāsa said :

1. After staying in the householder's stage of life thus in the second part of life, one should pass on to the stage of the forest hermit, accompanied by his wife or (alone but) maintaining the sacrificial fires.

---

1. This is normally the third stage in life and the rules etc. pertaining to it are given in the Dharma Sūtras of Āpastamba (II. 9. 21. 18), Baudhāyana (III. 3), Viṣṇu (95) and Smṛtis like Manu VI. 1-32, Yājñavalkya III. 45-55, in Mahābhārata *Śānti* 245-1-14, *Anuśāsana* 142 and Purāṇas like *AP*. ch. 160., *Bh. P.* VII. 12. 17-31, *NP*. I. 27. 85-106. Many verses are common to Smṛtis and Purāṇas *inter se* but that is inevitable in such works dealing with the same topic.

2-3. Or he should go to the forest after entrusting his wife to the care of the sons.[1] After seeing his grandchild, the old man with his body weak and shattered should go to the forest in the course of Uttarāyaṇa (Northern transit of the sun) on any auspicious morning in the bright half of the month. After going to the forest, he should observe all regulations and perform penance with great concentration.

4. He should take to a fruit diet after collecting holy fruits and roots. He should worship the *Pitṛs* and the deities with what constitutes his controlled diet.

5. He should always worship the guests; after taking bath he should worship the gods. With great composure, he should eat only eight mouthfuls out of what he brings from the house.

6. He should always wear the matted hair. He should not cast off (i.e. pare off) nails and hairs. He should always maintain (continue) the study of the Vedas; on other occasions he should observe restraint on his speech.

7. It is with food proper for sages, with various vegetables, fruits and roots grown in the forest that he should perform his daily fire-worship and also the five (great) sacrifices (*pañca-mahā-yajñas*).

8. He should always wear bark-garments. He should be pure, taking bath three times a day. He should be kind and considerate towards all living beings. He should avoid taking *Pratigrahas* (monetary gifts).[2]

9-10a. The Brāhmaṇa should perform regularly the sacrifices (specifically meant for) on Darśa and Paurṇimā (New Moon and Full Moon) days, on the proper Nakṣatra, as also the Āgrayaṇa *iṣṭi* Cāturmāsya sacrifices. He should observe (the holy rites) in the period of summer and winter solstices.

10b-12a. He should prepare separately *Puroḍāśas* (sacrificial offerings of ground rice offered in earthen dishes—*Kapālas*) and *Caru* (oblation of boiled rice and barley) with pure (offerable as oblations in sacrifice) wild grains (rice grown naturally in spring and Autumn) and gathered by himself.

---

1. Cf. Manu VI. 3, Yājñavalkya III. 45.
2. Cf. Manu VI. 5 and 7, Yāj. III. 46.

Having offered those highly sacred *Havis* (oblations) of the products of the forest to the deities, he should partake of the remainder for himself with the salt prepared by himself.[1]

12b-13. He should avoid wine and meat and the mushrooms growing on the Earth; 'earth-grass' i.e. *Andropogon Schoenanthus*; the fruit of the trees Śiśuka (Śigruka and Sleṣmātaka (*Cordia Latifolia*); he shall never eat anything cultivated (after ploughing the earth) with the ploughshare. Nor shall he eat anything abandoned by anyone.

14. Even when distressed, he should not make use of the flowers and fruits produced in the villages.[2] He should maintain and venerate the holy fire as per injunctions in the Vaikhānasa Sūtra.

15. He should not cause injury to any living being. He should be free from *Dvandvas* (mutually clashing opposites like pleasure and pain) and be free from fear as well. He should not take food during the night and be engaged in meditation during the night.

16. He should be one who has conquered the sense-organs and restrained anger. He should ponder over the perfect knowledge of Reality. He should always be celibate and not approach carnally even his wife.

17. The Brāhmaṇa, who, after going to the forest indulges in sexual intercourse with his wife passionately, violates his holy vow and has to perform expiation.

18. The child born thereby cannot be touchable by Brāhmaṇas. He is not authorised in the study of the Vedas. All the persons born in his family shall also be so.

19. He should invariably sleep on the ground below. He should be devoted to the *Japa* of the Sāvitrī Mantra. He should afford shelter unto all living beings and share things with others.

20. He should avoid slandering and falsely accusing others; he should avoid (too much of) sleep and lethargy; he should maintain one single fire. He should have no fixed abode; he shall resort to a ground purified by sprinkling water.

1. Manu VI. 14
2. VV. 13-14; cf. Manu VI. 16.

21. One should freely roam about alongwith the deer or take rest alongwith them. With very great concentration, he should lie down on a slab of stone or on the gravels.

22. He should be one who washes off immediately (i.e. one who does not hoard anything) or he can hoard things necessary for a month; or he can have all the requisite things for six months or he may be one who hoards things necessary for a year.

23. In the month of Āśvayuja (September-October) one should throw away all one's hoarded things.[1]* He should also discard the old worn clothes, vegetables, roots and fruits.

24. He should be a *Dantolūkhalika* (one who uses the teeth as mortar for chewing the grains and eating them). He should follow the practice of a pigeon. He should be an *Aṣmakuṭṭa* breaking or pounding corns etc. on stones) or he should be one who eats only what is ripened in the course of time.

25. He should eat food at night what he gathered during the day, in accordance with his capacity. He should be a *Caturthakālika* (i.e. one who eats after missing three meal-times) or he shall be an *Aṣṭamakālika* (one who eats after missing seven meal-times.)

26. He should perform expiatory rites in accordance with the Cāndrāyaṇa rites during the bright and dark halves of the month. He should take once in a fortnight boiled rice (or barley) gruel).[2]**

27. Established in the doctrine of Vaikhānasas one should always subsist on merely flowers, roots or fruits which have naturally fallen and withered.

28. One should roll on the ground or stand on the fore part of the foot (i.e. tip-toe) throughout the day. One should

1. VV. 22-23, Manu VI. 15, Yāj. III. 47

*v.l. *Pūrva-sañcitam* is better and hence accepted. Veṅkt. Press reading *pūrva-cintitam* 'as thought of before' does not give the proper sense.

2. Manu VI. 20-21 and 31

**Veṅkt. text : *dvijāgrān kathitān* 'reporting to foremost Brāhmaṇas' is irrelevant. Hence the v.l. *Yavāgūḥ kvathitāḥ* is accepted.

be continuously engaged in standing or sitting but should not lose courage on any account.

29. Gradually increasing his intensity in austere penance, he should get himself scorched in five fires; in the rainy season he should expose himself to showering clouds (for his shelter). He should put on wet clothes during the winter.[1]

30. He should take ablutions thrice a day and propitiate the *Pitṛs* and Devas or he should stand on a single foot and imbibe the rays then.

31. He should get himself surrounded by five fires. He should be an imbiber of smoke, heat or Soma juice. He should drink milk (or water) in the bright half and *Pañcagavya* (cow-dung, urine etc. of cows) during the dark half of the month.

32. Or he should eat fallen and withered dry leaves or observe penance called *Kṛcchra*. He should always practise Yoga and recite Rudra (Sūkta).

33. He should study Atharvaśiras and be interested in practising the principles of Vedānta;[2] he should resort restraints (*Yamas*) continuously; and he should alertly practise *Niyamas* (observances and rites).

34-35. He should wear the skin of a black-antelope, the upper garment and the white sacred thread. He should then impose sacred fires on his Ātman; and be devoted to meditation. He should be devoid of fire (i.e. give up fire-worship etc.) and a fixed abode; he should be a silent sage engaged in endeavour for salvation. He should take alms necessary for his journey from saintly Brāhmaṇas.

36. He should receive the same from other Brāhmaṇa householders residing in the forest. Himself residing in the forest, he should eat eight mouthfuls of what he brings from the village.

37-38a. In a cup of leaves or holding the palms like a cup or on a potsherd (*Śakala*) (he should receive those things). For the realisation of the Ātman, he should perform Japa of the different Upaniṣads, different Mantras, the Sāvitrī Mantra or

1. Manu VI. 23-24, Yāj. III. 52.
2. Manu VI. 29-30.

Rudra Adhyāya.

38b-39. He should resort to the great Departure (*mahā-prasthāna*) or observe fast unto death. He should abide by the procedure of dedication unto the Brahman, and may enter fire.[1] Those who resort to this stage of life duly, this state of life that destroys unholy things, attain the region of Īśvara; they go to that region after their death.

CHAPTER TWENTYEIGHT

Duties of Yatis (recluses)

Vyāsa said :

1. After staying in the stage of life as the forest-hermit during the third period of his life, thus, he should spend the fourth period of his life by renunciation.

2. After having established the fires in the Ātman, the Brāhmaṇa should renounce and go away as an anchorite. He should be engaged in the practice of Yoga, be quiescent and be devoted to Brahmavidyā (the lore of the Brahman).

3. People wish for Sannyāsa (renunciation) when *Vaitṛṣṇya* (absence of thirst i.e. attachment) towards all worldly objects surges up in the mind. Otherwise one would be a fallen fellow.

4. After performing the *Iṣṭi* of pertaining to Prajāpati or Āgneya[2] (pertaining to the fire god), he should become a *Dānta* (one with self control.) His passions and sins get perished. He should then resort to the Brahmāśrama (the stage of renunciation i.e. *Sannyāsa*)

---

1. Manu VI 31. Yāj III. 55. But the writers on Dharmaśāstra do not favour such suicides. Also Mbh. *Ādi* 779. 20.

2. Manu VI. 38, Yāj III. 56 require the performance of Prājāpatyeṣṭi, while Jābālopaniṣad 4 recommends *Āgneyī iṣṭi*. KP synthesized both the views by giving an option.

5. Various types of Sannyāsins are mentioned : some of them are *Jñāna-sannyāsins*, others are *Veda-sannyāsins* while some others are *Karma-sannyāsins*.[1]

6. He who is free from all attachments, devoid of Dvandvas (mutually clashing opposites) and who is fearless is called the renouncer of Jñāna type (*Jñānasannyāsin*). He is stabilised in his own Ātman.

7. He who studies the Vedas solely every day, is devoid of Dvandvas and who accepts nothing (or is propertyless or has nothing) is called the renouncer of the Veda type (*Veda-Sannyāsin*). He is one who has conquered the sense organs and is desirous of liberation.

8. The Brāhmaṇa who absorbs the sacrificial fires into the Ātman and who is interested in dedicating everything to Brahman, should be known as the renouncer of Karmans—as one devoted to great *Yajñas*.

9. Among these three, the Jñānin is considered to be the superior-most. He is a scholar who has no function to be performed nor has he any symbol.

10. He would be devoid of myness; should be fearless and quiscent; he should be above Dvandvas and free from acceptance (of gifts) (or possession-less). He should wear only a ragged loin cloth or he may be naked, but he is devoted to meditation.

11. He should be a celibate; take in only limited mouthfuls of food. He should get his food from the village. He should be engaged in reflecting on the spirit. He should not have worldly attachments. Nor does he take meat.

12. He should seek happiness and move about here with only the Ātman to assist him. He should not speak in appreciation of either death or life.

13-14a. He should wait only for the time of his death just as a servant waits for (his master's) order. He has never anything worth studying or hearing. He thus qualifies himself to be identical with Brahman.

---

1. VV. 5-9 KP gives a different classification of Sannyāsins. Mbh. *Anuśāsana* 141. 89 followed by AP. 161. 18 give (1) Kuṭicaka, (2) Bahūdaka (3) Haṁsa and (4) Paramahaṁsa as the usual classification of Sannyāsins.

14b-16. Either he may wear a single cloth or he may wear a loin cloth. The scholar may have either a tonsured head or a tuft of hair on the head. He should have three staffs. He should be free from acceptance of gifts. He should always wear ochre-robes. He should be engaged in the path of meditation. He should stay at the outskirts of the village or at the root of a tree or in the temple. He should view the enemy and the friend alike. He should face both honour and disrespect equally.

17-18a. He should maintain himself on alms. He should not take the food of only one man at any place. If, out of delusion or for any other reason, the ascetic takes the food from one person, no expiation has been mentioned for him in the Dharmaśāstras.

18b-19a. He should consider a lump of clay, a stone and a piece of gold (of the same value) equally. His soul should be free from passion and hatred. He should desist from injuring living beings and observe silence. He should be devoid of desires.

19. One should set foot after purifying the place with the vision (look carefully before treading on a place) ; he should drink water purified by means of a cloth; he should speak words purified by a knowledge of the scriptures; he should act with a pure conscience.

20. Except during the rainy season, a mendicant should not stay for long in a single place. He should take ablutions regularly and observe cleanliness. He should always have the waterpot in the hand. He should be clean.

21. He should perpetually be devoted to celibacy and should always stay in the forest. He should be devoted to the scriptures on salvation. He should be celibate and should keep his sense-organs fully conquered.

22. He should be free from haughtiness and egotism; he should be devoid of censure and backbiting. An ascetic endowed with the quality of the (realization of) knowledge of the Ātman shall attain salvation.

23. After taking bath he should perform the *Ācamana* rite according to injunctions. Thus purified he should always study (ponder over) the eternal Veda called *Praṇava* i.e. *OM* (sitting) in a temple. etc.

24-25. Wearing a sacred thread, with the Kuśa grass in his hand, wearing a clean washed ochre-coloured garment and his body smeared with ashes covering the hairs and with a quiescent soul and concentrated mind, he should continuously perform *Japa* of Brahman (Veda) pertaining to Yajña (sacrifice) or pertaining to divinity or concerning the soul described in the Upaniṣads.

26. The ascetic observing silence and celibacy may stay with his sons[1] also. If he practises the study of Vedas always, he shall attain the greatest goal.

27. These are particularly his vows viz. : non-violence, truthfulness, non-stealing, celibacy, greatest penance; (austeremost) forbearance, mercifulness and contenment.

28. He should adhere to the Vedantic knowledge with great concentration; he should perform the five Yajñas (Pañcamahā Yajñas) It is not for the sake of alms that he should be endowed with Jñāna and meditation.

29. He should always perform the Japa of the Homa mantras at the proper time with great concentration. He should read the Vedic passage every day. He should repeat the Sāvitrī Mantra at the junctions (morning and evening).

30. Thereafter he should meditate on Lord Parameśvara in a secluded spot. During secluded life one should avoid passion, fury and acceptance of monetary gifts.

31. The scholar who wears one or two garments, a tuft of hair (on the head), a sacred thread and holding a Kamaṇḍalu (water-pot) in hand and three staffs attains the greatest Being.

---

1. This is strange. The recluse has to leave home. wife, children, property etc. *vide* Manu VI-41, 43-42.

CHAPTER TWENTY-NINE

Duties of an Ascetic

Vyāsa said :

1. In this way the sustenance of ascetics of restrained soul (mind) who strictly adhere to the stage of their life, has been declared to be on begging alms or on fruits, roots etc.

2. He should beg for alms only for once. He should not indulge in it for long. Since, if an ascetic is attached to alms, he becomes involved in worldly affairs.

3. He should beg for alms only at seven houses.[1] If nothing is received he should begin begging for alms once again. He should wash the vessel and take food in it. Then once again, he should wash it with water.

4. Or he should take another vessel for collecting the alms and another for taking food everyday. After taking food he should wipe off that vessel and take food only to facilitate the journey of life. He should not be covetous.

5. The ascetic should go to collect alms when there is no smoke or burning coal, at a house where all the people have taken food and where the threshing rod is kept resting and the potsherds are disposed off.[2]

6. After saying "Bhikṣā" (alms) once, the mendicant ascetic should stand with the head bent (facing down) for a period of a *Godoha* (i.e. the time taken to milk a cow). (After receiving the alms) he should eat it silently. He should be pure and restrained in speech.

7. He should wash his hands and feet and perform the *Ācamana* rites in accordance with the injunctions. He should show food to the sun-god and partake of it facing the east. He should remain pure.

8. He should take in the five *Prāṇāhutis* (i.e. take the five particles of food while uttering *Prāṇāya svāhā* etc.). With concentration he should take in only eight mouthfuls of food.

---

1. Vasiṣṭha Dh. S. X. 7, Śaṅkha Smṛ. VII. 3
2. Manu VI. 56, Śaṅkha VII. 2

After performing the *Ācamana* rite he should meditate on Lord Brahmā, the great Īśvara.

9. Manu, the Prajāpati, says that the following four types of vessels may be used (for begging alms) by ascetics viz. : a gourd, a wooden vessel, a mud-pot or a bamboo pot.[1]

10. He should think of Īśvara always early in the night, in the middle of the night, at the close of the night and during the *Sandhyās* (i.e. dawn and dusk). During the *Sandhyās*, he should particularly make use of sacrificial fires.*

11-13. He should keep within the abode of the lotus of his heart, the deity named Viśva who is the cause of the birth of the Universe. He should remember the Ātman of all living beings—that which is stationed beyond darkness, the Ātman that is the support of all the brilliance, the unchanging bliss, that which is beyond Pradhāna and Puruṣa, Śiva (stationed in the) cavity of the sky, Īśvara of the form of Brahman, present within all beings. He should meditate on the lord devoid of beginning, middle and the end, the abode of the qualities such as bliss, etc.

14-15. He should meditate on the great Puruṣa, the Brahman, Brahmā, the unchanging truth, the universal formed Maheśa resembling the mid-day sun. He should stabilise the Ātman in the Supreme Ātman through Oṁkāra. He should meditate on Lord Īśāna present in the middle of the Ākāśa (firmament).

16. One meditating on the ancient pure Puruṣa, the cause of all beings, the only receptacle of bliss, shall be released from bondage.

17-18. Or he should ponder over the great firmament, the sole cause of all living beings, that which is present in the cavity of the heart, the abode of illusion for the universe; he should meditate on the enlivening force of all living beings, where the world gets dissolved; which, those desirous of liberation, see as the subtle bliss of Brahman.

---

1. Manu VI. 54 but there it is attributed to Svāyambhuva Manu

*v.l. *Sandhyāsvahni* '(especially) in the dawn, the dusk and at day' is better.

19. After pondering over the infinite real, Īśāna, the Brahman that is lying hidden in its middle, the Brahman characterised by perfect knowledge, he should sit with perfect self-control.

20. This is the greatest secret of all secrets imparted to ascetics by Maheśa. He who brings into practice the perfect knowledge, shall experience Yoga pertaining to Īśvara.

21. Hence, he should always be devoted to meditation; he should be devoted to the Ātmavidyā (knowledge of the soul). He should resort to the perfect knowledge of Brahman, whereby he shall be released from bondage.

22. Realising the non-identity of the self from all other things, and that the self is pure bliss, devoid of old age, one should meditate again on that Supreme knowledge.

23. He is, therefore, the Supreme Lord as from him all beings originate, by attaining him one is not born again. He is the God who transcends and rules over all.

24. That Lord is Maheśvara, the journey unto whom is mentioned to be perpetual and auspicious, and whom they call as the greatest.

25. Whatever holy main vows and subsidiary vows of the mendicant ascetics have been mentioned, if any of these are transgressed, expiatory rites are enjoined.[1]

26. After approaching a woman carnally, he should make amends as follows : He should control his mind, remain pure and perform Prāṇāyāma. He should then perform the expiatory rites called *Kṛcchra** and *Sāntapana*.

27. Thereafter he should remain with perfect mental control and regularly perform the *Kṛcchra* (expiatory) rite according to injunctions. The mendicant should come to the hermitage again and perform his regular duties with alertness.

28. Learned men say that a falsehood uttered for fun does not affect one adversely. Still it should not be pursued, as this is a serious incident.

---

1. VV. 25-36 enumerate the atonements or expiations for transgression of rules by a Sannyāsin.

*a better v.l. is *prāyaścittaṁ samahitaḥ* with concentrated mind take the *prāyaścitta*, as this avoids the duplication of *Kṛcchra prāyaścitta* in the next verse.

29. (If one speaks a lie even in joke) an ascetic desirous of piety should fast for one night and perform one hundred Prāṇāyāmas.

30. One should not commit theft even if one loses one's interest* (?). The Smṛti states that there is no other act of irreligion than theft.

31. It is spoken of as another kind of violence. It deprives one of the knowledge of the self. What is called wealth is the externally wandering life of man.

32. He who deprives a man of his wealth, deprives him of his life. If one commits it, that extremely wicked person, fallen from his pious way of life, gets his sacred vow violated. (Repenting again if) he feels despondent, he should perform *Cāndrāyaṇa* vow.

33. Śruti says that he should perform (the *Cāndrāyaṇa* rite) for a year in accordance with the injunctions in the scriptures. If the mendicant ascetic should repent again, he should perform his vow alertfully.

34. If the mendicant ascetic commits violence accidentally he should perform the expiatory rite of *Kṛcchrātikṛcchra* or *Cāndrāyaṇa*.

35. If, on seeing a woman, an ascetic involuntarily discharges his semen virile due to his weakness, he should perform sixteen Prāṇāyāmas.

36. If the involuntary emission of the semen takes place during the day time, he should perform hundred Prāṇāyāmas every day for three days. If one takes to wine and flesh in secret, or takes salt openly during Navaśrāddha (first Śrāddha after a person's death) *Prājāpatya* vow is the expiatory rite.

37. All the sins of a person engaged always in meditation perish. Hence, one should be engrossed in meditation on Maheśvara after realising him.

38. That which is the greatest Brahman, the brilliantmost light, the imperishable and unchanging support of all and is immanent in everything, should be known as Maheśvara.

---

*A better v.l. is *param āpadgatenāpi na kāryaṁ steyam anyataḥ* One should not perform theft from others even if he is in extreme difficulty'.

39. This lord Mahādeva is the pure and the greatest Śiva. He alone is the non-dualistic imperishable deity within the orb of the sun.

40.* (Defective verse) Since the lord is very great and is stationed in the principle called Ātmayoga and termed Svadhā, Agni (fire) and (knowledge) Jñāna, he is known as Mahādeva.

41. He who does not see any other lord than Mahādeva, he who realises him as the Ātman, attains the greatest region.

42. Those who consider their own Ātman different from Parameśvara do not realise tne lord. Their effort is futile.

43. The only Brahman is the supreme Brahman. That should be known as the unchanging principle. That lord is Mahādeva. By not realising this, one is fettered.

44. Hence, an ascetic of controlled mind should worship invariably. He should be quiescent, devoted to Mahādeva and engaged in the path of knowledge.

45. O Brāhmaṇas, thus the auspicious stage of life of the ascetics has been detailed to you. This has been formerly expounded to the sages by lord Pitāmaha (god Brahmā).

46. This excellent knowledge, the auspicious thing based on the duties of the ascetics, imparted by the self-born deity, shall not be given to anyone else except to sons, disciples and Yogins.

47. Thus the rules governing the rites of the ascetics have been described. It shall be the sole cause of the propitiation of Paśupati. Those who practise this every day with concentration of the mind are not reborn nor shall they face destruction.

---

*Veṅkt. Press text is full of misprints : The Crt. edition reads : *yasmān mahīyate devaḥ svadhāmni jñāna-sañjñini ātma-yogāhvaye tattve Mahādevas tataḥ smṛtaḥ* 'Inasmuch as the lord enjoys in his abode called (spiritual) knowledge and the reality called the Yoga of Ātman, he is said to be "great God".

CHAPTER THIRTY

Rules of expiation

Vyāsa said :

1. Henceforth I shall expound auspicious procedure of expiation[1] for the welfare of all Brāhmaṇas (v.l. people) and for dispelling sins.

2. By not doing the enjoined holy rite and by doing what is prohibited, a person incurs sin. The expiatory rite is the way of absolvement from sin.

3. No Brāhmaṇa should ever remain (anywhere) without performing the expiatory rite. He should perform what quiescent, scholarly Brāhmaṇas advise.[2]

4. What a quiescent Brāhmaṇa, who is the most excellent among the knowers of the meanings of the Vedas, who loves *dharma* (virtue) and who maintains (sacrificial) fires, does, shall be the greatest virtue even if it be that he alone performs it.

5. If there are three Brāhmaṇas who though they do not maintain sacrificial fire are but past-masters of Vedic interpretation and love Dharma, what they say should be ragarded as means of Dharma.

6-7. If there is a group of seven Brāhmaṇas who are experts in many scriptures on Dharma-śāstra and are proficient

---

1. Chs. XXX—XXXIV of KP deal with rules of *Prāyaścitta* or expiation from sin. The concept of sin is beyond the scope of annotations (For the concept of sin *vide* Hasting's *Encyclopaedia of Religion and Ethics* vol. XI article on "sin"). The concept of sin was well-developed in Ṛgvedic times (vide A. B. Keath—*The Religion and Philosoyhy of the Veda and Upanishads*, pp. 245-9, 264-8, 310-12 etc.).

The term *Prāyaścitta* means 'that whereby the *citta* (the mind) of the repentant is generally (*prāyaḥ*) free (from the oppressive sense of guilt) by the Parṣad assembly of Brahmin Pandits; a smṛti quotation in Parāśara Mādhava II. 1. p. 3)

The idea that a sin can be wiped out by *Prāyaścitta* gave rise to a vast literature from the time of ancient Dharma-sūtras down to mediaeval writers of digests (*Nibandhas*). Purāṇas as a part of Dharma-śāstra had dealt with them in details *vide* AP chs. 169-174, VP. I. chs. 14, 15 and 30.

2. VV. 3-8 state who should be regarded as authority in religious matter (as to what atonement be made etc.)

in logical reasoning of pros and cons and endowed with Vedic studies, these seven are glorified as authority on Dharma-Śāstra.

8. If there be twenty-one Brāhmaṇas who know the truth about the knowledge of Mīmāṁsā and are experts in Vedānta, can lay down the expiatory rite.

9. He who associates with the fallen sinners for one year by sharing their vehicles, beds and seats, with full knowledge thereof, shall also become fallen[1]

10. A Brāhmaṇa who officiates as a priest contracts a marriage with the fallen out-caste and teaches them Veda or dines with them, instantly becomes fallen.

11. The Brāhmaṇa who teaches them out of delusion or not knowing (their sins) or learns alongwith them shall become fallen in the course of a year.

12. The slayer of a Brāhmaṇa[2] should construct a hut in the forest and live therein for twelve years. For self-purification, he should beg alms with the skull of the dead as a symbol on the flag.

13. He should avoid the abodes of the Brāhmaṇas and the shrines of deities. He should remember that Brāhmaṇa constantly and censure himself.

14. He should quietly and slowly enter seven houses (for begging) the worthiness of which was not (previously) considered and which are free from smoke and fire (extinguished) and inmates whereof have taken their meals.

15. He should beg for alms only once. He should proclaim his sin to all men. Or he should maintain himself with fruits and roots obtained from the forest and subsist on them.

16. He should hold the skull and the Khaṭvāṅga (a staff with a skull at the top) in his hands. He should observe celibacy. When the twelfth year is completed in this manner, he shall become free from the sin of Brāhmaṇa-slaughter.

---

1. VV. 9-11 state the conditions under which even an innocent man is treated as 'falllen'.

2. Slaying of a Brāhmaṇa was regarded as a serious sin (*mahā-pāpa*). VV. 12-26 describe different atonements for this great sin.

17. When the sin has been committed unintentionally, this is the auspicious expiation. It should be remembered that if the sin is done intentionally, the purification is only after death, and not by any other means.

18. He should observe *Anaśana* (fast unto death) or *Bhṛgupatana* (fall off from a precipice) or he shall enter the burning fire or water.

19. In order to wipe off the sin of Brāhmaṇa-slaughter, he should discard his life for the sake of a Brāhmaṇa or a cow or for the sake of the dead.

20. The sin of Brāhmaṇa-slaughter is dispelled by curing a Brāhmaṇa of his chronic illness or by giving food to a very learned person.

21. Or a Brāhmaṇa is absolved of the sin of Brāhmaṇa-slaughter by taking the concluding ablutions of a horse sacrifice or by giving all his possessions to a Brāhmaṇa who has mastered the Vedas.

22. A Brāhmaṇa should observe fast for three nights and then take three baths in the world-famous confluence of the river Sarasvatī with the Aruṇā and he shall be purified.

23. By going to the holy place Rāmeśvara, and by taking bath in the great ocean or by seeing Rudra, he shall be rid of the sin if he observes celibacy.

24. There is the holy centre of lord Śūlin (Śiva) named Kapālamocana. By taking bath and propitiating the *Pitṛs* and Devas, one dispels the sin of Brāhmaṇa-slaughter.

25. It was there that the skull of Parameṣṭhin Brahmā was formerly deposited by Bhairava, the overlord of Devas, of unmeasured splendour.

26. By worshiping Mahādeva there, in the form of Bhairava, after the bath and after performing the *Tarpaṇa* rites to the Pitṛs one is freed from the sin of Brāhmaṇa slaughter.

CHAPTER THIRTYONE

Importance of Kapāla-mocana Tīrtha:[1] *Emplacement of God Brahmā's Skull*

The sages said :

1. Formerly, how was the skull severed from the body of Brahmā, placed on the Earth by Lord Rudra, Śaṅkara, of excessive brilliance ?

Sūta narrated :

2. O sages, listen ye all to the meritorious story that dispels sins, and the greatness of the intelligent Mahādeva, the lord of Devas.

3. Formerly, on the peak of Meru, the great sages bowed to the lord Pitāmaha, the primordial cause of the worlds, and said :- "What is that one immutable Principle ?"

4. The deity from whom the worlds originated was deluded by the Māyā of Maheśa. Not realising the greatest Being, he was over-bearing (enough) to say that he was (the unchanging principle).

5. "I am the Creator, the source of the origin of the Universe. I am the single self-born Īśvara. I am the beginningless greatest Brahman. By worshipping me, one is liberated.

6. I am the deity who makes all Devas function as well as desist (from functioning). There is no one in the worlds superior to me."

7-8. While he was professing like this, a portion of Nārāyaṇa was born and spoke these words laughingly- "The three-eyed lord is annoyed. O Brahmā, what is the reason for this ?

1. That *Vyāsa Gītā* is an interpolation by Pāśupatas becomes evident when in place and out of place they bring their favourite Deity. This chapter illustrates how the sin of *Brahma-hatyā* (killing a Brāhmaṇa) was absolved by taking a bath in a holy centre (Tīrtha) at Vārāṇasi and why it came to be named as *Kapāla-mocana* (reliever from the contact of a skull). The glorification of Śiva by embodiments of Vedas and amputation of the arrogant head of god Brahmā and the final emancipation from that sin of beheading Brahmā and physical separation of Brahmā's skull from Bhairava's hand—all is for the glorification of Śiva.

You are overpowered with ignorance. The qualities you have been boasting are not present in you. (v.l. This is not proper).

9-10. I am lord Nārāyaṇa, the primordial maker of the worlds, the Yajña incarnate. Without me, the whole universe cannot exist at all anywhcre. I alone am the Supreme brilliance. I alone am the greatest goal. It was after being urged by me that the sphere of the Universe has been created by you.

11. While these two deities were arguing with a desire to subdue the other, the four Vedas came to the place where these two deities were present.

12. On seeing lord Brahmā and the lord identical with Yajña (i.e. Nārāyaṇa) seated (there), (the Vedas) with a painful heart declared the reality of the Supreme Lord.

Ṛgveda said :

13. It is lord Maheśvara, within whom are stationed all living beings from whom everything functions and which they call the Supreme principle.

Yajurveda said :

14. It is the Pināka-bearing deity Śiva who is worshipped by means of all the Yajñas and the Yoga and whom they call Lord Īśvara.

Sāmaveda said :

15. That great Deva is Śaṅkara by whom this Universe revolves, who is the auspicious deity within the firmament and who is the principle Reality known and realised by the Yogins.

Atharvaveda said :

16. That is lord Bhava whom the ascetics visualize and worship as the great lord of Devas, as the great Puruṣa, as the great Ruler Rudra.

17. On hearing this auspicious utterance of the Vedas, lord Brahmā laughed utterly deluded, the Ātman of the Universe (i.e. Brahmā) then said :

18. "Why does that great Brahman who ought to be devoid of all attachments, sport about alongwith his wife and the excessively arrogant Pramathas (attendants) ?"

19. When this was uttered, the eternal lord, of the nature of *Praṇava* (OM), who is really formless, became embodied and spoke these words to Pitāmaha (god Brahmā).

Praṇava said :

20-21. "Indeed this lord Īśa, Rudra never sports about with a goddess who is different from himself. Maheśvara is of that sort. He is that lord Īśa, the eternal and the self-luminous. The goddess Śivā is one who has become his Bliss (i.e. his aspect called blissfulness) and not extraneous (coming from outside)."

22. Even when this was explained, the ignorance of Aja (Brahmā) whose body is Yajña, was not dispelled due to the Māyā of Īśvara.

23. In the meanwhile Viriñca (i.e. god Brahmā) the conceiver of the universe saw a divine wonderful and great brilliance filling up the space of the sky.

24. In the middle of it (that light) was stationed a sphere of brilliance shining with splendour. O excellent Brāhmaṇas, a divine splendour in the middle of the firmament appeared in front of him.

25. On seeing that divine face over his head, the grandfather of the worlds saw a sphere of splendour spotless and terrible.

26-27. The fifth head of Brahmā blazed with great fury. Instantaneously the great Puruṣa, Nīlalohita, the tawny coloured trident-bearing lord, having the serpents for his sacred thread was seen. Lord Brahmā spoke to Śaṅkara, Nīlalohita.

28. (Defective verse) * O Śaṅkara, you are born of my forehead formerly for the sake of knowledge (?) You are called Maheśāna. Hence, seek refuge in me."

29. On hearing the arrogant words of the lotus-born deity, Īśvara depatched his man Kālabhairava, the burner of worlds

*KP. Crt. ed. reads *jānāmi bhavataḥ pūrvaṁ lalāṭād eva Śaṅkara prādurbhavam* / "O Śaṅkara, I know your birth from my forehead formerly."

30. After fighting a great battle with Brahmā, Kāla-Bhairava slit the fifth face of Viriñca (Brahmā.)

31. Brahmā whose face was cut by lord Śambhu, died; but by means of the Yogic power of Īśa, the holder of the universe (Brahmā) regained his life.

32. Then he saw Īśāna, the eternal Mahādeva seated alongwith the great goddess and stationed in an other sphere of light.

33. He had the royal serpents for his bracelet; the crescent-moon as an ornament; he resembled a crore of suns (in brilliance), he shone with his matted hair.

34. He was clad in the hide of a tiger; he was bedecked in divine garlands; he held the trident in his hand; he was a Yogin who could not be looked at (due to his brilliance.)

35. He saw the primordial deity, the first deity, great lord whom those who are stabilised in Yoga see within their hearts as Īśvara and Brahman.

36. Verily, the great Lord whose supreme power, the goddess, is designated as the sky (v.l. established in the firmament) and whose Yogic soul (?) infinite *aiśvarya* (divine potencies like omniscience, omnipresence etc.) is seen indeed.

37. That Rudra, on merely bowing to whom once, the deluding seed of the entire universe gets dissolved, is seen indeed.

38. (Defective Verse). Those who do not strictly abide by rules of good conduct but who are only great devotees of him are liberated by the Ātman of the worlds. That Lord is now seen, indeed.

39. That Śiva whose Liṅga is always worshipped by Brahmā and other Devas as well as by the sages, the expounders of Brahman, has indeed become visible.

40. That Śaṅkara is seen whose side (i.e. proximity) is never left off by Īśvara*, the cause of origin of the entire universe and whose body is *Vijñāna* (Perfect knowledge).

---

*Īśvara not leaving the side or proximity of Śaṅkara is confusing. *Īśvarī* would be a better reading as that would qualify *tanu* 'body' and mean 'whose divine body.'

41. That Īśvara is indeed seen—Īśvara, the son of Hiraṇyagarbha, in whose circular halo of light is seen the Lord who is accompanied by Vidyā.

42. Indeed that Rudra is seen—Rudra at whose feet (if) anyone were to pour water or place a flower or a leaf, he crosses the ocean of existence.

43. Due to his presence, the eternal Time controls the entire universe (and Time-units ?). The god whose soul is Yoga and who is the governor of Kāla*

44. That Soma (god Śiva who is accompanied by Umā) is seen—the god whose ornament is Soma (the moon)—the life of all the worlds and an ornament unto the three worlds.

45. The great God (Mahādeva) whose natural eternal union with goddess Umā is ever seen and the great liberation (on seeing him) is extolled (as being attained) is now seen.

46. (Defective) Yogins, well-versed in the principles of Yoga, always meditate upon his union with the goddess, though he always faces separation** from the world (?) That Yogin is indeed seen.

47. On seeing the eternal Mahādeva seated in an excellent seat along with the great goddess, he attained the greatest perfect recollection.

48. Gaining the divine recollection pertaining to Maheśvara, lord Aja (Brahmā) propitiated the moonbedecked lord, the bestower of boons who was accompanied by Umā.

Brahmā said :

49. Obeisance to the great God. Repeated bows to the great goddess. Hail to Śiva the quiescent; perpetual obeisance unto Śivā (goddess Umā).

50. Om bow unto you the Brahman, obeisance, obeisance to you who are the Vidyā (Māyā), Obeisance to you

---

**Kālaḥ Kālo* in Veṅkt. Edt. is rather obscure. If emended as *Kāla-kālo* it means 'God who is the *Kāla* (destroyer and hence controller) of *kāla* (of time or god of death.)'

***viyogābhimukho'niśam* (Veṅk. Text). If emended as *viyogābhimukhā aniśam* will mean 'yogins who set their face against (the world)'. The metrical defect can be condoned by a double-sandhi *mukhāniśam.*

the great Īśa. Hail to the Primordial Prakṛti—the root cause of the universe.

51. Salutation to one whose body is *Vijñāna*; obeisance, obeisance to you *Cintā* (goddess of contemplation); Hail to the destroyer of Kāla; obeisance again and again to Īśvara (the goddess).

52. Obeisance, again and again to Rudra; salutations again and again to Rudrāṇī; obeisance, obeisance to you, Kāla (Time or Death); Repeated bows to you, the Māyā (the Deluding Potency).

53. Obeisance to the controller of all effects; obeisance to her who agitates. Hail to you, the Prakṛti and obeisance to Nārāyaṇa.

54. Obeisance to you the bestower of Yoga. Salutations to the preceptor of Yogins; obeisance to one abiding in the world* (?). Bow to the source of origin of the world.

55. Obeisance be to the lord of perpetual Bliss; Hail to one whose very form is Bliss; obeisance to one devoid of actions; salutation to the material cause of the universe.

56. Obeisance to you whose body is Oṁkāra; obeisance to you stationed therein. Hail to you stationed in the firmament; obeisance, again and again to the Śakti (potency) of the firmament.

57. Making obeisance thus to Īśa by means of "Somāṣṭaka" (eight verses eulogising the lord accompanied by Umā) god Brahmā fell on the ground like a piece of log, repeating the *mantras* of *Śatarudrīya*.

58. Then Lord Mahādeva, Hara, the remover of the distress of those who bow to him, raised him by means of his hands and said : "I am now pleased with you."

59. After bestowing great Yoga and the great unequalled *Aiśvarya* (prowess) on him (Brahmā) he (god Śiva) spoke to Rudra, Lord Nīlalohita who was standing in front of him.

60. This is god Brahmā. He is the most venerable one unto this universe. He is the first one to stay in this universe; He is elder to you by means of the Guṇa; He is to be protected by you. He is your father.

*v.l. *saṁsāra-nāśaka* 'destroyer of saṁsāra).

61. He is the ancient Puruṣa; O sinless one, he should not be killed by you. Thanks to the greatness of his Yoga and *Aiśvarya* (divine powers and faculties), he has sought refuge in me alone.

62. And he is sacrifice and that is his pride (v.l. He is the venerable sacrifice himself). His pride is to be chastened by you. You have to carry with you Brahmā's head.

63. Demonstrating to the world the expiatory rite for dispelling the sin of the slaughter of a Brāhmaṇa, go abegging. You should establish Devas and the Brāhmaṇas."

64. After addressing these words to Parameśvara (i.e. Rudra), the supreme lord went to his divine natural abode, the greatest region.

65. Thereafter, lord Īśa, Nīlalohita of matted hair made Kālabhairava hold god Brahmā's head.

66. For the purpose of quelling the sin (of Brāhmaṇa-slaughter) you perform the beneficial holy rite in the world. With the skull in the hand, you beg for alms all round."

67. After saying thus, he sent his daughter well known as *Brahmahatyā* whose face was terrible due to the curved fangs and who had clusters of flames for ornaments.

68. Assuming a terribly hideous form follow the trident-bearing deity as long as he enters the divine city of Vārāṇasī."

69. After saying this, he spoke to Kālāgni (Kāla bhairava) the great Īśvara of the worlds—"At my behest, wander over all the worlds seeking alms.

70. When you will meet Nārāyaṇa, the lord of Devas, free from ailments, he will tell you clearly the means of expiation for the sin."

71. On hearing the statement of the Lord of the deities, Lord Hara, the Ātman of the universe wandered over the three worlds with the skull in his hand.

72. He assumed a hideous dress and form. He shone by means of his own brillance. His form was holy, comely and endowed with glory. He had three eyes.

73. That great god with eyes like the fire of universal destruction, who was surrounded by Siddhas and the leaders of Pramathas (attendants) shines (shone dazzling) like crore of suns.

74. After imbibing the divine nectar, the bliss of Parameṣṭhin, the lord full of shining sports and pastimes, came down to the world.

75. On seeing Śaṅkara, the black-faced Kāla Bhairava, endowed with beauty and comely form, hosts of women followed him.

76. They began to sing different kinds of songs; they began to dance in front of the lord; looking at his smiling face, they knitted their eyebrows.

77. After passing through the lands of Devas, Dānavas and others, the trident-bearing lord went to the region of Viṣṇu where Puruṣottama stayed.

78. After reaching the divine abode, Śaṅkara, the benefactor of the worlds, began to enter it along with the Prominent Bhūtas.

79. Without knowing the divine and great being of Parameśvara, the powerful gatekeeper prevented the trident-bearing lord.

80. He was famous by the name of Viṣvaksena. He was born of a part of Viṣṇu. He held conch, discus and the mace in his hands; he was mighty armed and clad in yellow robes.

(Verse in the bracket)

Then the gatekeeper, born of Viṣṇu fought with the terrible-looking attendant of Śiva, called Kālavega (who attacked him) by the order of Bhairava.

81. After routing Kālavega, the gatekeeper with his eyes turned red due to fury, rushed against Rudra and hurled the Sudarśana disc against him.

82. Lord Mahādeva, the conqueror of foes, the trident-bearing god, the destroyer of the Tripuras, contemptuously looked at him, as he rushed against him

83. In the meanwhile, a great goblin comparable to the fire at the end of the Yugas, pierced his heart by means of the trident and felled him to the ground.

84. Mortally struck down by the trident (the gatekeeper) lost all his great strength and abandoned his life like persons afflicted by sickness on seeing death.

85. After killing the servant of Viṣṇu and taking his

body with him, Rudra entered the inner apartment alongwith the leading Pramathas.

86. On seeing Īśvara, the cause of the universe, Lord Hari broke a vein in his forehead and let the blood flow out.

87. "O suppressor of the Tripuras, O excessive splendoured, (O deity of unmeasured splendour), accept alms (offered) by me. No other kind of alms is worthy of you."

88. The blood continued to flow out in a continuous stream for a thousand divine years. Still that skull of Brahmā, Parameṣṭhin could not be filled up.

89. After eulogising him with different emotional ways (?) (v.l. with various Vedic mantras) and great respect, lord Hari Nārāyaṇa spoke to Kālarudra.

90. "Why are you carrying this skull of Brahmā ?" Maheśvara, the lord of Devas, recounted everything that happened.

91. Acyuta (Viṣṇu), Hṛṣikeśa (Lord of senses) called Brahmahatyā (the evil spirit of the slaughter of a Brāhmaṇa) and requested her "Please let go the trident-bearing deity."

92. Though requested by the enemy of Mura (i.e. Viṣṇu), she did not leave off his (Rudra's) side. After meditating on the source of origin of the universe, the omniscient Lord spoke to Śaṅkara.

93. "O lord, go unto the auspicious divine city of Vārāṇasī where Īśvara (god Śiva) quickly destroys the sins of the worlds."

94. Thereafter, the lord sportively went to the holy centres and shrines with a desire for the welfare of all the worlds.

95. Here and there, he was eulogised by the Pramathas of great Yogic power. The great Yogin with the dead body on his hands danced.

96. Assuming another form, lord Hari, Nārāyaṇa followed him, desirous of seeing his dance.

97. On seeing Govinda, the bull-bannered lord of infinite Yogic soul, danced again and again smilingly.

98. Following Rudra, Hari with the Dharma as his carrier, reached the city of Mahādeva, well-known as Vārāṇasī.

99. As soon as the lord of the universe with matted hair

entered the city, Brahmahatyā cried out, "Alas, Alas !" loudly, and entered the nether-worlds highly distressed.

100. After entering the greatest abode, lord Hara, Śaṅkara, placed the skull of Brahmā in front of the attendants.

101. After placing it (the skull), Mahādeva, the ocean of mercy, handed over the dead body to Viṣṇu with the words "May this come to life."

102. "Those who always remember this Kāpāla dress of mine find their sin here and hereafter perish quickly.

103. After coming to the excellent holy centre and performing the ablutions duly, one should propitiate the *Pitṛs*, manes and Devas after which one is liberated from the sin of slaughter of Brāhmaṇa.

104. Realising that the world is transient, ye all go to the greatest city. At the time of death the perfect knowledge imparted by me yields the highest region."

105. After saying this and embracing Janārdana (Viṣṇu), the lord instantaneously vanished alongwith the leading attendants.

106. After regaining his servant Viṣvaksena from the trident-bearing lord, the lord Kṛṣṇa silently went back to his land. (?)

107. Thus the meritorious story that quells great sins has been recounted to you. The holy centre Kapālamocana is very auspicious and is extremely liked by Sthāṇu.

108. He who reads this chapter in the presence of Brāhmaṇas is released from all sins mental, verbal and physical.

CHAPTER THIRTY-TWO

Expiatory rites

Vyāsa said :

1. An (otherwise) excellent Brāhmaṇa taking to wine-drinking[1] should drink it fiery-red (i.e. red hot). His body being scorched with the same, he shall be liberated (from that sin).

2. He should drink cow's urine of the colour of fire or the diluted cow's dung or milk, water or ghee. Then he shall be liberated from the sin.

3. Clad in a wet cloth, he should meditate on Nārāyaṇa, Hari, with great (mental and physical) purity. For the absolvement of sin, he should perform the holy rite in expiation for the sin of Brahmahatyā (Brāhmaṇa-slaughter).

4. A Brāhmaṇa stealing gold[2] should approach the king and confess his guilt. He should request, "Your Majesty should chastise me."

5. The king should take a threshing rod and should himself strike him with it once. Ordinary thief becomes pure on being killed and a Brāhmaṇa by means of penance.

6-7. He should take a threshing rod or a staff of Khadira wood, or a sharp pointed Śakti (spear) or an iron club on his shoulders. He should then rush to the king with dishevelled hair. He should confess that sin of his saying "I have committed such and such a sin. Chastise me."

8. Either by chastisement or through release the thief is liberated of the sin of theft. By not chastising him, the king incurs the sin of the thief.

9. A Brāhmaṇa desirous of wiping off the sin incurred from the theft of gold by means of penance should wear bark-garments and perform the expiatory rite of a slayer of a Brāhmaṇa.

---

1. VV. 1-3 wine-drinking is another great sin (*mahāpāpa*), its expiation being by the same rite as of Brahma-hatyā.

2. VV. 4-11 deal with the expiation for the third great sin—stealth.

10. Or the Brāhmaṇa should become purified by taking bath in the *Avabhṛtha* (concluding ablution) of the horse-sacrifice. Or he should give his own weight in gold to Brāhmaṇas.

11. The Brāhmaṇa who has stolen gold should observe celibacy and perform the *Kṛcchra*[1] rite for a year, in order to quell that sin.

12. If a Brāhmaṇa being infatuated with lust commits adultery with the wife of his preceptor,[2] he should embrace a red hot and fiery image of a woman made of black iron.

13. Or he should himself cut off his penis and scrotum, hold them in his palms and walk straight towards the southern direction till he falls down dead.

14-15. The defiler of a preceptor's bed should perform the expiatory rite of a slayer of a Brāhmaṇa for the purpose of purification; or he should lie on the ground for a year embracing the thorny branch of any tree with mental purity. The defiler of the preceptor's bed is then absolved of the sin. Or the Brāhmaṇa should wear bark-garments and with great concentration, he should perform the Kṛcchra rite for a year.

16-17. Or having taken the *Avabhṛtha* bath in a horse-sacrifice, the Brāhmaṇa becomes pure. He should take his meal on the eighth occasion after missing seven meals. He should observe celibacy and perform Sadāvrata (perpetual rite). *He should pass three days by standing and sitting strenuously. He should then lie down on the bare ground. Within three years, the sin is dispelled.

18. Or he should observe four or five Cāndrāyaṇa[3] vows.

---

1. *Kṛcchra* or *Prājāpatya* is a general term for several kinds of expiations. It has about 12 varieties. (For details vide Kane—H. D. Vol. IV, pp. 120, 132-133).

2. Adultery (esp. with one's preceptor's wife) was another great sin. VV. 12-18 give various expiations of unequal intensity for it.

3. In this expiation the intake of food—one morsel on the 1st *tithi* (lunar day) increases every day by one morsel upto 15 morsels on the full-moon day and decreases by one morsel every day in the dark half with complete fast on amāvāsyā (the new moon) day. As this expiation depends on the increase or decrease of the digits of the moon it is called Cāndrāyaṇa.

*Veṅk. text reads : *Sthānāśanābhyāṁ viharanstrirahno'bhyupa yatnataḥ* / *aśana* is emended as *āsana* (Crt. ed. supports this reading).

I shall now mention the expiation for a person who is in intimate contact with fallen persons[1] (or out-castes).

19. If a Brāhmaṇa has close intimacy with a fallen fellow, he should perform the expiatory rite enjoined for that person, for the purpose of wiping off that sin.

20. If the close intimacy is of six months duration, he should perform *Taptakṛcchra* rite alertfully for a year, as an expiatory rite.

21. The great sinners, wipe off their sins and impurities by means of these holy rites. Or the expiation on the Earth (can be achieved) by visiting holy centres.

22-24. A Brāhmaṇa who commits heinous sins like Brāhmaṇa-slaughter, drinking of wine, theft of gold, sexual intercourse with the wife of the preceptor or contact with the sinners of these crimes (will-fully) should observe fast. He should then remain in the holy centre with concentration of mind. He should meditate on lord Śiva (god with matted hair) and enter the blazing fire. No other means of expiation is observed by sages, the expounders of Dharma. Hence by burning his body in holy centres he shall become pure.

CHAPTER THIRTYTHREE

Narration of Expiatory rites (continued)

Vyāsa said :

1. The definite decision is this that a Brāhmaṇa who knowingly indulges in sexual intercourse with his daughter, sister or daughter-in-law should enter the blazing fire.

2. If one cohabits with one's mother's sister or the wife of the maternal uncle, or the sister of one's father or a niece, one should perform the expiatory rites of Kṛcchra and Atikṛcchra.

---

1. VV. 19-24 prescribe practically the same rites of expiation for those who live in contact with the great sinners and are fallen.

3. In order to quell that sin, one should observe the Cāndrāyaṇa vow meditating on lord Hari, the source of origin of the universe, the lord devoid of beginning and end.

4. For the destruction of the sin of cohabiting with one's own brother's wife, one should, with great concentration perform four or five Cāndrāyaṇa rites.

5. If one commits adultery with father's niece or mother's niece or the daughter of the maternal uncle one shall perform the Cāndrāyaṇa rite.

6. If one cohabits with the wife of friend or the sister of one's own wife one should observe fast for a day and a night and then perform the Kṛcchra rite.

7-8a. If a Brāhmaṇa carnally approaches a woman in her monthly course, he becomes pure only after three days. Three Taptakṛcchra rites have been enjoined (as atonement for) sexual intercourse with a Cāṇḍāla woman. By observing *Sāntapana*[1] vow (in addition), he becomes pure. Otherwise no expiation is prescribed in Smṛtis.

8b-9. For committing adultery with a woman from his maternal *gotra* (line of ancestors) or one belonging to his own *Pravara* lineage, he becomes pure if he observes with self-control and concentrated attention, the Cāndrāyaṇa vow. If a Brāhmaṇa has sexual intercourse with a Brāhmaṇa woman (other than his wife), he should perform one Kṛcchra expiation.

10-11. After committing the sin of raping a virgin, one should perform the Cāndrāyaṇa expiation. For the sin of discharging the semen virile in the lower animals, in a man, in a woman in her monthly course, in non-vaginal parts or in the water, one should observe the Kṛcchra rite. If a Brāhmaṇa ravishes an old woman, he shall be pure only in three days.

12. If one cohabits with a cow, one should observe the Cāndrāyaṇa rite. By cohabiting with a prostitute, a Brāhmaṇa (incurs sin and), he should perform the Prājāpatya vow.

---

1. *Sāntapana* is generally expiation for acts of Jātibhraṁśakara (pollution of castes). It lasts for two days and one has to take in *pañcagavya* on the first day and observe a fast on the second day.

13. By carnally approaching a fallen woman, one shall become sinful and be purified only by three Kṛcchra rites. To wipe off the sin of cohabiting with a Pulkasī (Cāṇḍāla woman), one shall observe the vows of Kṛcchra and Cāndrāyaṇa.

14. By cohabiting with a dancing woman, or an actress, or a washer-woman selling bamboos or working in hides for livelihood, one should perform Cāndrāyaṇa rite.

15. If a religious student being deluded by passion indulges in sexual intercourse with a woman, he should wear the skin of a donkey and beg for alms at seven houses.

16. He should perform ablutions three times a day, proclaiming his sin. He should be released from that sin in the course of a year.

17. An *Avakīrṇin* (a religious student violating the rules of chastity) should perform the expiatory rite for Brāhmaṇa-slaughter for the period of six months. Such a person gets relieved of the sin if he abides by the advice of Brāhmaṇas.

18. One should perform the expiatory rite for the sin of discharging semen virile. He should not beg for alms for seven days nor should he worship the fire.

19. He should repeat always (the seven) great Vyāhṛtis beginning with Oṁkāra, for the period of a year. He should take food only at night. He should not be pure and should partake of the alms received after begging.

20. With his anger shed off, he should perform the Japa of Sāvitrī (Gāyatri, Mantra) rapidly (?) on the bank of the river or holy places. He is thereby absolved of his sin.

21. If a Brāhmāṇa unintentionally murders a Kṣatriya, he should perform the expiatory rite of a Brāhmaṇa-slayer for six months or make a gift of five hundred cows.

22. Or he should remain in a forest performing meditation with great concentration and perform Prājāpatya,[1] Sāntapana or Taptakṛcchra rite for a year.

1. *Prājāpatya*—the same as *Kṛcchra*, but it is normally prescribed for unintentional sexual offences. Here it is prescribed for homicide (For details vide HD IV, pp. 145-146).

23. Either by mistake or wantonly, if he happens to kill a Vaiśya, he should perform the expiatory rite of a Brāhmaṇa-slayer and make gifts of a thousand cows and a fourth of it (i.e. two hundred and fifty).

24. After killing a Śūdra by mistake, one should perform expiatory rites for a year. He should perform the rites Kṛcchra and Atikṛcchra or the rite of Cāndrāyaṇa.

25. For wipping off the sin of killing a Kṣatriya, a Vaiśya or a Śūdra, the expiatory rite in order is the gift of a thousand or five hundred or two hundred and fifty cows. Or he shall perform the expiatory rite of a Brāhmaṇa-slayer for eight or three years.

26. After killing a Brāhmaṇa woman, a Brāhmaṇa should perform the expiatory rite for eight years; after killing a Kṣatriya woman, he should perform the expiatory rite for six years; after killing a Vaiśya woman, he should perform the expiatory rite for three years.

27. After killing a Śūdra woman, an excellent Brāhmaṇa shall become pure within a year. A twice-born should give something as a gift for a twice-born to wipe off the sin of killing Vaiśya woman.

28. After the murder of the outcaste also, one should perform the Cāndrāyaṇa rite. God Brahmā says that he will regain purity by means of the expiatory rite called Parāka.[1]

29. After killing a frog, a mungoose, a crow, a cat, a mule or a mouse or a dog, a Brāhmaṇa should perform a sixteenth of the Mahāvrata (great vow).

30. After killing a dog, one should alertfully drink milk (or water) for three days (?). After killing a cat or a mungoose, one should walk a distance of a Yojana (=12 km).

31. On killing a horse, a Brāhmaṇa should perform the expiation called Kṛcchra for twelve nights. On killing a serpent, the excellent Brāhmaṇa should make a gift of an image made of iron.

---

1. *Parāka* is called *Kṛcchra* by some and is said to remove all sins. It constitutes of not taking food for twelve days and remaining self-controlled and vigilant (Manu XI. 215, AP. 171. 10).

32. On killing a eunuch one should make a gift of a palāla (weight) of straw and a Māṣa weight of lead. On killing a boar, one should gift away a jar or ghee and on killing a Tittira bird, one should make a gift of a *Droṇa* measure of gingelly seeds.

33-34. On killing a parrot, a calf of two years, a Krauñca bird of three years, a swan, a crane, a stork, a peacock, a monkey, a vulture, or the bird Bhāsa, one should give away a cow to a Brāhmaṇa. On killing beasts of prey, one should gift away a milch cow.

35. (Defective) On killing non-meat-eating (herbivorous) animals, one should gift away a heifer. On killing a camel one should gift away gold weighing a Guñjā seed (?). On killing animals with bones (? backbones), some gift must he made over to a Brāhmaṇa.

36. On causing violent injury to the boneless animals, one becomes pure by performing "Prāṇāyāma; for wiping off the sin of cutting fruit-bearing trees, one should perform the Japa of hundred Ṛks.

37. Drinking of ghee is the expiatory rite for the sins of cutting hedges, creepers and turning plants, flower-laden plants and trees, of killing birds of all types and the living beings born of sweat and destroying the outcome of fruits and flowers.

38b-39. On killing elephants, the expiatory rite is Taptakṛcchra. On killing a cow due to mistake, the expiatory rite is Cāndrāyaṇa or Parāka. There is no atonement if the cow is killed wantonly.

CHAPTER THIRTYFOUR

Expiatory rites[1] (*continued*)

Vyāsa said :

1. For the sin of abducting men or women, of seizing a house, well, tank or a water (reservoir), the purificatory rite is Cāndrāyaṇa.

2. After committing the petty theft, of article of no great worth from the houses of others, one should perform the expiatory rite of Sāntapana and Kṛcchra for the purpose of self-purification, after the restitution of the same (to the owner).

3. After committing the theft of grains, cooked food and cash intentionally from the houses of his fellow-caste men, an excellent Brāhmaṇa shall become purified by Kṛcchrārdha (half a Kṛcchra) vow.

4. Drinking the Pañcagavya[2] is the expiation for the theft of food-stuffs and edibles, of vehicles, beds and seats, of flowers, roots and fruits.

5. The expiation for the theft of grass, fuel and timber, of raw rice and jaggery, of robes, hides and meat, is fasting for three nights.

6. The expiation for the theft of jewels, pearls and coral, of copper and silver and of magnetic stones is eating of food-particles for twelve days.

7. As an expiation for the sinful act of stealing cotton, eleven-hoofed or single-hoofed animals, of flowers, scents and medicines, one should drink water (or milk) for three days.

8-9a. After eating human flesh, one should perform the expiatory rite of Cāndrāyaṇa. After eating a crow, a dog, an elephant, a boar, or a cock, one becomes purified through Taptakṛcchra.

9b-10a. After taking in the flesh of beasts (and birds) of prey, their faeces or urine, as well as those of cow, jackal and

---

1. This chapter prescribes expiation for petty sins. It is interesting as it throws a flood of light on what the ancient elites in India regarded as unbecoming, offensive or, and sinful, before the 10th cent. A.D.

2. *Pañcagavya* is a liquid preparation of five products of the cow, viz. cow's urine, dung, milk, curds and ghee. It is to be taken at the end of each *Prāyaścitta*. It removes all petty sins (For details vide H. D. Vol. II., pp. 773-774).

monkey one should perform the same (viz. Tapta-kṛcchra) rite of expiation.

10b-11. After eating the Gangetic porpoise and the blue jay as well as fish, one should observe fast for twelve days and perform Homa with ghee and Kūṣmāṇḍa (white gourd). After eating a mungoose, an owl and a cat, one should perform Sāntapana rite.

12. After eating a beast of prey, camel or a mule (or donkey), one is purified by means of Taptakṛcchra vow. He shall perform all rites in accordance with the procedure mentioned before.

13. After eating the flesh of a crane, a stork, a swan, the Kāraṇḍava duck and the Cakravāka (ruddy goose) bird, one should not take food for twelve days.

14. After eating the dove, the Ṭiṭṭibha, the parrot, the drake, the owl and the web-foot, one should perform the same expiatory rite.

15. After eating the Gangetic porpoise, the blue jay, the flesh of fish and Katāhāra (i.e. a jackal or a crow that is feasting on dead bodies), one shall perform this expiatory rite alone.

16. After eating the cuckoo, the fish (animals and birds), the frog and the serpent, one shall become pure within a month, if one takes in barley boiled in cow's urine as food.

17. On eating acquatic beings, animals born in water, gallinaceous birds (such as domestic owl, porridge etc.) red-footed parrots, one should observe this vow for seven days.

18. On eating dog's flesh and dried meat and on even getting them made ready for oneself, one should perform this expiatory rite for a month, in order to quell that sin.

19. On eating brinjals, earth-grass, horse-radish, a tree called Kuṭaka, Caṭaka (a sparrow), the Khaḍga (rhinoceros) and Kumbhīra (a plant *Rottleria tinctoria*), one shall perform the expiatory vow called Prājāpatya.

20. On eating garlic and onion, one should observe the Cāndrāyaṇa vow, (on eating) Nālikā (lotus-stalk) and Taṇḍulīa, one becomes pure by means of the Prājāpatya rite.

21. On eating the Aśmāntaka plant and the young shoot of any plant, one becomes pure by means of Taptakṛcchra rite. On eating safflower, one shall become pure by means of the expiatory rite of Prājāpatya.

22-23a. On eating the bottle-gourd and Kiṁśuka also one should perform the same (above) rite. On drinking the squashes and decoctions (?) of these out of delusion, one should subsist on barley cooked in cow's urine for seven days, after which one would become pure. On eating Udumbara (Indian fig) at will, one becomes purified by means of Taptakṛccha.

23b-24a. After eating in a Śrāddha at the end of the 1st year or during the period of impurity due to death or birth, a Brāhmaṇa of great concentration and purity shall become purified by means of the Cāndrāyaṇa rite.

24b-25a. In case a Brāhmaṇa eats the food of a person who performs Homa everyday but does not make (even the slightest) gift of cooked food, he shall perform the Cāndrāyaṇa rite neatly.

25b-26. On eating the cooked food that is forbidden or that is served by low-caste fellows), one becomes pure by means of Taptakṛcchra. On eating the food of a Caṇḍāla, a Brāhmaṇa shall observe the Cāndrāyaṇa vow properly.

27. If he takes that food wantonly and deliberately, he should perform the Kṛcchra rite for a year and he has to undergo consecration rites once again. (Defective) After taking in an intoxicating drink other than wine, he should perform the Cāndrāyaṇa expiation.

28. On eating forbidden food, one becomes pure by means of the Prājāpatya vow. If one (unknowingly) drinks urine, semen virile or faeces, one shall perform this rite in expiation.

29a. If (the duration of expiation or fast) is not enjoined the expiatory rite must really be performed everywhere for one day.

29b-30a. On taking in the faeces and urine of the filthy pig, donkey, camel, jackal, monkey and crow, a Brāhmaṇa should perform the Cāndrāyaṇa expiatory rite.

30b-31a. The three twice-born castes (i.e. the Brāhmaṇa, the Kṣatriya and the Vaiśya) deserve to be consecrated once again, if they unwittingly take in the urine and faeces in contact with urine.

31b-32. If out of delusion, an excellent Brāhmaṇa takes in the faeces and urine of the carnivorous birds, he should perform the expiatory rite of Mahāsāntapana. If he takes in the urine and faeces of the vulture, frog, sparrow and the domestic fowl, he should perform the Kṛcchra rite.

33-34a. A person (Brāhmaṇa ?) is purified by observing the Prājāpatya vow, if he happens to eat the leavings of food (*ucchiṣṭa*) of a Brāhmaṇa. (In case he eats) the *ucchiṣṭa* of a Kṣattriya, Tapta-kṛcchra expiation should be performed, and Ati-kṛccha expiation, after eating a Vaiśya's *ucchiṣṭa*. Having eaten the leavings of food of a Śūdra, a Brāhmaṇa should observe the Cāndrāyaṇa vow.

34b. After drinking water from the pot of wine, one should perform the vow of Cāndrāyaṇa.

35. If a Brāhmaṇa eats the leavings of the food (of unspecified persons), he becomes purified by drinking cow's urine, eating (for food) barley cooked in cow's urine or by drinking the water that remains after cows have drunk.

36. If one takes in water defiled by urine, faeces etc., the expiatory rite for the sin is Sāntapana or Kṛcchra.

37. If a Brāhmaṇa, knowingly, drinks water from the well of a Cāṇḍāla or his water-pot, he should perform the rite of Sāntapana or Kṛcchra. That is the way to atone for the sin.

38. On drinking the water touched by a Cāṇḍāla, an excellent Brāhmaṇa becomes purified by means of Pañcagavya (preparation of the five products of cows viz. urine, faeces, milk, curds and ghee) as well as the chief expiatory rite for three days.

39. If a Brāhmaṇa knowingly or out of delusion touches a great sinner and takes food with him, he should take bath and perform Taptakṛcchra.

40. If one touches a great sinner, a Cāṇḍāla, or a woman in her monthly courses and unwittingly takes food, he shall become pure (after observing fast for) three nights.

41. If a man fit to take bath (i.e. one who should take bath) takes food, without bathing), he shall become pure (by observing a fast) in the course of a day and a night. If he does

so wilfully, the lotus-born lord says that he should perform the rite of Kṛcchra.

42. On eating stale food-stuffs or those defiled by cows, etc, one should observe fast or perform a fourth of the Kṛcchra expiation.

43. At the end of every year, a Brāhmaṇa should observe the Kṛcchra vow again for the purification of the sin due to the eating of forbidden things unwittingly and particularly those taken in wantonly.

44. After performing the Yajñas on behalf of Vrātyas (the people of the three castes who have become outcaste) and the obsequies of others as well as for exorcising (for malicious purpose), one becomes purified by means of three Kṛcchras.

45. On performing the cremation and other rites for Brāhmaṇas and others who are killed, a Brāhmaṇa becomes pure by means of Prājāpatya expiation and eating barley cooked in cow's urine.

46. A person who has besmeared himself with oil or vomitted, passes urine or discharges faeces or shaves himself or indulges in sexual intercourse, becomes purified by observing a fast for a day and a night (i.e. one full day).

47. If one abandons fire (worship) or makes another to neglect it for one day, he becomes purified (by fasting) for three nights. And (for the negligence of fire-worship) for three nights, he (should observe fast) for six days.

48. If out of blunder he forsakes the fire worship for ten days or twelve days, he should perform the Kṛcchra and the Cāndrāyaṇa expiatory rites to quell that sin.

49. On accepting a gift of wealth from a fallen man, one will become pure by abandoning the same. But lord Manu says that he should observe Kṛcchra vow duly.

50. Persons who have desisted from (and hence violated) the vow of fasting (before its completion) and those who have finished (i.e. abandoned) their order of mendicancy (i.e. Sannyāsa) should perform three Kṛcchra and three Cāndrāyaṇa vows.

51. They should again get consecrated by purificatory rites beginning with *Jāta-karma*. Sanctified thus the Brāhmaṇas

become purified. Persons knowing Dharma should observe that vow properly.

52. A person who did not perform the Sandhyā worship should observe fast for the day and remain controlled in mind. If he does not perform the Sandhyā worship at night the same (i.e. fast at night) should be continued for that night.

53. A person who has not gathered sacrificial twigs and performed the Yajña should, for the purpose of purification, repeat the Gāyatrī Mantra a thousand and eight times taking bath and remaining pure, with concentration of mind.

54. (Defective verse) If out of blunder, a householder does not perform the Sandhyā prayer he should take bath and observe fast. He shall become pure immediately. If he be exhausted (and does not perform Sandhyā-prayer), he should remain perfectly self-controlled.

55. Having dropped off the daily (sacred) duties prescribed in the Vedas, a *Snātaka* (one who has completed the period of studentship and is due for marriage) who (thus) violates his vow, should observe fast on that day.

56. An excellent Brāhmaṇa who exterminates another* (?) should perform the Kṛcchra vow for one year. A Vrātya should observe the Cāndrāyaṇa Vrata and give a cow a gift whereby he becomes purified.

57. If a Brāhmaṇa does anything (indicating) atheism, he shall perform the Prājāpatya rite. If he does anything injurious to Devas or the preceptors, he will become pure by means of Tapta Kṛcchra.

58. If one willingly travels by a camel-cart or a donkey cart, or enters water in the nude, he shall become pure only (by fasting for) three nights.

59. The expiatory rite for *Apāṅktas* (outcastes i.e. those who are not eligible to sit in the same rows for meals with others) is missing five meals and taking meal only on the sixth occasion, for one month. The Japa of the Saṁhitā and the Homas as per procedure laid down by Śākala, every day.

---

*The reading should be probably *agnyutsādī* and not *anyotsādī* as in Veṅk. Ed. *agnyutsādī* means 'one who has destroyed (given up fire worship by extinguishing) the sacred fire."

60. On wearing a blue or red cloth, a Brāhmaṇa should observe fast for a day and a night and drink Pañcagavya. He shall then be pure.

61. If one explains the Vedas, the Dharmaśāstras and the Purāṇas to a Cāṇḍāla, he shall become pure only by means of the Cāndrāyaṇa rite. There is no other means of expiation for him.

62. On touching a Brāhmaṇa killed by hanging etc. the purity can be regained by Cāndrāyaṇa or Prājāpatya vows.

63. If a Brāhmaṇa defiled by Ucchiṣṭa (i.e. with food particles in the mouth and on hands and) has not performed *Ācamana* (the concluding sipping of water after meal) touches a Cāṇḍāla and others unwittingly, he should take bath and repeat the Gāyatrī Mantra a thousand and eight times.

64. Or he should repeat the Drupadā Mantra a hundred times. He should maintain celibacy and good concentration of mind. He should observe fast for three nights strictly. He shall then become pure by means of the Pañcagavya.

65. A Brāhmaṇa, while Ucchiṣṭa (with particles of food in the mouth or on hand) willfully touches Cāṇḍālas or fallen persons (outcastes) should observe the Prājāpatya vow for purification.

66. On touching a Cāṇḍāla, a Sūtakin (one having the impurity due to birth or death of a relative) or a dead body, a woman in her monthly course and a fallen fellow a person touched by them, one should take bath for the sake of purity.

67. If one touches a person touched by a Cāṇḍāla, Sūtakin and a corpse, one should take bath and perform Ācamana and Japa with great concentration.

68. An excellent Brāhmaṇa who knowingly touches these persons or is touched by them, should take bath and perform *Ācamana* rite for the sake of purity. So says lord Pitāmaha.

69. If a Brāhmaṇa, taking food is accidentally touched, he should perform Śauca (purificatory rite) and then observe fast. After that he should take bath and perform Homa. This is the holy rite.

70. On touching the dead body and a Cāṇḍāla (v.l. dead body of a Cāṇḍāla) one shall perform the Kṛcchra rite,

one shall become pure. On touching a person who has anointed his body.* (?) one becomes pure within a day and a night (after observing fast).

71. On touching liquor, a Brāhmaṇa should perform three Prāṇāyāmas and he shall become pure. On touching garlic and onion, he should drink ghee and he shall become pure.

72. If a Brāhmaṇa is bitten by a dog, he should drink milk for three days in the evening. If he is bitten above the umbilical region, he should increase (the quantity of milk) twofold.

73. This quantity of milk shall be increased threefold if he is bitten on the arms and if bitten on the head, this shall be fourfold. Or an excellent Brāhmaṇa bitten by dogs, should take bath and perform Japa of the Sāvitrī Mantra.

74. If an excellent Brāhmaṇa who is not sick and who has the means but does not perform great Yajñas but partakes of food (and enjoys) he shall become pure by performing half of a Kṛcchra rite.

75. If a man maintaining sacred fires does not worship them on the *Parvan* days or if a person does not go unto his wife during the prescribed days after menstruation, he should perform half a Kṛcchra.

76. (Defective) If person even though not sick (simply) puts his body into the water without using water (for washing himself?), he should take a dip into water alongwith clothes and touch a cow and then he becomes pure.

77. (If any sin is committed) knowingly, a Brāhmaṇa should perform the japa after the sun has arisen, remaining in the water itself. He should then repeat the Gāyatrī a thousand and eight times. He should observe fast for three days.

78. On following the dead body of a Śūdra out of his own free will, an excellent Brāhmaṇa should take ablutions, in rivers and perform the Japa of a thousand and eight Gāyatrī Mantra.

---

*v.l. *Saṁspṛśyam* (after touching) an untouchable (who has besmeared himself with oil).

79. After swearing an oath with the delimitation of another Brāhmaṇa* (?), a Brāhmaṇa should perform the Cāndrāyaṇa rite by means of cooked barley food.

80. After serving food irregularly (partially to persons sitting) in the same line, one becomes purified of the sin by means of kṛcchra rites. On treading the shadow of a Cāṇḍāla, one shall take bath and drink ghee.

81. If in the stage of impurity, one looks at the fire or the moon he should look at the sun (for expiation). On touching a human bone, one should take bath and he becomes pure thereby.

82. Having done a false study, one should beg for alms for a year. An ungrateful person should stay in a Brāhmaṇa's house and perform sacred rites for five years.

83. After producing *Huṁ* sound against a Brāhmaṇa and after using *Tvam* (you in singular) in respect to elderly persons (i.e. instead of using *Bhavān*—your 'honour'), one should take bath and spend the remainder of the day without taking food. He should then bow down and propitiate those persons.

84. If one beats (the elders) even with the blade of a grass, if one binds their neck with a piece of cloth and if one conquers them in an argument, one should propitiate the other one.

85. On intimidating (by threat) a Brāhmaṇa with the intention of killing him, one should perform the kṛcchra rite; on felling a Brāhmaṇa to the ground, one should perform the Atikṛcchra rite, and on spilling the blood of a Brāhmaṇa, one shall perform both the expiatory rites of kṛcchra and Atikṛcchra.

86. After uttering a lie to or for reviling an elderly person (or a teacher) one should perform the expiatory rite by refraining from taking food for one night (v.l. or three nights) for dispelling that sin.

87. If one spits at or reviles in front of Devas and the sages, one should burn one's tongue by means of a firebrand. Gold too should be given as gift.

88. If any Brāhmaṇa passes urine in the garden of Devas (i.e. in the precincts of shrines) even for once, his penis

*v.l. *vadha-saṁyutam* "concerning the murder of . . ."

should be cut off for the sake of expiation and he should perform Cāndrāyaṇa rite.

89. If out of delusion, an excellent Brāhmaṇa passes urine in the *sanctum sanctorum* of a temple; his penis should be cut off. He should perform the Cāndrāyaṇa rite.

90. After blaspheming and rebuking the deities, Devas and the sages, an excellent Brāhmaṇa must duly perform the Prājāpatya vow.

91. On conversing with them (i.e. such) sinners one incurs sins for which he should take bath and worship the Lord. On seeing them, he should look at the sun and on remembering them he should remember Viśveśvara (in order to wipe off the respective sins.)

92. Even in hundreds of years it is impossible to redeem that person from sin who censures god Śiva, the ruler of the universe, the over-lord of all living beings.

93. At the outset, he should observe the Cāndrāyaṇa vow, then Kṛcchra as well as the Atikṛcchra. He should then seek refuge in the Lord whereby he shall be released from that sin.

94. The gift of all (one's) possessions duly is the means of expiation for all sins. He should perform the rites of Cāndrāyaṇa duly, as well as those of Kṛcchra and the Atikṛcchra.

95a. The pilgrimage to holy centres is the means of expiation for all sins.

95b-96. The person who propitiates Bhava (Śiva) on the New Moon day, is released from all sins on worshipping the Brāhmaṇas.

97. By worshipping Mahādeva on the eighth day and the fourteenth day in the dark half of a month through a Brāhmaṇa, one is released from all sins.

98. By seeing the three-eyed Īśa with offerings in the first Yāma (period of three hours) of the night on the thirteenth day, one is released from all sins.

99-101a. One should observe fast on the fourteenth day in the dark half. With great concentration, he should then offer seven libations of water along with gingelly seeds in each handful to Yama, Dharmarāja, Mṛtyu, Aṇtaka, Vaivasvata, Kāla and

Sarvaprāṇahara. He should offer these libations in the forenoon after taking his bath. He is then released from all sins.

101b-102a. During the performance of all holy rites one should be quiescent with controlled mind. He should observe celibacy and fast. He should worship Brāhmaṇas. He should lie down on the ground at night.

102b-103a. With god Brahmā, the grandsire of the world, in view, one should worship three Brāhmaṇas on the new moon day. He is released from all sins.

103b-104a One should observe fast on the sixth *Tithi* in the bright half of the month, with great concentration and worship lord sun on the seventh *Tithi*. He is released from all sins.

104b-105a. One should worship Yama on the fourth day (*Tithi*) or in the constellation Bharaṇī or on Saturday (s) and he is released from the (accumulated) sin of seven births.

105b-106a. One should refrain from taking food on the *Ekādaśī* (eleventh) *Tithi* and worship lord Janārdana on the twelfth day of the bright half. He is released from great sins.

106b-107a. The following, during eclipse and other (auspicious) occasions, is the means of expiation for great sins : penance, Japa, visiting holy centres and the worship of Devas and the Brāhmaṇas.

107b-108a. Even though a man be defiled by all sins, if he abandons his life after the holy observances in the holy centres, he is absolved of all sins.

108b-109. A woman who enters the funeral pyre along with her husband, shall uplift him even if he is a Brāhmaṇa-slayer, an ungrateful fellow or one defiled by great sins. Learned men know this to be the greatest expiation for women.

110. If a woman is chaste and is engaged in serving her husband, she does not incur any sin either in this world or in the other.

(*Verse in brackets*)

No hesitation need be felt in this matter that if a woman is endowed with the quality of chastity and is eager to serve her husband, she has no sin either in this world or in the other and that, she is relieved of all sins.

111. A chaste woman devoted to piety (*dharma*) shall always attain welfare and happiness. No man can, by any means, create discomfiture for her.

112. Just as in the case of Śītā,[1] well-known in the three worlds, as the charming and beloved wife of Rāma, the son of Daśaratha, she conquered the king of Rākṣasas.

113. Urged by Kāla (Death), Rāvaṇa, the king of Rākṣasas, desired Sītā, the wide-eyed beautiful wife of Rāma.

114. It is reported that by means of his Māyā, he disguised himself (as) an ascetic and determined to abduct that beautiful lady while she was strolling (solitarily) in the tenantless forest.

115. The lady of pure smiles realised his intention. Remembering her husband, the son of Daśaratha, she sought refuge in the Āvasathya (household) fire.

116. With her palms joined in devotion, Rāma's wife worshipped the great Yogī, (the fire-god), the destroyer (scorcher) of the worlds, as if he was her husband Rāma incarnate (and prayed) :

Eulogy of the Fire-god.

117. I bow unto Kṛśānu (fire) of the form of Kāla, of great Yogic power, the greatest riddle, the destroyer of all living beings.

118. I take shelter in lord Pāvaka (the purifying deity), the eternal deity of universal forms, the Yogin who wears the (elephant) hide, the lord of the goblins the Supreme god.

119. I resort unto the Ātman of radiant blazing body abiding in the hearts of all living beings. I seek refuge in the Lord whose form is the universe, the source of all that fiery, brilliant, I resort to the fire-god, the Lord of great Yogins, the sun, the supreme god.

---

1. VV. 111-140 tell us a different story of the abduction of Sītā than the one given by Vālmīki. According to KP. real Sītā was protected by Agni (the fire-god) the *Āvasathya* (Household sacrificial) Fire and it was the illusory Sītā) created by Agni that was abducted by Rāvaṇa. The Chāyā-sītā entered the fire for 'purification' and real Sītā came out of the Fire-god and was accepted by Rāma.

120. I seek refuge in Rudra, the great swallower (destroyer), the trident-bearing Lord, the fire of the Universal destruction, the Lord of Yogins, the dispenser of fruits (in the form) of enjoyment and liberation.

121. I resort unto you the diverse-eyed deity with the forms of *Bhūḥ*, *Bhuvaḥ* and *Svaḥ*, one who is lying hidden in the golden abode, the great one of unmeasured splendour.

122. I resort to Vaiśvānara abiding in all living beings, the lord who conveys *Havyas* and *Kavyas* (i.e. offerings) (to gods and Pitṛs). I resort to Lord Vahni.

123. I resort to that Supreme reality, the excellent and auspicious principle of the sun. I resort to the Agni ascending to heaven, the greatest splendour, the imperishable conveyor of oblations to gods.

124. After repeating (the prayer in) these eight (?) verses on Vahni, the famous wife of Rāma mentally meditated on Rāma and remained silent with her eyes closed.

125. Then out of the Avasathya (household) fire, Lord Maheśvara (the great god), the bearer of sacrificial oblations, of resplendent soul manifested himself as if burning with his own refulgence.

126. Desirous of getting Rāvaṇa killed he created an illusory Sītā. Taking the real Sītā the beloved of Rāma, the fire-god vanished there.

127. On seeing such a Sītā (i.e. the illusory one) Rāvaṇa the lord of Rākṣasas, took her and went to Laṅkā situated within the ocean.

128. After killing Rāvaṇa, Rāma took Sītā and (came back) accompanied by Lakṣmaṇa. His mind became agitated due to suspicion.

129. For convincing the living beings, the illusory Sītā entered the fire; immediately she was consumed by the fire.

130. After burning the illusory Sītā, the lord fire-god of hot rays, showed the real Sītā to Rāma. The fire-god (the purifier) became a beloved of Devas.

131. Catching hold of the feet of her husband, the daughter of Janaka the lady of beautiful middle, made obeisance to Rāma on the ground.

132. On seeing it Rāma was delighted in mind. Surprise was evident in his eyes. After bowing to the Vahni with bent head, Rāghava propitiated him.

133. The lord spoke to Vahnī; Was this fair-complexioned lady burned by you before, as she has been seen come to my side again?

134. Lord Fire-god, the scorcher of the worlds, spoke to the son of Daśaratha, telling him everything as it had happened in the presence of all living beings.

135. "This beloved of yours is highly chaste as goddess Pārvatī. She is the greatest favourite of the goddess whom she had propitiated by means of penance (?)

136. This chaste lady of good conduct is endowed with the readiness to serve her husband like Bhavānī in regard to Īśvara. She was protected by me because she was desired by Rāvaṇa.

137. But Sītā who was abducted by the lord of Rākṣasas was the illusory Sītā created by me with a desire to get Rāvaṇa killed.

138. On that account, Rāvaṇa, the wicked king of the Rākṣasas and the destroyer of the worlds, had been killed. The Māyā has also been withdrawn.

139. "Accept this pure Jānakī at my instance. See lord Nārāyaṇa your own self the source of origin and the place of everything".

140. After saying this, the fierce lord fire-god whose flames spread everywhere and who had faces on all sides was duly honoured by Rāghava and the other people and he vanished.

141. Thus the greatness of chaste ladies has been described by me. This (narrative) is remembered to be the expiatory rite for ladies. It absolves one from all sins.

142. Even a person full of all sins shall be released from sin, if he controls himself well and abandons his body in the holy centres.

143. A Brāhmaṇa or any man is released from all sins accumulated by him by taking bath in all holy centres in the world.

Vyāsa said :

144. Thus, the Dharma propounded by Manu has been propounded to you by me. The eternal path of knowledge (has also been narrated) for propitiating Maheśa.

145. One should pursue the path of knowledge with the assistance of Yogic practice. He then sees Mahādeva. No one else can see Him even in hundreds of Kalpas.

146. A person who establishes the great Dharma and that Jñāna (knowledge) pertaining to Parameśvara (Supreme God Śiva) is considered to be the greatest Yogin and there is no one in the world superior to him.

147. If a person is competent to establish both Dharma and Jñāna, but does not do so out of delusion, he is not a great favourite with the Lord, though he may be endowed with Yoga (Yogic Powers).

148. Hence gifts should always be given to Brāhmaṇas particularly to those who are endowed with piety and faith and those who are quiescent.

149. He who reads this dialogue between you all and me shall be free from all sins and shall attain the greatest goal.

150. A wise and intelligent person should read this in the presence of Brāhmaṇas during Śrāddhas and during rites concerned with gods. It should be listened to by all twice-born ones.

151. A person who ponders over the meaning and narrates this with concentrated mind to pure Brāhmaṇas shall be released from the coverings of sins and faults and attains Lord Maheśvara.

152. After saying this much, the holy son of Satyavatī, sage Vyāsa, consoled the sages and Sūta and went away in the same manner as he had arrived.

CHAPTER THIRTYFIVE

The Greatness of Gayā and other sacred places[1]

The sages requested :

1. O Romaharṣaṇa, now please recount to us the great Tīrthas (sacred places) that are well-known in the world.

Romaharṣaṇa narrated :

2. Ye all listen. I shall recount the different kinds of holy centres described in the Purāṇas by sages, the expounders of Brahman.

3. O excellent sages, every one of these holy rites, viz. Ablution, *Japa*, *Homa*, *Śrāddha*, *Dāna* (charitable gift) etc. performed (at these places) sanctifies the family upto the seventh generation.

4. The well-known holy place of Brahmā the Supreme god Parameṣṭhin viz Prayāga extends to five Yojanas (1 Yojana = 12 kms). Its greatness has already been described (vide Supra I. chs 36-39).

5. Another excellent Tīrtha is that of the Kurus (i.e. Kurukṣetra). It is respected by Devas. It is spotted with the hermitages of the sages and it dispels all sins.

6. After performing ablution therein, one becomes pure-souled, devoid of arrogance and rivalry. Whatever little he gives as gift, sanctifies both (paternal and maternal) families.

7. The holy centre of Gaya[2] is highly mysterious. It is a rare spot for the rites of the *Pitṛs*. A man who offers Piṇḍas there is not born again.

---

1. After the section called Vyāsa-Gītā (chs. 12-34), KP. describes various holy places and Tīrthas. Visit to Tīrthas is a way of expiation of sins, hence this section. All these Tīrthas belong to North or rather Aryan-speaking area in India. In Part I chs. 30-39 KP describes mainly Vārāṇasi and secondarily other holy places like Prayāga.

2. VV. 7-15 describe Gayā. By Gayā, KP. implies the area between Ramaśilā hill on the North and Brahmayoni hill on the south and on the bank of the Phalgu. The ancient town of Gayā is on the southern side. Viṣṇupada (which is called Rudrapada here) is in the ancient part. The present temple was built some two centuries ago by the Maratha queen Ahalyabai Holkar of Indore.

8. All the *Pitṛs* are redeemed by him who goes to Gayā and offers Piṇḍas even once. They will attain the greatest goal.

9. For the welfare of the worlds, his foot had been imprinted by Rudra[1] the great Ātman. One shall propitiate the *Pitṛs* there.

10. If a person who is competent to go to Gayā does not go there, the *Pitṛs* bewail him because all his efforts will be in vain.

11. The *Pitṛs* sing songs and the great sages glorify—"Whoever goes to Gayā will redeem us."

12. "Even if he is endowed with sins, even if he is devoid of adherence to his own duties, if anyone goes to Gayā, he will redeem us.

13. Many sons endowed with good behaviour and virtues should be sought after so that at least one in that group may go to Gayā."*

14. Hence one, especially a Brāhmaṇa, shall assiduously and duly offer Piṇḍas with great concentration, after going to Gayā.

15. Blessed are those men who offer Piṇḍas at Gayā. They shall uplift seven generations of both the families (i.e. of the father and of the mother) and shall attain the greatest goal.

16. There is another excellent Tīrtha which is called the residence of the Siddhas. It is well known as Prabhāsa[2] and Lord Śiva abides there.

17. By performing ablutions there and thereafter Śrāddha and the worship of the Brāhmaṇas, a Brāhmaṇa attains the ever-lasting and excellent world.

---

1. KP cannot be charged with Brahmanising an ancient Buddhist locality, as it was already Brahmanised before the Chinese traveller Hiuen Tsiang visited it in A.D. 637. But vicinity of Bodh-gayā, Asoka's dedication of caves in Barabar Hill to Ājīvakas and the caves in Nagarjuni hills to Śramanic Asoka's grandson Daśaratha show that formerly it was a centre of Ājīvakas by religion.

It is, however, called *Viṣṇupada* for the last many centuries.

*The same as Yama quoted in *Tristhalīsetu*, p. 330.

2. Prabhāsa (Devapaṭṭana, Verwal) in Saurastra (Gujarat) has the famous shrine of Somanatha, one of the twelve jyotir-liṅgas. The shrine which was demolished by Mahmud of Gazni in A.D. 1025 was reconstructed again after Indian Independence.

18. There is the holy place named *Traiyambaka*[1] which is bowed to by all Devas. After worshipping Rudra there, one shall get the fruit of the Jyotiṣṭoma sacrifice.

19. After worshipping the golden-eyed Mahādeva, the god with matted hair, and honouring Brāhmaṇas, he will obtain the chieftainship of the attendants of Śiva.

20. Someśvara is the excellent holy Tīrtha of Rudra, the Parameṣṭhin. On seeing Rudra, the ultimate cause,* it shall remove all ailments.

21. There is an auspicious sacred place, the holiest among all other holy places, known as Vijaya. There is a famous Liṅga of the great Lord, known as Vijaya.

22. O excellent Brāhmaṇas, having stayed there for six months on regulated abstemious diet, observing celibacy and with great concentration of mind, the person goes to the supreme position (viz. liberation).

23. There is another auspicious excellent Tīrtha in the eastern lands. It is the solitary (v.l. Ekāmra)[2] holy centre of the lord of Devas. It bestows the benefit of chieftainship of Śiva's attendants.

24. By giving some auspicious plot of land to the devotees of Śiva at this place, a king shall become an emperor. One who is desirous of liberation, shall attain salvation.

25. The waters of Mahānadī are holy and destructive of all sins. By plunging therein at the time of eclipse, one is released from all sins.

26. There is another river named Virajā.[3] It is well known in the three worlds. By taking bath there, a Brāhmaṇa or any man, is honoured in the Brahmaloka.

---

1. Tryambakeśvara near Nasik at the source of Godāvari. This is one of twelve Jyotirliṅgas in India.

*v.l. *rudra-sāyujya-kāraṇam* 'the cause of giving the identity with god Rudra.)

The site of Kṛṣṇa's death is near here.

2. Ekāmra—the same as modern.

Bhuvaneshwar in Orissa. It is a Rudra Tīrtha also called Kṛttivāsa (Bm. p. 34. 6). This place, equal to Vārāṇasī in sanctity, came to be called *Ekāmra(ka)* due to a famous mango tree in the previous kalpa. BM. P. 41. 12.

3. A river in Orissa.

27. There is another holy centre of Nārāyaṇa named Puruṣottama.[1] It is there that Nārāyaṇa the glorious and great Puruṣa resides.

28. By taking bath there and worshipping the great Viṣṇu as well as by worshipping Brāhmaṇas, an excellent Brāhmaṇa shall attain Viṣṇu's region.

29. The holy centre named Gokarṇa[2] is the greatest of all holy centres and is well-known. It is destructive of all sins. It is the abode of Śambhu, Parameṣṭhin.

30. On seeing the greatest and excellent Liṅga Gokarṇa of the lord, one shall attain all cherished desires and shall be a favourite of Rudra.

31. By worshipping the Liṅga of the trident-bearing lord Mahādeva in the northern Gokarṇa, one shall attain *Sāyujya* (identity) with Śiva.

32. Lord Mahādeva there, is well known as Sthāṇu. On seeing him, a man is released from all sins instantaneously.

33. Another holy centre of Viṣṇu, the great Ātman, is Kubjāśrama.[3] By worshipping the Puruṣa, Viṣṇu, one is honoured in the Śveta Dvīpa.

34. It was here that Lord Nārāyaṇa was let off by Rudra, the enemy of the Tripuras, after destroying the Yajña of Dakṣa.

35. All around it, within the radius of one Yojana, is a sacred place resorted to by multitudes of Siddhas and sages. There is a holy shrine of Viṣṇu where the Supreme Person resides.

---

1. Jagannātha Puri in Orissa. Its glory is described in Bm. P. Chs. 45-51, 69, 177.

2. A place sacred to Śiva on the West-coast in Kumta Tehsil of North Kanara Dist. (Karnataka). This is the Ātma-liṅga of god Śiva which while being taken away by Rāvaṇa, was duped away by Gaṇeśa and established here.

There are two Gokarṇas—Northern and Southern (LP. I. 92-134-135). KP. mentions northern Gokarṇa in v. 31 below.

3. The mention of the destruction of Dakṣa's sacrifice shows that this must be Kanakhala near Haridwar.

36. At Kokāmukha[1] there is another holy centre of Viṣṇu of miraculous activities. If a person dies here* a man is freed from sins, and he attains the Sārūpya (similarity in form) of Viṣṇu.

37. Śāligrāma[2] is a great holy centre that increases the pleasure of Viṣṇu. A man abandoning his life there, observes Hṛṣīkeśa (the lord of sense-organs).

38· There is an auspicious and beautiful abode of the Siddhas, well-known as Aśvatīrtha. Lord Nārāyaṇa himself stays there always as Horse-headed deity.

39. There is a holy centre well known in the three worlds. It is a very auspicious abode of the Siddhas. That merit bestowing holy place of Brahmā, the Parameṣṭhin is there.

40-41a. (the holy centre) Puṣkara[3] is destructive of all sins. It accords Brahmaloka to persons who die here. The excellent Brāhmaṇa who mentally remembers Puṣkara is purified of all sins. He rejoices alongwith god Indra.

41b-42a. There, Devas, Gandharvas, Yakṣas, serpents, Rākṣasas and Siddhas worship the lotus-born deity viz. Brahmā.

42b-43a. Having performed ablution, one should become pure and after worshipping god Brahmā, the highest deity and also an excellent Brāhmaṇa, he sees god Brahmā.

43b-44a. Approaching lord of Devas, Indra, the blameless one, a man assumes his (Indra's) form and attains all desires.

44b-45a. The Saptasārasvata[4] holy centre is the greatest one, resorted to by Brahmā and others. By worshipping Rudra there, one derives the fruit of a horse-sacrifice.

---

1. Varāha-Kṣetra in the district of Purnea in Bengal on the Triveṇī (the confluence of Tambar, the Aruṇā and Suna) above Nathpur.

*the v.l. *mṛto'tra pātakair muktaḥ* is preferred here to *muktotra martyaḥ* |

2. A sacred place near the source of the Gaṇḍaka river. Sages Bharata and Pulaha practised penance here. The sacred pebbles called Śālagrāmas are obtained here.

3. A lake, sacred to god Brahmā. It is six miles from Ajmer (Rajasthan).

4. In Kurukṣetra, the story of Maṅkaṇaka is repeated in Mbh. *Vana.* 83-115, *Śalya* 38. 4-13. The collective name seven Sarasvatīs is given in Mbh. *ibid* as follows: Suprabhā, Kāñcanākṣī, Viśālā, Manoramā, Oghavatī,

45b-46. It was here that (sage Maṅkaṇaka propitiated the bull-bannered Śiva, Rudra, the Supreme Lord, by means of penance. Thereafter, sage Maṅkaṇaka blazed by means of his penance.

47. On knowing that Rudra had come, he danced due to ecstatic delight. Lord Rudra spoke to him—"Why did you dance?"

48-49. Even after seeing the god Īśāna (Śiva), he danced again and again. On seeing him puffed with pride Lord Īśa, in order to subdue his arrogance, slit open his own body and pointed out the heap of *Bhasma* and said "O excellent Brāhmaṇa, see this heap of *Bhasma* originating from my body."

50. "O leading sage, this is the greatness of penance, there is also another person like you, wherefore did you dance?

51-53a. This is not proper in an ascetic. I am even superior to you." After saying this to the excellent sage Rudra, the seer of the entire universe, narrated to him the great reality of the universe. Hara then danced, taking up a form with a thousand (i.e. innumerable) heads, a thousand eyes and a thousand feet. His face was terrible due to the curved fangs. He appeared ferocious with wreaths of flames.

53b-54. Then he saw by the side of that Trident-bearing Lord, a gracious-looking, wide-eyed auspicious goddess Śivā with resplendent charming sportfulness, comparable in size (v.l. brilliance) to crores of suns.

55. On seeing the lord of the Universe smiling and standing there resplendently, the heart of the leading sage became agitated due to fright and he trembled.

56. He bent down his head before Rudra and with self-control he repeated the verses of Rudrādhyāya. The three-eyed lord Īśa, favourably disposed towards his devotees, became delighted.

57-59. He assumed his previous form. The goddess disappeared. Embracing the devotee who was bowing to him,

---

Sureṇu, and Vimalodakā. These are sacred rivers in different parts of the country viz. Pushkar, Naimiṣāraṇya, Gayā, Kośala Kurukṣetra Haridvāra and the Himālayas respectively but the Sarasvatī is supposed to have been there in that river-form.

Śiva, the lord of Devas himself, said "O dear one, do not be afraid. What shall I give unto you ? Then the delighted sage desirous of asking him bowed down his head before god Hara, the Lord of mountains, and the slayer of the Tripuras, and submitted "Obeisance be to you O Mahādeva; salutations to you O Maheśvara.

60-61. What is this lordly form with faces all round, yet very terrible ? Who has that lady who stood shining by your side and who vanished very suddenly. I wish to know everything." When this was enquired of, Lord Hara spoke to Maṅkaṇaka :

62. The great Lord, the fire (the destroyer) of the three cities, explained to him (Maṅkaṇaka) his own (path of) Yoga and about the goddess :

"I am the thousand (innumerable)-eyed god, the soul of all and have faces on all sides.

63. I am the scorcher of all bonds. I am Kāla (Time, Death), Hara and the cause of Kāla. Everything consisting of the sentient and the non-sentient is urged by myself.

64. I am that Person (soul) who is immanent in all and I am verily the Supreme Person. The deluding Potency (Greatest Māyā) is the Prakṛti consisting of the three Guṇas.

65. She is described by the sages as Śakti (Potency), the eternal source of origin of the universe. The creator of the universe enchants the universe by means of the Māyā.

66. The Śruti states that the Supreme, unmanifest Nārāyaṇa is of the form of Māyā. In this way, I always establish the entire world.

67-68. I Unite with Prakṛti, the twentyfifth Principle known as Puruṣa. That pure, omnipresent, immovable unborn god in union with her Prakṛti creates this whole universe from Prakṛti which is his own form.

He is the illustrious god Brahmā, of the form of the Universe, the grandsire of the world.

69. This creatorship of the great Ātman has been clearly narrated to you. I am the sole lord, beginningless, the primordial Kāla. the all-pervading lord, the destroyer (of the Universe).

70. (While creating and destroying) I assume the greatest form. I am mentioned as Rudra by the learned men. That supreme Potency (Parā Śakti), well-known as goddess Vidyā, belongs to me alone.

71. The person of Vidyā has indeed been visualised by you. So also these principles the Pradhāna, the Puruṣa and Īśvara.

72. The Śruti says : Viṣṇu, Brahmā and lord Rudra (are) Kāla (?). These three deities are beginningless and endless. They are stabilised in the Brahman alone.

73. The Śruti says that it is unmanifest, imperishable and everything has that as its soul. The great principle is Ātman and Bliss. It is consciousness alone, the greatest region.

74-75. It is the entire firmament, the Brahmā, nothing is other than it. After realising this and resorting to the path of devotion, I should be honoured and worshipped. Thereafter you will see Īśvara." After saying this much, Lord Hara disappeared.

76. The sage propitiated Rudra in that very same place by means of the path of devotion. This holy centre is unequalled, sacred and resorted to by Brahmarṣis. By resorting to this, a scholarly Brāhmaṇa is released from all sins.

CHAPTER THIRTYSIX

Glory of Sacred Places : the death of Kāla

Sūta said :

1. There is another large and highly sacred place of the Supreme deity Rudra. It is famous as Rudrakoṭi[1], in all the three worlds.

1. A sacred place of this name is found under Kurukṣetra, Vārāṇasi and the Narmadā. It is probably the one at Kurukṣetra. That is implied here as Śiva assumed one crore forms for sages. This is mentioned in Mbh. *vana*. 82. 118-124, Pd. P. I. 25. 25-30.

2. Formerly, in the holiest of the times, a crore Brahmanical sages of great self-control (desirous of seeing the lord) came to that great land.

3. "I will see the Pināka-bearing lord Giriśa at first" (Thus they vied with one another). A great dispute arose thus among them who were endowed with devotion.

4. On seeing their devotion, Rudra, the Lord of mountain, the preceptor of Yogins, assumed a crore forms. Thus he became Rudrakoṭi (A crore of Rudras).

5. All of them saw the consort of Pārvatī, the great god Hara, resident in the mountain cavity. They became delighted and well-nourished in their minds.

6. With the devotional feeling : "O I have seen at the outset the Lord, the great god devoid of beginning and end" all of them dedicated their minds unto Rudra with devotion.

7. Then they saw a mass of brilliance in the firmament. They were desirous of attaining the greatest region.

8. Where the lord thus revealed himself and stayed, it is considered to be an auspicious and very holy centre. After visiting this and worshipping the Rudra the devotees shall attain the Sāmīpya (nearness) of Rudra.

9. There is another auspicious and excellent Tīrtha by the name of Madhuvana.[1] A person who observes rules and regulations after going there, shall attain half the throne of Indra.

10. There is another city named Padmanagarī. The land is auspicious and highly meritorious. After going there and worshipping the Pitṛs, one will redeem a hundred members of his family.

11. Kālañjara[2] is a great holy centre in the Rudraloka* Maheśvara is the deity, Hara is fond of the devotees who worship lord Kālañjara.

---

1. Near Mathurā, so called as it was once the haunt of demon Madhu. It is identified with present Maholi five miles to the south-west of Mathurā.

2. A hill and a fort in Bundelkhand, the capital of Chandellas. If the temple of Kāla Bhairava in the fort be related to the story of King Śveta given here, this identification is probable. Kane includes this Tīrtha under Vārāṇasī (HD IV. 766) The story of Śveta is narrated in LP. chs. I. 30-34 but he is a sage there.

*Veṅkt. text reads: *rudra-loke maheśvaraḥ*/If emended as *loke rudro maheśvaraḥ* in the world where Rudra is the great god.'

12. Formerly there was an excellent saintly king named Śveta. He was a devotee of Śiva. He worshipped the trident-bearing lord with obeisances unto him and expecting his blessings.

13. He installed Rudra in accordance with the injunctions, given priority to the path of devotion. With his mind dedicated unto Rudra, he performed the *Japa* of Rudra always.

14. Seizing a dazzling terrible trident made of steel, Kāla came to that spot where the king was standing, in order to take him away.

15. On seeing the terrible and ferocious Kāla, the destroyer of all, approaching with the trident in his hand, the king was overwhelmed with fear.

16. With both of his hands the King caught hold of the excellent Liṅga and bowed down to Rudra with his bent head. He repeated the Śatarudrīya Mantra.

17. Standing in front of the King, Kṛtānta (God of Death) laughingly said to the king who was bowing down and performing the Japa of Bhava mentally "Come away, come away."

18. The king who was terribly afraid but was devoted to Rudra requested him, "Kill others after leaving off one who is engaged in the worship of Īśa."

19. The lord (i.e. Kāla here) said to him who was frightened and spoke as mentioned above—"Who is there who does not stand under my control whether he is engaged in worshipping Rudra or not?

20. After saying thus, Kāla, the destroyer of the worlds. bound that king by means of nooses. The king on his part continued the Japa of Śatarudrīya.

21. Then he saw in the Firmament the enormous and brillant ancient mass of splendour of the lord of goblins. It was surrounded with clusters of flames and pervaded the universe.

22. In the middle thereof he saw a brilliant form a Puruṣa of golden colour. The lord was accompanied by the goddess. His body shone with the digit of the moon. He became much delighted. He thought that the Lord was coming to him.

23. On seeing Rudra, the great Lord, the lord of everything, coming at not a great distance, accompanied by the goddess, the royal sage became free from fear. Kāḷa rushed at the saintly king to take him away.

24. (Defective verse) On seeing him, Lord Rudra, the ancient leader of the goblins, of fierce activities said to Kāla—"Give unto me my devotee quickly, the devotee who remembers me, O Kāla. He remembers my form (?)"

25. On hearing the statement of Śiva (lord of the Bull), the Ātman of Kāla of the form of Rudra* (?) considered (his nature (himself) too high. He bound the devotee again by means of nooses. Then Rudra** rushed at him with great velocity.

26. On seeing him (Kāla) coming towards (himself to attack), the Lord then glanced at Umā, the daughter of the mountain (Himālaya). The knower of the procedure of all Māyās (Śiva) contemptuously struck Kāla with his left foot, while he (King Śveta) was looking on.

27. That extremely terrible fellow died on being struck by the foot of Maheśa. The Pināka-bearing great God stood shining alongwith Umā.

28. On seeing the Lord Īśvara, Hara, the imperishable deity, the prominent saintly king became delighted in his mind then and bowed unto him.

Eulogy of Śiva

29. "Obeisance to Bhava, the cause (of the universe) to Hara, who wishes for the welfare of the whole universe. Salutation to Śiva, the intelligent one. Obeisance to the bestower of Salvation.

30. Obeisance again and again (innumerable times) to the great superhuman power and prosperity. Obeisance to you, the overlord of men, of the form that is devoid of division.

31. O lord of Gaṇas, obeisance be to you. Hail to you, O deity that dispel the misery of those who resort to you, salutation to you of eternal (primordial) beginningless prosperity, to one that holds the horn of a boar.

*v. l. *ugra-bhāvaḥ* 'of terrible intention.'

**If emended as *Rudram* 'Kāla rushed at Rudra', it will suit the next verse and obviate the contradiction therewith.

32. Obeisance to you the bull-bannered Lord, bow to one that has a wreath of skulls. Salutation to you of great mountain (v.l. great actor); obeisance to you auspicious Śaṅkara."

33. Śaṅkara then blessed the king engaged in obeisance; then he bestowed on him the chieftain-ship of his own Gaṇas and then (finally) his own form (identity with him).

34. Instantaneously Hara who was saluted by the leading ascetics and the Siddhas became invisible along with Umā, his attendants and the leading king.

35. When Kāla was killed by Maheśa, god Brahmā the lord of the worlds, begged of Rudra the boon—"May he (Kāla) come back to life.

36. O bull-bannered Īśāna, it is not the slightest fault of Kṛtānta the god of Death. He was appointed on that job (of taking away the lives of beings) by you."

37. At the instance of the lord of Devas, Hara, the lord of the chief of Devas, the Ātman of the universe said—"So be it." He (Kāla) too became like that (i.e. revived).

38. Thus is the holy centre well known as Kālañjara. On going there and worshipping Mahādeva one attains the chieftain-ship of the Gaṇas.

CHAPTER THIRTYSEVEN

The Glory of Mahālaya and other holy centres

Sūta said :

1. This is another holy spot that is very great and very mysterious and full of miracles, pertaining to Lord Mahādeva. It is well known as Mahālaya.[1]

1. Mahālaya—The same as Oṁkāranātha. 2 in Vārāṇasi, De (p. 117).

2. There, on a rocky surface, his footstep was imparted by Rudra, the enemy of the Tripuras, the primordial lord of Devas. It is a proof pointed to the atheists.

3. The quiescent devotees of Paśupati, with their bodies dusted with holy ashes and engaged in the study of the Vedas, worship Mahādeva there.

4. One who takes his bath, sees the foot-print of god Śiva with great devotion and makes obeisance with bowing head, shall attain Rudra's proximity (i.e. liberation called *Samīpatā*).

5. There is another abode of Śambhu, the great Ātman the lord of Devas. It is very auspicious and is well known as Kedāra.[1] It is the home of Siddhas.

6. One who takes bath there, worships the bull-bannered Mahādeva and drinks the pure water, shall attain the chieftainship of the Gaṇas.

7-8. After performing *Śrāddha*, *Dāna* (religious gifts) and other rites, one attains everlasting benefit. There is a holy centre called Plakṣāvataraṇa[2] that destroys all sins. It is resorted to by excellent twice-born ones and the Yogins who have subdued their minds. By performing the worship of god Viṣṇu, one is worshipped in Viṣṇu's region.

9. Another holy spot is Magadhāraṇya. It bestows good goal on all the people (v.l. giving access to heavenly region). On going there, an excellent Brāhmaṇa attains everlasting heavenly pleasures.

10. The meritorious holy centre Kanakhala[3] is destructive of great sins. It was here that the sacrifice of Dakṣa was destroyed by Rudra.

---

1. Kedāranātha, a *Jyotir-liṅga* in the district of Garhwal in U. P. and on the southern side of the Mandākinī and Dūdhagaṅgā—De. p. 97.

2. Plakṣāvataraṇa—the source of the river Sarasvatī, in Sirmur hills of Sewalik range of the Himalayas. The fountain from which the river takes its rise was at the foot of a Plakṣa tree, hence it is called Plakṣāvataraṇa or Plakṣa-prasravaṇa.

3. Kanakhala—the place of Dakṣa's sacrifice destroyed by Rudra. It is at a distance of two miles to the east of Hardwar on the confluence of the Gaṅgā and Nīladhārā.

11. By bathing in the river Gāṅgā there, a pure man endowed with noble feelings, is freed from all sins and he shall stay in the region of god Brahmā.

12. The holy centre well-known as Mahātīrtha is sacred and a favourite of Nārāyaṇa. One who worships Hṛṣīkeśa (Viṣṇu) there goes so Śvetadvīpa (the abode of Nārāyaṇa).

13. Another excellent holy centre is the auspicious one by the name Śrīparvata.[1] On abandoning the vital airs here, one shall become the beloved of Rudra.

14. Rudra, Maheśvara, is ever present there accompanied by the goddess. Bathing there and offering Piṇḍas etc. shall be excellent and everlasting.

15-16a. The river Godāvarī is holy and destructive of all sins. On bathing there and duly performing Tarpaṇa rites to the Pitṛs and Devas, one shall purify one's soul of all sins and shall attain the benefit of the gift of a thousand cows.

16b-17. The sacred river Kāverī has holy waters and is very large. After observing fast for three days or (at least) one day, one should bathe there and offer water libations. One is released from all sins.

18-19a. The mode of resorting to holy centres by the twice-born is now narrated. He whose mind and speech are pure and whose hands and feet are stabilised (i.e. do their respective functions,) is non-greedy and celibate shall attain the benefit of holy centres.

19b-21a. The great holy centre called Svāmitīrtha[2] is well-known in the three worlds. Skanda respectfully bowed to by the immortal beings, is ever present there. On bathing in the Kumāradhārā and performing the Tarpaṇa rites for Devas and others, and one propitiating lord Ṣaṇmukha (the six-faced deity), one rejoices with Skanda.

---

1. Śrīparvata or Śrīśaila—A hill in Karnool district on the southern side of the river Kṛṣṇā which makes her way through a gorge in Eastern ghats. It is the site of Mallikārjuna, a famous Jyotir-liṅga. It was once a centre of Tāntrikas.

2. Svāmi-tīrtha. De (p. 107) identifies it with the temple of Kumārasvāmī situated about a mile from tiruttani on the Southern Railway.

21b-22. The river named Tāmraparnī is well-known in the three worlds. There is no doubt in this that on taking bath there and on performing the Tarpaṇa rites to the Pitṛs in accordance with the injunctions, one shall redeem even those Pitṛs who had committed sins.

23. At the source-place of Kāveri, there is a well-known holy centre named Candratīrtha. What is given in that holy centre is of ever-lasting benefit. It yields good goal i.e. the heaven to those who die there.

24. O Brāhmaṇa, those devotees who see Sadāśiva the lord of Devas at the foot of the Vindhyas, do not see the face of Yama (the god of Death).

25. At Devikā[1] (?), there is the holy centre named Vṛṣa. It is resorted to by Siddhas. One who takes bath there and libation, attains perfection in Yoga.

26. The holy centre Daśāśvamedhika is destructive of allusions. A man obtains the benefit of performing ten Aśvamedhas (horse-sacrifices) therein.

27. The holy centre named Puṇḍarīka is beautified by the Brāhmaṇas. A person of self-control approaching it, shall obtain the benefit of Puṇḍarīka (sacrifice).

28. The grestest among the holy centres is named Brahmatīrtha.[2] On worshipping god Brahmā here, one is honoured in the world of Brahmā.

29. There are some holy centres as these: The Vinaśana[3] where the river Sarasvatī lost itself in the sand, the auspicious Plakṣa-prasravaṇa (the source of the Sarasvatī), that which is known as Vyāsatīrtha[4] and the excellent mountain Maināka.[5]

---

1. Devikā—Modern Deig, a tributary of the Rāvī in Punjab (HD IV p. 746, De. p. 55).

2. It is mentioned as a sub-tīrtha under various holy places and rivers like Vārāṇasī, Gayā, Narmadā (KP. II 41. 56) Godāvarī, Sarasvatī. De. (p. 40) identifies it with Puṣkara lake in Rājasthān.

3. Vinaśana—the spot in the sandy desert of Ambala and Sirhind district of Punjab. The exact location of Vinaśana is presumed to be near Sirsa.

4. Vyāsa-tīrtha—Kane locates this in Kurukṣetra HD IV. 824. It is under the Narmadā *infra* ch. 41. 25-27.

5. Maināka is located at Badari, west of Gujarat and near the Sarasvatī. Dey (p. 121) regards the range of Sewalik hills from the Gaṅgā to the Beas.

30-31a. The source of origin of Yamunā is destructive of all sins. The river, the daughter of the Pitṛs, is well known as goddess Gandhakālī. He who bathes in it goes to heaven, after death. He will be able to remember his previous birth.

31b-32a. The holy centre of Kuberatuṅga[1] is resorted to by the Siddhas and the Cāraṇas. One who abandons his life therein, shall become a follower of Kubera.

32b-33a. The holy centre well known as Umātuṅga is the place where the beloved of Rudra (performed her penance). On worshipping the great goddess there, one shall attain the benefit of the gift of a thousand cows.

33b-34a. It is my opinion that the penance or Śrāddha performed in Bhṛgutuṅga, or the charitable gifts made there sanctifies seven generations in both the families (i.e. that of the father and that of the mother).

34b-35a. The great holy centre of Kāśyapa is well known as Kālasarpis. With the desire for the diminution of sins, one should offer Śrāddhas there every day.

35b-36a. The Śrāddha, Dāna, Homa, Japa and penance performed in Daśārṇa are of everlasting benefit and inexhaustible for ever.

36b-37a. The Tīrtha named Kurujāṅgala[2] resorted to by the twice-born is famous. On making charitable gifts there in accordance with the injunctions, one is honoured in the Brahmaloka.

37b-39a. Whatever is offered in the great Tīrtha, in Vaitaraṇī,[3] in the Svarṇavedī, in the Dharmapṛṣṭha,[4] in the great and auspicious head of Brahmā, in the holy hermitage of Bharata, in the auspicious and sacred Gṛdhravana, in

1. KP. and Vāyu mention Kubertuṅga, Umātuṅga, Bhṛgu-tuṅga as the best places for Śrāddha but their location is uncertain.

2. It is between the Sarasvatī and Dṛṣadvatī, Sirhind in Punjab (HD IV. 773).

3. Vaitaraṇī—A river in Orissa rising in the Vindhya-mountain Jaipur stands on this river.

4. Dharma-pṛṣṭha, the same as Dharmāraṇya of Buddhists—4 miles from Bodha Gayā, De. p. 56.

Mahāhrada[1] and in the Kauśikī[2]—whatever is offered in these places—is of everlasting benefit.

39b-41a. His footstep was imprinted on Muṇḍapṛṣṭha,[3] by the intelligent Mahādeva, for the welfare of all living beings and as a proof to be pointed out to the non-believers. A man devoted to Dharma shall within a short time, abandon his sin like the serpent casting off its slough.

41b-42. The holy centre named Kanakanandā[4] is well-known in the three worlds. It is to the North of Brahmapṛṣṭha and is resorted to by groups of Brāhmaṇa sages. On taking holy dip there, the twice-borns go to heaven along with their physical bodies.

43. The Śrāddha offered there is cited to be everlasting. On taking the bath, a man reduces his sins and he is freed from the threefold indebtedness to god, sages and manes.

44. By means of ablution in the Mānasa-lake one shall obtain half the throne of god Indra. On going to the Uttara-mānasa one achieves very excellent Siddhis (mystic powers).

45. Hence, one should perform Śrāddha in accordance with one's capacity and physical strength, thereby he obtains divine pleasures and attains the means of salvation.

46. The mountain named Himavān is bedecked with different kinds of minerals. That mountain is eighty thousand Yojanas in length.

47. Siddhas and Cāraṇas live therein and the mountain is resorted to by the groups of Devas and sages. There is a beautiful Puṣkariṇī (holy lake) there named Suṣumṇā.

48. On going there, a scholarly Brāhmaṇa leaves off (is relieved of the sin of) Brāhmaṇa slaughter. The Śrāddha offered there is inexhaustible and highly flourishing.

49. He shall redeem the Pitṛs of ten previous generations and ten later generations. The Himavān is sacred everywhere. The Gaṅgā is sacred all round.

---

1. Mahā-hrada—near Badrinath (also Mbh. *Anuśāsana* 25.18).
2. Kauśikī, Mod. Kusi (Kosi) which flows through Nepal, Tirhut and joins the Gaṅgā below Patna.
3. Muṇḍa-pṛṣṭha—A hill situated on the Western bank of the Phalgu river at Gayā.
4. Kanakanandā—a river to the north of Muṇḍa-pṛṣṭha at Gayā.

50. All the rivers flowing into the ocean are sacred and those oceans are particularly holy. On reaching the hermitage —Badaryāśrama,[1] one is released from all sins.

51. There stays the eternal lord Nārāyaṇa along with Nara. The charitable gift as well as the Śrāddha offered there, is of everlasting benefit.

52. That is a holy centre liked by Mahādeva. It is particularly sanctifying. On offering Śrāddha with great concentration, one shall redeem the Pitṛs.

53. The holy centre Devadāruvana[2] is sacred. It is resorted to by the Siddhas and the Gandharvas as well as by the great lord of Devas. What is offered there is highly flourishing.*

54. After fascinating the sages and on being worshipped by everyone, the delighted lord Īśa spoke to the leading sages who had been sanctified.

55. "You all shall always stay here in this beautiful and excellent hermitage, with the devotion centering on me. Thereby you shall obtain Siddhi.

56. Those who are devoted to Dharma in the world worship me. I grant unto them the eternal great chieftainship of the Gaṇas.

57. I will stay here for ever alongwith Nārāyaṇa. A man abandoning his life here, is not reborn.

58. O excellent Brāhmaṇas, those people who have gone to the other lands but who remember this holy centre, will have all their sins dispelled by me.

59. Here all these holy rites are to be performed. If performed, *Śrāddha*, *Dāna*, *Tapas* (penance), *Homa*, *Piṇḍas*, meditation, *Japa* and other observances are of everlasting benefit.

---

1. Badaryāśrama—The same as Badrīnāth in Garhwal, U.P.

2. Devadāruvana—Kane regards this in the Himālayas near Badrināth. (HD IV p. 745). De (p. 54) thinks it to be the same as Dāruvana in which Badarikāśrama is situated. The story about the introduction of Phallus-worship in the next two chapters shows that this Dāruvana must be in the Himālayas.

*a better v.l. *mahad-varam* 'a great boon was given by the great god.'

60. Hence the holy Devadāruvana, resorted to by Mahādeva should be visited by the twice-born by every means.

61. Wherever there is Mahādeva or Viṣṇu, the Supreme Person, the Gaṅgā, the holy centres and the shrines are present there.

CHAPTER THIRTYEIGHT[1]

The description of Dāruvana

The sages said :

1. O Sūta, how did the bull-bannered lord reach Dāruvana and how did he fascinate the leading Brāhmaṇas ? It behoves you to narrate it.

Sūta said :

2. Formerly, in the beautiful Dāruvana resorted to by Devas and Siddhas, thousands of sages performed penance and lived along with their wives, sons, and other kinsmen.

3. They were engaged in doing various religious rites in accordance with the scriptural injunctions. The great sages performed various sacrifices and penances there.

4. Desirous of pointing out their defects as they were attracted to the path of action, the trident-bearing Hara went to Dāruvana.

5. In order to establish Nivṛttivijñāna (the perfect knowledge of renunciation), lord, the great god Śaṅkara, went there keeping Viṣṇu, the preceptor of the universe, at his side.

1. This chapter traces how worship of Śiva's Phallus (Liṅga) came to be established. The story of falling of Śiva's Phallus in Dāruvana is found in Śiva P. IV. 12. 4. 54 and Brahmāṇḍa P. ch. 27.

6-8. The Lord of the Universe disguised himsel as a man of twenty years with a majestic (respectable) personality (v.l. mysterious disguise), sportive languidness (?), big arms, stout (muscular) limbs, beautiful eyes, golden complexion, glory and face like the full moon. His gait was like an intoxicated elephant. The naked Lord of the world was wearing gold necklace embellished with all kinds of precious stones. Lord Īśa (Śiva) arrived there smilingly.

9. Hari, the infinite Puruṣa, the unchanging source of origin of the worlds, Viṣṇu, assumed the guise of a lady and followed the trident-bearing lord.

10-12. The female form (disguise) had the face resembling the full moon, the breasts plump and elevated, face lit up with bright smiles. The two anklets produced tinkling sound. It was clothed in Divine yellow garment. It was dark complexioned and beautiful-eyed; the gait resembled that of the elegant swan. It was very charming and coquettish. Thus the lord Hara, Īśa roamed about the forest of Devadārus alongwith Hari fascinating the universe by means of his Māyā.

13. On seeing the Pināka-bearing lord of the universe walking here and there, the women were deluded by his Māyā. They followed the lord of Devas.

14. All those chaste ladies being afflicted with passion, abandoned their sense of bashfulness and with their ornaments slipping down, those coquettish women began to go with him.

15. The sons of sages, the youngsters who had not yet subdued their minds, followed Hṛṣīkeśa (who was dressed like a woman), afflicted by passionate love.

16. On seeing the sole hero Īśa, very comely and loveable, accompanied by his wife, the groups of women began to sing and dance in their sportive dalliance. They embraced him too.

17. The sons of sages too coming in groups began to sing songs smilingly; on observing the consort of Padmā, of auspicious limbs, the primordial God, others in a group began to walk around with him.

18. Viṣṇu (the slayer of Mura), the son of Vasudeva, the master of Māyā (illusive potency) entered their minds,

whetted their inclination to enjoyment. They seemed to experienee Māyā as if it was real.

19. The lord of the universe and all the immortal beings, accompanied by Mādhava and seated in the midst of the group of women appeared to be accompanied by all Śaktis, although the lord of Devas (is usually) accompanied by only one Śakti (Umā).

20. Then again mounting back, he created the permanent great principle Pradhāna.* Lord Viṣṇu also re-assumed his original nature (followed ?) such (dancing) primordial Deity.**

21. On seeing the groups of women, Rudra, their sons and Keśava who fascinated them, the excellent sages became excessively angry.

22. Deluded by his Māyā, they spoke extremely harsh words to lord Kapardin (Śiva), they swore at and cursed him with various words.

23. Just as the stars in the sky remain invisible in the presence of the sun, so also when Śaṅkara came there their penances were repelled.

24. After reproaching him, the Brāhmaṇa ascetics approached the bull-bannered deity. Deluded by him they asked the lord of Devas—"Who are you, Sir ?"

25. The lord replied—"O sages of holy rites, I have now come here to your land to perform penance alongwith my wife."

26. On hearing his statement Bhṛgu and other leading sages said: "Perform penance after putting on a garment and after abandoning your wife."

27. Thereafter, the Pināka-bearing lord Śiva (Nīlalohita) smiled. Then looking at Janārdana who was sitting by his side and who was the source of origin of the worlds, he said:—

28. "How is it that you, knowers of religion, quiescent-minded sages, are eager to maintain your wives, while you advise me that I should abandon my wife ?"

---

*v.l. *nṛtyan parama-prabhāvam* is better. It means "Again re-gaining his original great nature, he began to dance."

**v.l. *tadīśavṛttāmṛtamādidevaḥ* "followed the act of dancing of that Lord Śiva."

The sages said :

29. "This has been stated by us that wives who lead a lecherous life should be abandoned by the husbands. Loyal wives of good features and behaviour like these (our women) do not deserve abandonment."

Mahādeva said :

30. "O Brāhmaṇas, this lady never even mentally wishes for anyone else. Nor do I leave her off at any time."

The sages said :

31. "O base man, she was seen by us, behaving in an unchaste manner. You have told a lie. Go away quickly."

32. When addressed thus, Mahādeva replied: "Only truth has been spoken by me. It is your imagination that she appears to you." Leaving them, he moved away.

33. In the company of Hari, Parameśvara (Śiva) who sought for alms, went to the holy hermitage of Vasiṣṭha, the great souled leading sage.

34. On seeing the lord arrived begging for alms, Arundhatī, the beloved wife of Vasiṣṭha, respectfully welcomed him and bowed to him.

35. She washed his feet and offered him excellent seat. On seeing his body languid and enfeebled as a result of the thrashing indulged in by the Brāhmaṇas, the chaste lady, with countenance cast down (due to dejection) in her face, applied medicines and healed his wounds.

36. She worshipped him richly and imploringly asked him,—"Who are you, Sir ? Where did you come from, in the company of your wife ? What are your customs and manners ? May these things be mentioned." The Lord replied: 'I am the most excellent among the siddhas.

37. You see yonder, the pure shining sphere of the Brahman. This is my deity. I owe to this always."

38. After saying this and blessing the chaste lady, the glorious lord to whom the Brāhmaṇas beat with sticks and their own fists and lumps of clay, went away.

39. On seeing Giriśa walking about in the nude and characterised by hideousness, they said—"O wicked minded fellow, uproot this your *Liṅga* (phallus)."

40. Śaṅkara, the great Yogin, said to them—"I will do so if you have hatred towards my *Liṅga* (phallus)."

41. After saying so, the lord who had gouged the eyes of Bhaga, uprooted the *Liṅga.* Instantaneously they could see neither the lord nor Keśava nor the Liṅga.

42. Evil omens occurred indicating danger and fear to the worlds. The thousand-rayed sun did not shine. The earth quaked again and again. The planets became lustreless. The great ocean was agitated.

43. Anasūyā, the chaste wife of Atri, saw a dream. Highly agitated in all her senses, she narrated it to the Brāhmaṇas.

44. "Illuminating everything with his lustre, indeed it was Śiva who was seen in our abodes begging for alms, accompanied by Nārāyaṇa."

45. On hearing her words the sages who became terrified, went upto Brahmā of great Yogic power, the creator of the universe.

46. The lord was being worshipped by pure Yogins who were the most excellent among the knowers of Brahman. He was accompanied by the four Vedas in their embodied form as by Sāvitrī.

47. He was seated on a beautiful seat full of miracles : it shed forth myriads of rays and it was associated with Jñāna (perfect knowledge), Aiśvarya (prowess and glory) and other qualities.

48-49. He was shining in his body, with gentle smiles and brilliant eyes. On seeing the four-faced, mighty-armed, great Aja (unborn) identical with the Vedic metre, possessing divine body with delighted face, they knelt on the ground, touching the Earth with their heads and propitiated the Lord.

50. With delighted mind the four-faced deity of four forms spoke to them—"O excellent sages, what is the reason for your visit ?"

51. With palms joined in reverence above their heads, all intimated to the Supreme-souled Brahmā of what happened.

The sages said :

52. A certain highly brilliant person has entered the holy Dāruvana alongwith his wife, who was very beautiful in all her limbs. But he was naked.

53. The Lordly person fascinated our entire women and daughters, with his charming personality. While his beloved* defiled our sons.

54. We heaped various imprecations and curses on him but they were defied and set at nought. He was beaten soundly by us. His Liṅga was struck down.

55. That lord vanished alongwith his wife and the Liṅga. Terrible omens ensued, terrifying all the living beings.

56. O excellent among men, who is this lordly person ? We are all frightened. O Unerring being, we have sought refuge in you.

57. Indeed, you know whatever happens in this universe. Protect and save us with your blessing."

58. Thus informed by the groups of sages, the lotus-born deity, the Ātman of the universe meditated on the trident-bearing lord with palms joined in reverence and said :

Brahmā said :

59. Alas ! Woe unto you ! What happend today is destructive of everything of yours. Fie upon your strength and power. Fie upon your penance. It has become useless and false in regard to you in this matter.

60. After obtaining greatest of all treasures, thanks to the favourable impressions (results) of all (previous) merits it has been neglected by you all who are deluded and whose practice of good conduct has become useless.

61. It is for this treasure that all yogins seek and desire and all the ascetics aspire. Alas ! after obtaining that very same treasure, you have neglected and lost it.

**Priyo* in the Text should be *Priyā* in this context.

62. A great treasure, to acquire which, the propounders of the Vedas worship by means of various Yajñas, has been neglected and lost by you, after attaining it.

63. I have acquired this lordship of the universe after continuously worshipping the lord. But after seeing that lord you have missed him like those who are devoid of good luck (who may see) a treasure (but lose it instantaneously.)

64. You had come across that treasure-*Brahman* in whom divine Supremacy has been vested and who is the imperishable deity; but alas you have rendered it futile after attaining it.

65. This god Mahādeva is the great deity who should be known and realised. There is no other greater region than his that can be attained.

66-67. He is the most eternal of all deities, sages and the Pitṛs. At the end of a thousand Yugas, at the time of the final dissolution, Maheśvara, assuming the form of Kāla, destroys all embodied beings. It is he alone who creates the subjects by means of his splendour.

68. He is *Cakrin* (one armed with the discus); he is the Supreme Ruler. He is characterised by the Śrīvatsa mark. This god is a Yogin in Kṛta-yuga, Yajña (sacrifice) in Tretā, the Lord Kāla in Dvāpara and in the Kaliyuga, he is the banner of virtue (*Dharmaketu*).

69. Rudra has three Mūrtis (forms) by whom the universe is pervaded. The Smṛti says : "Agni (The fire god) is the Tamas form, Brahma is the Rajas form and Viṣṇu is the Sattva form.

70. It is stated in Smṛti that he has another eternal auspicious form having the quarters for garments(i.e. nude), where abides Brahman endowed with Yoga.

71. The lady, his wife, who was seen by you near his side, and who was conversed with (v.l. seen) by you is lord Nārāyaṇa, the eternal Supreme Ātman.

72. All this is born of him. It shall get dissolved only in him. He (alone) can liberate all. He alone is the great goal.

73. The Śruti says that Nārāyaṇa is the thousand- (i.e.

innumerable) headed Puruṣa, with thousand eyes and thousand feet. He has one horn and is the great Ātman.

74. The semen virile* becomes the foetus in him. The lord is of illusory aquatic body (?). He is being eulogised by means of various kinds of Mantras by Brāhmaṇas who seek salvation.

75. At the end of the Kalpa, the Supreme Person withdraws the entire universe in him and after drinking the Yogic nectar, he lies down to sleep in the greatest region of Viṣṇu.

76. Viśvadṛk (the seer of the universe) is neither born nor dies nor increases in size. The unborn deity is sung about as the unmanifest original Prakṛti, by the followers of the Vedas.

77. When the night passes on, Maheśvara becomes desirous of creating the entire universe and then sows the seed in the umbilical region of the unborn.

78. Know me to be the Supreme Ātman, Brahma with faces on all sides, the great Puruṣa, Universe, the excellent foetus of water.

79. You had been deluded by his Māyā, so you do not realise that progenitor, Mahādeva, the lord of Devas, Hara, the lord of all living beings.

80. This lord Mahādeva is the beginningless Lord Hara. In association with Viṣṇu, he creates and dissolves the Universe.

81. Actually he has no task to be performed; there is no greater being than he. He, of illusory Yogic body, gave the Vedas unto me, formerly.

82. He is the wielder (master) of Māyā and through Māyā, he makes and dissolves everything. Seek refuge in that Śiva alone; after realising that he alone is conducive to salvation."

83. On being advised thus by the lord, the sages, the chief of whom was Marīci, bowed down to lord Brahmā and asked him with great concentration.

---

*better v.l. : *ṛtasya* Then the line means "in the womb of Ṛta."

CHAPTER THIRTY-NINE

The Entry into the forest of Devadāru

The sages said :

1. O lord of all immortal beings, tell us, how we can see that Pināka-bearing lord once again. You are the saviour of of those who seek refuge.

Brahmā said[1] :

2-3. Make an excellent *Liṅga* of the Lord resembling the *Liṅga* which was seen by you all and struck down on to the ground, and observing celibacy, worship it with respect along with your wives and sons, through the various Vedic observances.

4-5. Instal it with the Mantras pertaining to Śaṅkara and taken from Ṛk, Yajus and Sāman Saṁhitās. Undertaking great penance and reciting the Śatarudrīya Mantras, all of you worship the trident-bearing deity with great concentration, alongwith your sons and kinsmen. With the palms joined in reverence, seek refuge in the trident-bearing lord.

6. Thereby, you will see the lord of Devas, rarely visible to those who are not self-possessed. On seeing him, all ignorance and unrighteousness perish."

7. Thereafter, they bowed down to Brahmā of unmeasured prowess and the granter of boons. Delighted in their minds, they went to the forest of Dāruvana once again.

8. Although they did not know the great Being, they with their passions and jealousy eschewed, began to propitiate Śiva as instructed by god Brahmā.

9. They (stationed themselves) in the different kinds of pieces of grounds, caves of mountains and the auspicious lonely banks of the rivers.

10-11. Some maintained themselves by eating the moss; some of them lay beneath the water; some of them exposed themselves to the rainy clouds and some stood on the tips of their big toes. Some were *Dantolūkhalins* (eaters of food-grains

---

1. VV. 2-6 explain briefly the method of the worship of Śiva-liṅga.

using the teeth as mortar). Others were *Aṣmakuṭṭas* (who pound grains, etc. by means of stones, for eating); some had only vegetables and leaves to eat. Some performed prescribed ablutions, while some were drinkers of rays.

12. Some had their abodes at the roots of trees; others used rocky grounds as their beds. Worshipping Maheśvara, they spent their days in penance.

13. Thereafter, the bull-bannered lord Hara felt inclined to favour them with enlightenment, since he is one who removes the distress of those who seek refuge in him.

14. In the Kṛta Age, God Śiva the delighted Supreme Lord arrived at the forest of Devadāru trees on the auspicious peak of the Himālayas.

15. He was naked and bore hideous marks. He had smeared ashes (*Bhasma*) all over his body. He held firebrands in his hands. His eyes were red and tawny-coloured.

16. At some places he used to laugh terribly; in some places he used to sing in surprise; sometime he used to dance with amorous passion; sometimes he cried frequently.

17. The mendicant roamed round the hermitages and begged for alms frequently; the lord took up an illusory guise and came to that forest.

18. The Pināka-bearing lord kept Gaurī, the daughter of the mountain, by his side. As before, the goddess of Devas, came to the forest of Devadārus.

19. On seeing the lord with matted hair arrived along with the goddess, they bowed down their heads to the ground and propitiated Īśvara.

20. They worshipped Bhava (Śiva) with various Vedic Mantras and auspicious hymns pertaining to Maheśvara, as other sages propitiated him with Mantras of *Atharvaśiras* :

Eulogy of Śiva

21. "Obeisance to the overlord of Devas, Hail to you, Mahādeva. Salutation to you the three-eyed deity holding the excellent trident.

22. Obeisance to you having the quarters for clothes, Bow to the Pināka-bearing lord of hideous forms. Obeisance to

the lord bowed to by all but not bowing down himself to anyone.

23. Obeisance to you the annihilator of the god of death. Hail to you, the destroyer of all. Obeisance to one whose sport is dance. Bow to one of terrible forms.

24. Obeisance to one with the form (body) of a man as well as of a woman (i.e. half man and half woman). Obeisance to one with self control. Salutations to the quiescent ascetic Hara.

25. Obeisance to you, Rudra, the terrible; obeisance to you clad in elephant hide; salutation to *Lelihāna* (frequently licking the tongue). Obeisance to you Śrīkaṇṭha.

26. Obeisance to one of Aghora and Ghora (nonterrible and terrible) form. Obeisance to Vāmadeva; salutation to one of golden necklace; obeisance to one who does things pleasing to the goddess.

27. Obeisance to the highest deity Śambhu, the supporter of the waters of the Gaṅgā; obeisance to the overlord of the Yoga and the over-lord of living beings.

28. Obeisance to the *Prāṇa* (vital airs), obeisance to one who bears *Bhasma* marks on the body; obeisance to you *Havyavāha* (the fire-god) with curved fangs; obeisance to *Havyaretas* (having Havya as the semen virile).

29. Obeisance to one who cut off the head of Brahmā; obeisance to you *Kālarūpin* (having the form of Kāla). Never, never do we know either your arrival or your departure.

30. O! Lord of the Universe, O Mahādeva! whatever you may be, our obeisance be to you. Obeisance to the lord of the Pramathas and the bestower of auspicious riches.

31. Obeisance to you, holding skull in the hand. Obeisance to you, the most pleased one. Obeisance to the gold-complexioned one. Obeisance to you having the aquatic *Liṅga*.

32. Obeisance to one having fire and the sun for his *Liṅga*. Obeisance to you with *Jñāna Liṅga*; obeisance to one having serpents as garlands; to one who is fond of the Karṇikāra; obeisance to you, wearing crown and earrings; salutation to the destroyer of Kāla.

33. O Mahādeva, O Mahādeva, O three-eyed lord of Devas. May what is done due to delusion be forgiven; you alone are the refuge unto us.

34. Your activities are wonderful, mysterious and inscrutable. Indeed Śaṅkara is incomprehensible to Brahmā and all others.

35. Knowingly or unknowingly whatever a man does is actually done by the lord through his Yogic Māyā."

36. After eulogising Mahādeva conscientiously and with concentration like this, they bowed to Giriśa and said—"May we see you as before."

37. On hearing their eulogy, the moon-bedecked lord accompanied by Umā, Śaṅkara himself showed his great form to them.

38. On seeing the Pināka-bearing lord alongwith the goddess, those Brāhmaṇas stood delighted in their minds as before and bowed to him.

39-40. All those sages viz :—Bhṛgu, Aṅgiras, Vasiṣṭha, Viśvāmitra, Gautama, Atri, Sukeśa, Pulastya, Pulaha, Kratu, Marīci, Kāśyapa and Saṁvartaka of great penance bowed to the lord of the chief of Devas and spoke these words :

41. "O Lord of Devas, how shall we worship you always, by means of the path of action or by means of the path of knowledge ?

42. By means of what divine path is the lord to be worshipped here ? What is it that should be resorted to ? What is it that should not be resorted to ? Please mention all these to us :

Śiva said[1] :

43. O great sages, I shall expound to you the excellent incomprehensible secret formerly narrated by Brahmā to Mahādeva.

44. The means of salvation of men should be known

1. VV. 43-65 explain the Puranic Pāśupata Yoga. KP. disapproves of the 'left' or 'non-Vedic Pāśupata, and other sects. The influence of Kevalādvaita on KP. is obvious.

as two-fold, one of Sāṁkhya and the other of Yoga. Sāṁkhya associated with Yoga is the bestower of liberation on men.

45. The great Puruṣa is not seen by Yoga alone. But Jñāna (knowledge) by itself is the bestower of salvation.

46. Eschewing the pure Sāṁkhya and depending solely on Yoga, ye all made your attempts for salvation.

47. For this reason, O Brāhmaṇas, I came here to this land to point out the delusion arising in those men who depend on Karman alone.

48. Hence, the perfect knowledge that is devoid of impurity and that is the means of salvation should be seen, heard and realised assiduously by you all.

49. The Ātman is one and only one, omnipresent. It is of the nature of pure consciousness and bliss, free from impurity and eternal. This is indeed the Philosophy of the Sāṁkhyas.

50. This alone is the greatest knowledge. This is being sung about as Liberation. This is described as the pure Kaivalya and *Brahmabhāva* (the state of Brahman).

51. Resorting to this greatest stand-point, the great-souled ascetics strictly adhering to it and holding on to it, see me the Viśva (the universe), the Īśvara.

52. This is that greatest knowledge, the absolute *Sat* (Reality) that is unsullied. I alone am the lord to be realised. This Śivā is my form.

53. O leading Brāhmaṇas, many means to *Siddhi* (realisation) have been mentioned; of them all, my perfect knowledge is the most superior.

54-55. Ascetics strictly adhering to the path of knowledge, are quiescent, who sincerely seek refuge in me, who apply the sacred *Bhasma* over them (their bodies) and who always meditate on me in their hearts and who are interested in my devotion have exhausted all their sins. Ere long, I annihilate their terrible cavity of worldly existence (?) (v.l. ocean of Saṁsāra).

56. Indeed the holy Pāśupata vow has been formerly designed by me for the achievement of liberation. It is the gteatest of all secrets. It is the subtlest essence of the Vedas.

57. One who performs Pāśupata vow, shall be quiescent; he must have perfect self-control; he should dust his body with sacred ashes; he should observe celibacy and remain naked.

58. Or he should wear a loin-cloth or a single garment; he should be silent and engaged in the study of Vedas. The scholar shall meditate on Śiva as Paśupati.

59. Śruti states that this Pāśupata Yoga should be resorted to by the seekers of liberation; that those who maintain Pāśupata rite should be free from desire.

60. Freed from passion, fear and anger, filled with me, taking refuge in me, purified by penance in the fire of spiritual knowledge, many have entered my Being.

61. There are other scriptures opposed to the Vedic view. They have been propounded by me alone and they are very fascinating in this world.

62. Those cults are—Vāma, Pāśupata, the Soma cult, the Lākura (Lākula) and the Bhairava and such other cults which are opposed to Veda should not be resorted to.

63. O Brāhmaṇas, I am the embodiment of Vedas. My form cannot be understood by those who know the meanings of other scriptures. Except the eternal lord* no one knows it.

64. Ye all establish this path; worship Maheśvara. There is no doubt in this that ere long the perfect knowledge will dawn.

65. O excellent ones, may ye have extensive and deep devotion unto me; O excellent sages, I shall grant you my presence, the moment I am meditated upon.

66. Having said this, the lord vanished there itself along with Umā. The sages remained in Dāruvana and continued the worship of Śaṅkara.

67-68a. (Some) noble-souled sages, engaged in strict observance of celibacy, quiescent, interested in the path of knowledge, came together and held many discussions concerning the knowledge of the soul :

What is the cause of this world : Our Soul.

There must be a cause of creating these things. What can it be : God (Īśvara).

**deva* in Veṅk. Text. v.l. *Veda* is better: It means 'with the exception of the eternal Vedas none knows it'.

68b-69. While they were pondering over this, after resorting to the path of meditation, the great goddess, the daughter of the most excellent mountain, appeared before them.

70. She resembled a crore suns. She was engulfed in a cluster of flames. With her pure brilliance, she filled the whole firmament.

71. They sought and saw the incomprehensible daughter of the mountain, encircled in the halo of a thousand flames. They bowed to this lady, the wife of the lord of all. They knew her as the seed of the Supreme.

72. "This is the spouse of our Supreme Lord. She is our abode (goal) and soul. Her (other) name is Firmament; seeing in her their own selves and the entire universe, the sages were overjoyed.

73. They were seen by the wife of the great lords. In the meanwhile, they saw the lord, the cause of everything, Śambhu, the wise sage Rudra, the lord, the ancient Puruṣa.

74. On observing the goddess and the lord Īśa they bowed down and attained the greatest bliss. Thanks to the favour of the lord, the perfect knowledge, the cause of the destruction of subsequent births, dawned in them.

75. This potency of Lord Śiva is the only source of the universe, is the Ātman of all; controller of everything and beginningless, she is termed *Vyoma* (firmament) and she appears to shine in the heaven.

76. The great Parameṣṭhin, Maheśvara who is beyond everything, the sole Śiva, Rudra, the lord of Devas created the universe in her after mounting over the Māyā that is existing in the great Śakti. (?)

77. The Lord is one. He is hidden in all living beings. Rudra, the wielder of Māyā, is entire and undivided. He and the goddess are not different or separate. On realising this, people attain immortality.

78. Lord Maheśa then vanished. The over-lord of the Devas vanished alongwith the goddess. The dwellers of the forest propitiated again Rudra, the primordial lord.

79. Thus the story of all the former exploits of the lord

Devas in the forest of Deva-Dārus has been narrated to you all according as I have heard about them in the Purāṇas.

80. He who reads or listens to this everyday, is liberated from all sins. He who recounts this to quiescent Brāhmaṇas, attains the greatest goal.

CHAPTER FORTY

The Glory of Narmadā

Sūta said :

1. This highly meritorious river goddess Narmadā,[1] resorted to by Devas and Gandharvas, is famous in the worlds. It is a river that is the most sacred of all holy rivers.

2. Listen ye all to its greatness as recounted by Mārkaṇḍeya to Yudhiṣṭhira. It is auspicious and destructive of all sins.

Yudhiṣṭhira said :

3. O sage, thanks to your favour, various items of virtue (*Dharma*) have been heard by me; so also the greatness of Prayāga and different kinds of holy centres.

4. The Narmadā has been mentioned by your holiness as the most important of all sacred rivers. O excellent sage, it behoves you to recount its glory now."

---

1. Next to Gaṅgā, Narmadā is a very sacred river, glorified in various Purāṇas like AP. ch. 113, Pd. P. *Svarga Khaṇḍa* ch. 13, Mt. P. chs. 185-193, NP. II. 77. The Skanda has devoted one book (Part) to its glorification. As compared with Sk. P. or Mt. P. KP. treats it briefly but succinctly. It is interesting to note that most of the verses on the glory of Narmadā in Pd. P. are the same as those of Mt. P. Even the KP. has borrowed a number of verses from the Mt. P. as shown below.

Mārkaṇḍeya said :

5. The Narmadā is the most excellent of all rivers; it flowed out of Rudra's body. It shall redeem all living beings mobile and immobile.[1]

6. I shall now recount the greatness of Narmadā, which I have heard from the Purāṇas. It is auspicious. Listen with single-minded attention.

7. Gaṅgā is auspicious in Kanakhala and Sarasvatī is meritorious in Kurkṣetra. But whether in the village or in the forest, Narmadā is meritorious everywhere.[2]

8. The holy water of Sarasvatī sanctifies one in three days; the water of Yamunā sanctifies one in seven days; the water of Gaṅgā sanctifies immediately; but the water of Narmadā sanctifies one at its very sight.[3]

9. In the western half of Kaliṅga, on the mountain Amarakaṇṭaka (it has its source). It is very holy. It is the most beautiful and charming in the three worlds.[4]

10. O leading king, Devas, Asuras, Gandharvas, saints and the ascetics have attained the highest *Siddhi* by performing penance on her banks.

11. O king, a person who takes his bath there, maintains all religious observances and has conquered the sense-organs shall redeem a hundred members of his family after observing fast for a night.

12. O leading king, it is heard that the excellent river is more than hundred Yojanas in length and its width is two Yojanas (1 Yojana = 12 kms).[5]

13. Sixty thousand holy centres and sixty crores of them are situated in Amarakaṇṭaka all round the mountain.[6]

---

1. The same as Mt. P. 190. 17.

2. Verse 7 in KP. is the same as Mt. P. 185.10.

3. This shows how Narmadā is superior to Gaṅgā, Yamunā and Sarasvati. A borrowal from Mt. P. 185.11.

4. Mt. P. 185.12.

5. The same Mt. P. 185. 23b-24a (More's edt.) Cf. AP 113. 2. Though the length of Narmadā is correct, its width viz 2 Yojanas, is wrong.

6. AP. 113. 2 and NP. II. 77.

14-15. O Sinless King ! Attentively listen to the fruit acquired if a person of very pure conduct—celibate, with anger controlled and sense-organs subdued, refrained from all types of Himsā (violence) and engaged in the welfare of all—abandons his life (there) in a state of purity.[1]

16. O son of Pāṇḍu, he rejoices in heaven for a hundred thousand years. He will be surrounded by divine damsels, the groups of Apsaras.

17. He will smear himself with divine scent and unguents. He will shine with divine flowers. He sports in the divine world and he rejoices alongwith Devas.

18. After falling off from heaven, he shall be born as a righteous king. He will obtain a house embellished in different kinds of gems and jewels.

19. The house shall be shining on being bedecked in diamonds and Lapis Lazuli. The columns therein shall be made of jewels. It shall be endowed with paintings, vehicles of brilliant appearance as well as hundred of maid-servants.

20. He shall be the emperor ruling over kings. He will be elegant and glorious and loved by all women. He will live for more than a hundred years enjoying all pleasures.

21. When (for ending his life) he enters fire or water or when he observes fast, his departure shall be with no return (to Saṁsāra) like that of the wind absorbed in the sky.

22. On the ridge of the western mountain, there is a lake named Jaleśvara. It is well known in the three worlds and is destructive of all sins.[2]

23. If one offers Piṇḍas there and performs the Sandhyā worship, it is as good as propitiating the (Pitṛs) for ten thousand years. There is no doubt about this.

24. On the southern bank of Narmadā, there is a great river named Kapilā. It is stationed not very far. It is covered by Juicy Arjuna trees.[3]

---

1. Committing suicide in a holy place was regarded as a means for Liberation. Mt. P. 193. 28b-29c.

2. Mt. P. 185. 50b-51.

3. Mt. P. 185. 53.

25. That is meritorious and highly blessed. It is well-known in the three worlds. O Yudhiṣṭhira, the holy spots there number to more than a hundred crore.[1]

26. The trees that fall into the holy river after growing for many years, attain great goal due to the contact of waters of Narmadā.[2]

27. A second holy river is the blessed and auspicious Viśalyakaraṇī. A man taking bath in that holy river becomes free from pains, sins and grief.[3]

28. Kapilā and Viśalyā are heard as the two excellent rivers mentioned by Īśvara formerly with a desire for the well-being of the worlds.

29. O lord of men, he who gives up food until death in that Tīrtha, shall have his soul purified of all sins. He goes to the region of Rudra.[4]

30. O king, on taking his bath there a man shall attain the fruit of a horse-sacrifice. Those who reside on the northern bank reside in the region of Rudra.[5]

31. As Śaṅkara told me, O Yudhiṣṭhira, the bath and the charitable gift at Sarasvatī, Gaṅgā, and Narmadā are of equal efficacy.[6]

32. He who abandons his life on the mountain Amarakaṇṭaka is honoured in the Rudraloka for hundreds of crores of years and more.[7]

33. On sprinkling the head with the holy and sacred water of Narmadā along with its foam one is relieved of all sins.

---

1. Mt. P. 185. 53.
2. Mt. P. 185· 54b-55a.
3. Mt. P. 185. 55b-56a.
4. Mt. P. 185. 62.
5. Mt. P. 185. 63b-64a.
6. Mt. P. 185. 64b-65a.
7. Mt. P. 185-65b-66a.

The above examples are enough to show that KP. has freely borrowed from the Mt. P. or both the Purāṇas had used a common *Narmadā-māhātmya* and hence the above textual identity of verses.

34. Narmadā is holy everywhere. It dispels sins of Brāhmaṇa-slaughter. By observing fast for a day and a night, one is absolved of the sin of Brāhmaṇa slaughter.

35. The most excellent holy centre jaleśvara is destructive of all sins. A man who observes religious regulation and restraints on going there, attains all desires.

36. On going to Amarakaṇṭaka during the lunar or solar eclipse, a man attains ten times the merit of an Aśvamedha (horse-sacrifice).

37. This excellent mountain is meritorious. It is resorted to by Devas and Gandharvas. It is full of various kinds of trees and creepers. It shines with different kinds of flowers.

38. O King, Maheśvara (the great God) is present there alongwith the goddess (Umā). Brahmā, Viṣṇu, and Rudra (Indra?) (are present there) alongwith the groups of Vidyādharas.

39. The man who circumambulates the mountain Amarakaṇṭaka attains the fruit of Pauṇḍarīka sacrifice.

40. The river Kāverī[1] is well-known as the destructive of sins. One should take bath there and worship the bull-bannered Mahādeva. (One who takes bath) at the confluence of Narmadā is honoured in the Rudraloka.

CHAPTER FORTYONE

The Glory of different sacred places on the Narmadā[2]

Mārkaṇḍeya said :

1. It has been told formerly by sages as well as by the self-born deity that Narmadā, the destroyer of all sins, is the best among all rivers.

1. This Kāverī is the northern branch of the Narmadā where the island Oṁkāra is situated (HD IV P. 705 footnote 1604).

2. This chapter gives only the important sacred places on the Narmadā. Mt. P. and Pd. P. states that there are ten crores of sacred places on

2. The excellent river Narmadā has been eulogised by the sages. It flowed out of the body of Rudra with a desire for the well-being of the worlds.

3. It is destructive of all sins for ever. It is bowed to by all Devas and is eulogised by Devas and Gandharvas as well as by Apsaras (heavenly ladies).

4. On the northern bank is the Tīrtha well-known in the three worlds, by the name Bhadreśvara.[1] It is holy, auspicious and destructive of all sins.

5. O king, man taking bath there, rejoices with Devas. O leading king, thereafter one should go to the excellent sacred place Vimaleśvara.

6-7a. O King, a man taking bath there shall attain the the benefit of the gift of a thousand cows. Thereafter, with self-control and regulated diet, one should go to Aṅgāreśvara. He shall wipe off all sins and be pure. He is honoured in the Rudraloka.

7b-8a. O leading king, thereafter, one should go to the meritorious spot named Kedāra. On taking bath and drinking the water, one shall obtain all desires.

8b-9a. Thereafter, one should go to Niṣphaleśa. It is destructive of all sins. O great king, on taking bath there, one is honoured in the Rudraloka.

9b-10a. O leading king, one should thereafter go to the excellent Bāṇatīrtha. One forsaking the life there, shall attain Rudraloka.

Narmadā, while AP. (113.2) and KP. *supra* 40.13 raise the number to sixty crores and sixty thousand and the NP. II. 77. 4 and 27-28 limits this number to three crores and a half.

Though many of the verses in this chapter are also common to Mt. P. and NP. II. 77, the similarities are not pointed out as this point has been proved in the last chapter.

1. There are a number of Tīrthas the geographical location of which is as yet to be ascertained and Tīrtha of the same name occurs in different sacred places like Vārāṇasī, Prayāga, Kurukṣetra or Gayā. For example Kedāra in v. 7b-8a is at Vārāṇasī, Garhwal UP. (the famous Jyotirliṅga), in Kashmir and at Gayā. Hence only out-standing Tīrthas are noted.

10b-11a. Thereafter, one shall go to Puṣkariṇī and perform the rite of holy ablution there. O king, on taking bath there a man shall be the lord of a throne.

11b-12a. Thereafter, one should go to Śakratīrtha on the southern bank. Immediately after the bath therein, a man shall attain half the seat of Indra.

12b-13a. O leading king, thereafter, one should go to Śūlabheda, so says the Śruti. On bathing and drinking water there, one shall derive the benefit of a thousand cows.

13b-14. A pure man should observe fast during the night after duly performing the ablution rite. Then he should propitiate the lord of Devas of great Yogic power. After attaining the the fruit of a gift of thousand cows, he goes to Viṣṇu's region.

15. Thereafter, he should go to Ṛṣitīrtha which is destructive of all sins of men. As soon as a man takes his bath therein, the man is honoured in Śivaloka.

16. There itself is the holy centre of Nārada. It is very auspicious. Immediately after the bath therein, a man obtains the fruit of a gift of a thousand cows.

17. It was here that formerly the divine sage Nārada performed penance. Maheśvara, the lord of Devas, became delighted and granted him Yoga.

18. A Liṅga installed by Brahmā is known as Brahmeśvara. O king, a man who takes his holy bath there is honoured in the Brahmaloka.

19. Thereafter, one should go to Ṛṇatīrtha (by visiting which) the man shall certainly be relieved from indebtedness. Thereafter, one should go to Vaṭeśvara. He shall derive sufficient benefit of the current life.

20. Thereafter, one should go to Bhīmeśvara. It is destructive of all ailments. Immediately after the bath there, a man is relieved of all miseries.

21. O leading king, thereafter one should go to the excellent Piṅgaleśvara. By observing fast for a day and night, one shall attain the benefit of Trirātra sacrifice.

22-23a. O leading king, he who makes a gift of a tawny-coloured cow, there, is honoured in the Rudra-loka as many thousand years as there are hairs on its body and on that of its calves.

23b-24a. O ruler of men, he who abandons his life there, rejoices indefinitely as long as the moon and the sun shines.

24b-25a. Those who stay on the banks of Narmadā go to heaven when they die just like the saintly men of good activities.

25b. Thereafter, one should go to Dīpteśvara. It is a penance grove otherwise called Vyāsatīrtha.

26. Formerly, the great river Narmadā had become afraid of Vyāsa. On being rebuked by Huṁkāra (i.e. the sound Huṁ) (by Vyāsa), the river receded from that place immediately (v.l. *dakṣiṇena* (flowed) to the South).

27. O Yudhiṣṭhira, if a devotee circumambulates that place, Vyāsa becomes delighted and he obtains the benefit desired.

28-29a. O leading king, thereafter, one shall go the confluence of the river Ikṣu. It is meritorious and well-known in the three worlds. Śiva is present there. O king, on taking bath there, a man shall obtain the chieftain-ship of Gaṇas.

29b-31a. Thereafter, one should go to Skandatīrtha that dispels all sins.* One who takes bath there dispels sins committed by him ever since his birth. Devas and Gandharvas worship lord Skanda, the bearer of Śakti, the noble-souled excellent son of Śiva.

31b-33a. Thereafter, one should go to Aṅgirasatīrtha and perform the rite of ablution there, getting thereby the merit of a gift of a thousand cows, he goes to Rudra's region. It was here that Aṅgiras, the son of Brahmā, propitiated the bull-bannered lord of Devas and the universe by means of penance and obtained the excellent Yoga.

33b-34a. Thereafter, one should go to Kuśatīrtha that dispels all sins. One should take the holy plunge there (whereby) he will obtain the benefit of a horse-sacrifice.

34b-35a. Thereafter one should go to Koṭitīrtha that dispels sins committed by him ever since his birth.

*The Veṅk. Text has an irrelevant line here : *ṛṇa-tīrthaṁ tato gacchet sa ṛṇān mucyate dhruvam* "one should go to Ṛṇa-tīrtha; one definitely gets rid of indebtedness."

35b-36a. Thereafter, one should go to Candrabhāgā and perform the rite of ablution there. Immediately after the bath there, the man is honoured in the region of the moon.

36b-37a. The excellent Tīrtha Saṅgameśvara is on the southern bank of Narmadā. O king, on taking bath there, the man derives the benefit of all *Yajñas*.

37b-40a. On the northern bank of Narmadā is the extremely splendid Tīrtha, the beautiful Ādityāyatana, as mentioned by Īśvara. O leading king, on taking bath there, and offering *Dānas* religious gifts according to one's capacity, one attains inexhaustible benefit, thanks to the power of the Tīrtha. Those who are indigent and sickly, those who commit evil deeds, are released from all sins. They go to Sūryaloka (the world of the Sun).

40b-41a. Thereafter, one should go to Mātṛtīrtha and perform the rite of ablution there. Immediately after the bath there, the man shall attain the heavenly world.

41b-43a. Thereafter, one should go westward to the excellent holy centre Marutāśaya. O leading king, one should take bath there and with purity and sound concentration one should give gold to an ascetic in accordance with the extent of his riches. He goes to Vāyuloka by means of the aerial chariot Puṣpaka.

43b. O leading king, thereafter one should go to the excellent Ahalyātīrtha. Merely by taking bath there, one rejoices with the Apsaras for an indefinite period.

44-45. On the Kāmadeva day which falls on the thirteenth day in the bright half of the month Chaitra, one should worship Ahalyā. Wherever he is born, the man shall be excessively loved by all. He shall be endowed with glory and will be loved by women like Kāmadeva.

46. Approaching the Saridvarā (the excellent river) (?) one should go to the well-known Tīrtha of Indra. Immediately after taking bath there, one attains the benefit of the gift of a thousand cows.

47. Thereafter one should go to Somatīrtha and perform the rite of ablution there. Immediately after the bath therein, the man is freed from all sins.

48. During the lunar eclipse, it is destructive of sins. O king, the Somatīrtha is wellknown in the three worlds and it yields great benefits.

49. He who observes the vow of Cāndrāyaṇa with great concentration in that holy centre, shall have his soul purified of all sins. He shall go to the Somaloka.

50. O ruler of men, he who immolates himself by entering fire at this holy centre; he who drowns himself in the water thereof or he who observes fast unto death there, is never reborn as a mortal being.

51. Thereafter, one should go to Stambhatīrtha and perform the rite of ablution there. Immediately after the bath there, the man is honoured in the Somaloka.

52. O king, thereafter one should go to the excellent Viṣṇutīrtha. That excellent abode of Viṣṇu is called (Yodhī-) Yodhanīpura.

53-54a. Crores of Asuras were fought therein by Vāsudeva (Viṣṇu) and so a sacred place came into being there. (One who bathes there) shall have the glory and splendour of Viṣṇu. By observing fast for a day and a night, one dispels the sin of Brāhmaṇa-slaughter.

54b-56a. On the southern bank of Narmadā there is an extremely splendid Tīrtha well-known as Kāmatīrtha. It is the place where Kāma worshipped Hari. A man, taking bath in that holy centre and devoutly engaged in observing fast, is honoured in the form of Kāma.

56b-57. O leading king thereafter one shall go to the excellent Brahmatīrtha. It is well-known as Umāhaka (?) (v.l. Amogha). One should perform a *Tarpaṇa* rite (offering of libations of water) there for Pitṛs. One should duly perform Śrāddha on the full moon day and on the new moon day.

58. In the middle of the water there is a rock in the form of an elephant. One should offer Piṇḍas therein, with great concentration (on any day) during the month of Vaiśākha.

59. After taking bath, with concentrated mind and being devoid of arrogance and jealonsy (if the above rite is

performed), his manes are satisfied as long as the earth exists (i.e. up to the end of the world).

60. Thereafter, one should go to the Tīrtha called Viśveśvara and perform the rite of ablution there. Immediately after the bath there, the man shall obtain the chieftainship of the Gaṇas (attandants of Śiva).

61. O leading king, thereafter one should go where Janārdana (Viṣṇu) is (in the form of a) Liṅga. A man who takes bath there devotedly is honoured in the Viṣṇuloka.

62. It is here that Nārāyaṇa manifested himself to the sages of sanctified souls, in the form of a Linga which is the highest abode.

63-64a. Thereafter, one shall go to Akolla which is destructive of all sins. The ablution, the Dāna rite, the feeding of the Brāhmaṇas and the offering of Piṇḍas performed here bestow infinite benefit after death.

64b.65. If a Brāhmaṇa prepares *Caru* with Traiymbaka (Narmadā) water and offers the Piṇḍas duly at the root of Ankolla plant (Alangium Hexapetalum) the Pitṛs shall be redeemed. They are satisfied as long as the moon and the stars shine.

66. O leading king, thereafter, one should go to the excellent Tīrtha Tāpaseśvara. O leading king, on taking bath therein, one shall attain the benefit of penance.

67. Thereafter, one shall go to Śuklatīrtha[1] that is destructive of all sins. O Yudhiṣṭhira, there is no other holy centre on a par with it on Narmadā.

68. Its sight, the touching, the ablution (therein), Dāna, Tapas, Japa, Homa, and observance of fast in the holy centre Śuklatīrtha yield great benefits.

69. The holy centre well known as Śuklatīrtha is said to be a Yojana in extent. It is resorted to by Devas and Gandharvas. It is destructive of all sins.

70. Even if the holy centre is seen from the top of a tree from far, it dispels the sin of Brāhmaṇa-slaughter. God Saṅkara, Bharga, stays there always with the goddess.

1. VV. 67-84 describe the importance of Śuklatīrtha—on the north bank of Narmadā about 10 miles north-east of Broach.

71. O king of holy rites, in the fourteenth day in the dark half of the Vaiśākha month, Hara comes out of his own world to be present here.

72. The leading gods, demons, divine minstrels, Siddhas, Vidyādharas, the attendants of Śiva and celestial damsels and the leading Nāgas stay there.

73. One dispels sins committed ever since one's birth in the Śuklatīrtha just as a coloured cloth turns white by washing in water.

74. The ablution, Dāna, penance and Śrāddha appear to be infinite. There will never be a holier Tīrtha than the Śuklatīrtha.

75. A man who commits sinful deeds earlier in his life dispels them by observing fast for a day and a night in Śuklatīrtha.

76-77a. One should observe fast on the fourteenth day in the dark half of the month of Kārttika and perform the ablution of god, the Supreme deity (Śiva) with ghee. He shall never fall off from the abode of Īśvara in the company of twenty one generations of his family.

77b-78a. One does not obtain by means of penance, celibacy or *Yajñas* or even *Dānas* that goal which one attains in the Śuklatīrtha.

78b-79a. The Śuklatīrtha is a great holy centre resorted to by the sages and Siddhas. O king, a man who takes bath there is not reborn.

79b-80. During the vernal and equinotical transit of the sun and on Caturdaśī (fourteenth) days, the devotee should, after the bath, observe fast. With good self-control and great concentration, he should make charitable gifts in accordance with his capacity. Hari and Śaṅkara will become delighted.

81-83a. By the power of the single Tīrtha, every thing shall be endless. Listen to the merit accruing to one who helps a helpless poor Brāhmaṇa or one with kinsmen to celebrate a marriage at this holy centre. He is honoured in the Rudraloka as many thousand years as there are hairs on his body and in those of his progeny.

83b-84. O leading king, thereafter, one should go to the excellent Yamatīrtha. O Yudhiṣṭhira, one who takes bath here in the fourteenth day in the dark half of the Māgha month and takes food only at night, never experiences the pain of being in the womb (i.e. is liberated).

85-87. O leading king, thereafter one shall go to the excellent Eraṇḍītīrtha.[1] The man (devotee) should take bath at the confluence and observe fast. If he should then feed a single Brāhmaṇa, it has the benefit of feeding a crore men. One endowed with the feelings of devotion should take bath at Eraṇḍī confluence. He should enter the water with clay applied to the head. When the waters of Narmadā (in the confluence) too touch him, he is freed from all sins.

88. O leading king, thereafter one should go to the holy centre Kallolakeśvara. There is no doubt in this that Gaṅgā descends into it on the auspicious days.

89. After bathing in it and drinking its water, one should make charitable gifts in accordance with the injunctions. He shall be freed from all sins and be honoured in the Brahmaloka.

90. Thereafter, one should go to Nanditīrtha and perform the rite of ablution there. Nandīśa is pleased and the devotee is honoured in the Somaloka.

91. O leading king, thereafter one should go to the auspicious Tīrtha Anaraka. O king, a man taking a bath there never sees hell.

92. O leading king, one shall deposit one's bones in that holy centre. He is born in the world again as a beautiful person endowed with riches and worldly pleasures.

93. O leading king, thereafter one shall go to the excellent Kapilatīrtha. O king, a man taking bath there shall obtain the benefit of the gift of thousand cows.

94-95. During the month of Jyeṣṭha, particularly on the fourteenth day, the man devotee should observe fast. He should make charitable gifts of lamps, along with ghee. He should perform ablution of Rudra with ghee. Then he shall attain riches as a benefit thereof. He should make the gift of a tawny-coloured cow embellished with bells and ornamens.

1. Eraṇḍī is a tributary of Narmadā in Baroda Dist. It is now called *Urī* or *Or*. Its confluence with the Narmadā is Eraṇḍi-tīrtha.

96. He shall himself become endowed with all ornaments, and will be respected by all Devas. He shall become strong as Śiva, and will be sporting always like Śiva.

97. On Tuesdays and Caturthī days in particular, one should perform ablution rite of Śiva and feed Brāhmaṇas.

98-99a. In an aerial chariot desired by all, he shall travel accompanied by all Devas. He shall go to the abode of Indra and rejoice alongwith him. After falling off from heaven, he shall be one endowed with fortitude and worldly enjoyments.

99b-100a. One shall perform the ablution rite of Śiva on Tuesdays, on the ninth day and on the new moon day assiduously. One shall become handsome and endowed with comely features.

100b-101. O leading king, thereafter one shall go to the excellent Tīrtha Gaṇeśvara on the fourteenth day in the dark half of the Śrāvaṇa month. Immediately after the bath, there the man is honoured in the Rudraloka.

102-103. After performing the Tarpaṇa rite of the Pitṛs, he is freed from the three debts. Near Gaṅgeśvara is the excellent Tīrtha called Gaṅgāvadana. A man who takes his bath there entertaining any desire of fruit or not, is freed from all sins committed ever since his birth.

104. Near it on the western side, not very far from it, is the Tīrtha Daśāśvamedhika which is well-known in the three worlds.

105. After observing fast for a night in the auspicious month of Bhādrapada, one should perform the ablution rite and the worship of the bull-bannered deity Hara on the new moon day.

106. He shall then go to Rudra's city by means of golden aerial chariot decorated with clusters of tinkling bells. He shall then rejoice with Rudra.

107. He should perform the rite of ablution on any day at any place. After performing Tarpaṇa rites for the Pitṛs, he shall derive the benefit of horse sacrifice.

CHAPTER FORTYTWO

The greatness of the various holy centres on Narmadā

Mārkaṇḍeya said :

1. O leading king, thereafter, one should go to the excellent Bhṛgutīrtha.[1] Formerly holy lord Bhṛgu propitiated Rudra there.

2. By visiting that lord, one is immediately freed from sins. This holy centre is very large and destructive of all sins.

3-4. Those who take bath there go to heaven. Those who die here are not reborn. In accordance with his (donor's) capacity, a pair of shoes, a chariot horse, gold, cooked food and full meal should be given. It (the *dāna* given here) is said to be everlasting. All (other) *dānas*, offerings, sacrifices and penance and rituals perish.

5-6a. O Yudhiṣṭhira, the penance performed in the Bhṛgutīrtha is imperishable. O Yudhiṣṭhira, the presence of Rudra, the enemy of the Tripuras, there, is due to his Bhṛgu's own severe penance. It is said so by Rudra, the enemy of the Tripuras.

6b-8a. O leading king, thereafter one should go to the excellent Tīrtha Gautameśvara. It was here that Gautama propitiated the Trident-bearing lord and attained Siddhi. O king, a man who takes bath there and is devoted to the observance of fast, goes to Brahmaloka by means of a golden aerial chariot. He is honoured in the Brahmaloka.

8b-9a. Thereafter, one should go to the Vṛṣotsarga Tīrtha. He shall attain the eternal region. Those foolish men deluded by the Māyā of Viṣṇu do not know the glory of this Tīrtha.

9b-10. Thereafter, one should go to the Dhautapāpā holy centre where the sins are washed by means of this meritorious act. It is situated on Narmadā. O king, it is

1. Bhṛgu Tīrtha—Bhera-ghat, 12 miles to the West of Jabalpur (De, p. 34). It has now a temple of 64 Yoginis. Here Paraśurāma regained his energy taken away by Rāma the son of Daśaratha.

destructive of all sins. A man taking bath in that holy centre, dispels the sin of Brāhmaṇa-slaughter.

11. O leading king, he who abandons his life there in that holy centre, shall be blessed with four arms and three eyes. He shall be as mighty as Hara.

12. He shall reside in the Śivaloka for ten thousand Kalpas and more with exploits similar to that of Śiva. After a long time, he is born on the Earth. He shall then be a sole Emperor over the world.

13. O leading king, thereafter, one should go to the excellent Tīrtha called Hastatīrtha (v.l. Haṁsa-Tīrtha). O king, a man who takes bath there, is honoured in the Brahmaloka.

14. O leading king, thereafter, one should go to that holy centre where Janārdana is settled. It is called Varāha tīrtha. It yields the capacity to go to Viṣṇuloka.

15-16a. O leading king, thereafter, one should go to the excellent Candratīrtha. One should perform the rite of ablution there, particularly on the full moon day. Immediately after the bath, a man shall be the sole emperor on the Earth.

16b-17a. Thereafter, one should go to Devatīrtha which is bowed by all the other holy centres. O leading king, on taking bath there, one rejoices alongwith the deities.

17b-18a. O leading king, thereafter one should go to the excellent Śaṅkhatīrtha. What is given as charitable gift there shall become a hundred million times (more beneficial).

18b-19a. O leading king, thereafter one should go to the auspicious Paitāmahatīrtha. The Śrāddha offered there shall wholly become inexhaustible in merit.

19b-20a. He who abandons his life after reaching the holy centre Sāvitrītīrtha shall shake off all sins. He is honoured in the Brahmaloka.

20b-21a. There itself the Manohara (charming) Tīrtha is extremely splendid. O king, a man taking bath there is honoured in the Rudraloka.

21b-23a. O leading king, thereafter, one should go to the excellent Kanyātīrtha. O king, a man taking bath there is freed from all sins. One shall perform the rite of ablution here on the third day in the bright half of the month. Immediately after the bath, the man shall become the sole Sovereign ruler over the Earth.

23b-24a. Thereafter, one should go to the holy centre Sarga Bindu which is bowed to by Devas. O king, a man who takes bath there, never sees mishaps and ill fortune.

24b-25a. Thereafter, one should go to Apsareśa. He should perform the rite of ablution there. He sports in the heavenly world and rejoices alongwith celestial damsels.

25b-26. O leading king, thereafter one should go to the excellent holy centre Bhārabhūti. He should worship the lord after the observance of fast. He is honoured in the Rudraloka. O king, one who dies in this holy centre, shall attain the chieftainship of the Gaṇas.

27. In the month of Kārttika, one shall worship the lord of Devas, the consort of Pārvatī. Learned men assert that it is ten times more beneficial horse-sacrifice.

28-29. He who gifts away a bull as lustrous (white) as the Kunda flower and the moon goes to the Rudraloka by means of a vehicle to which a bull is yoked. He who abandons his life after reaching the holy centre, shall be freed from all sins. He goes to Rudraloka.

30. O ruler of men, he who enters water (and drowns himself) in that holy centre goes to the heavenly world by means of a vehicle to which swans are yoked.

31. The Confluence of the rivers Eraṇḍi[1] and Narmadā is well-known in the world. That holy centre is also highly meritorious and destructive of all sins.

32. One who regularly observes fasts and performs holy rites devotedly, O king, is freed even from the sin of Brāhmaṇa-slaughter after taking bath there.

33. O leading king, thereafter one should go to the confluence of Narmadā and the ocean. It is famous as Jamadagni and there Janārdana is present.

1. Eraṇḍi-saṅgama—the confluence of Eraṇḍī (mod. Urī) and the Narmadā near Karnali in former Baroda State (now Gujarat)—De, P. 59.

34. O king, a man who takes bath in the meeting point of Narmadā and the ocean obtains three times the benefit of a horse-sacrifice.

35. O leading king, thereafter one should go to the excellent Piṅgaleśvara. O king, a man who takes his bath there, is honoured in the Brahmaloka.

36. He who visits Vimaleśvara after observing fast there, dispels sins committed in seven births and goes to Śiva's abode.

37-38a. O leading king, thereafter, one should go the excellent Ali tīrtha (v.l. Alakā-tīrtha). He should observe fast for a night with regulated conduct and diet. Thanks to the greatness of this holy centre, he is freed from the sin of Brāhmaṇa-slaughter.

38b-39a. These holy centres have been recounted to you in brief and in view of their importance. O son of Pāṇḍu, the number of the holy centres is big. They cannot be narrated in detail.

39b-41a. This large sacred river is well-known in the three worlds. Narmadā is the most excellent of all rivers. It is the beloved of Mahādeva. O Yudhiṣṭhira there is no doubt in this that he who mentally remembers Narmadā, obtains the benefit of a hundred Cāndrāyaṇa rites, or even more.

41b-42a. Those persons who do not have faith, those who have resorted to terrible non-belief, do fall in the terrible hell. So says Parameśvara.

42b. Lord Maheśvara himself resorts to Narmadā. Hence, this river should be known as very meritorious, and destructive of the sin of Brāhmaṇa-slaughter.

CHAPTER FORTYTHREE

Greatness of Naimiṣāraṇya[1] *and Japyeśvara*

Sūta said :

1. This excellent holy centre Naimiṣa is well known in the three worlds. Being more liked by Mahādeva (than any other Tīrtha), it is destructive of great sins.

2. O excellent Brāhmaṇas, it is the place created by the highest deity, god Brahmā for the performance of penance by the sages desirous of seeing Mahādeva.

3-4. The six Brāhmaṇa families viz : the Marīcis, the Atris, the Vasiṣṭhas, the Kratus, the Bhṛgus and the Aṅgiras formerly approached the lotus-born deity Brahmā, the four-faced, the four-formed god who bestows boons on all (or all boons). Bowing down to the unchanging creator of the universe they asked him. Ṣaṭkulīyas[2] (the sages belonging to the six families) said :

5. (Defective verse) O lord, obeisance to you. Please recount, by what means can we see the only lord Īśāna, the god with matted hair.

Brahmā said :

6. "Perform a *Satra* (a sacrificial session) of the duration of one thousand years with your speech and mind free from defects. I shall tell you the place where you will perform the same."

7. He touched the mind-wheel and let it go. Thereafter, he told them "This wheel has been discharged by me. Follow it. Do not delay.

8. Where the rim of this wheel gets shattered is the auspicious place for the purpose of penance."[3] Thereafter he let the wheel go and they followed it.

---

1. Naimiṣāraṇya is in a way 'the birth-place' of all Purāṇas. Its importance is described in Bd. P. I. 1. 156-174, *Śiva Vāyavīya Saṁhitā* 3. 52-63, Va. P. 1. 1. 166-167. KP. endorses what other Purāṇas state about this.

2. *Ṣaṭkulīyas* are Brāhmaṇas belonging to the families of the above-mentioned six sages viz. Marīci, Atri, Vasiṣṭha, Kratu, Bhṛgu and Aṅgiras.

3. Here Naimiṣa is etymologically connected with *nemi* 'rim' of a wheel. Bd. P. and other Purāṇas mentioned above endorse the same.

9. As it rolled on, its rim got shattered at a place which came to be remembered by the name Naimiṣa. It is very holy and is honoured everywhere.

10. It is full of Siddhas and Cāraṇas. It is resorted to by Yakṣas and Gandharvas. This excellent holy centre Naimiṣa is the abode of lord Śambhu.

11. Formerly, Devas, alongwith Gandharvas, Yakṣas, serpents and the Rākṣasas performed their penance here and attained excellent boons.

12. Resorting to this place, the Saṭkulīyas (the Brāhmaṇas of the six families) propitiated the lord of Devas with great concentration, by means of *Satra* and perceived Maheśvara.

13. Each of the following holy rites here shall destroy the sin committed in the course of seven births viz.=the *Dāna* rite, the penance performed, the Śrāddha offered and the Yajña performed.

14. Formerly, it was here that the lord, (Brahmā) recounted the Brahmāṇḍa Purāṇa[1] purified (sanctified) by the (description of the) Brahman, to the sages who were performing the Satra.

15. Even till this day, lord Mahādeva of universal vision sports about alongwith his spouse Rudrāṇi, while the Pramathas surround him as attendants.

16. Giving up their lives here by means of observances, the twice-born will go to the Brahmaloka, after which they are not born again.

17. Another excellent holy centre is what is well-known

Śrīdhara on Bh. P. I. 1. 4 quotes from Vr. P. and states that here Lord Viṣṇu killed the army of Asuras within the twinkling of the eye (*nimiṣa*) and hence, it came to be called "Naimiṣa".

Geographically it is the area round modern Nimsar at a distance of 20 miles from Sitapur and 45 miles to the North west of Lucknow. Nimsar is a railway station.

But KP emphasises its importance as a sacred place proper for Penance, performance of yajña and other religious rites.

1. Obviously KP is composed later than the Brahmāṇḍa Purāṇa.

as Japyeśvara.[1] It was here that Nandin the great Gaṇa (attendant) continuously performed the *Japa* of Rudra.

18. Mahādeva, the Pināka-bearing lord, became pleased with him alongwith the goddess. He granted him similarity with himself and ability to defy death.

19. There was a virtuous pious-souled sage named Śilāda. In order to acquire His blessing, he worshipped the the bull-bannered Mahādeva.

20. At the end of a thousand years since (Śilāda) he began his austere penance. Śarva, the sustainer of the universe, came to him accompanied by Umā and surrounded by the Gaṇas and spoke—"I am the granter of boons."

21. Of Īśāna, the foremost deity, the consort of the daughter of the mountain, he begged as follows :—'I request for a son like you who is not born from a womb and who is deathless (immortal).

22. Lord Maheśvara accompanied by the goddess said—'So be it'. Even as the Brahminical sage was looking on, Hara vanished from the scene.

23-25. Śilāda,[2] the most excellent among the knowers of Dharma, made use of that land. He ploughed the ground with a ploughshare. Breaking open the ground a splendid son with the brilliance of Saṁvartaka fire (i.e., the fire at the time of dissolution) came into view. He was smiling as it were. With this lustre he illuminated the quarters. He was richly endowed with handsome features and comeliness. He was on a par with

1. The location of Japyeśvara or Jāpyeśvara is doubtful. According to De, P. 81, Japyeśvara of the LP I.ch. 43 & *Śiva P.* is the same as Jalpiśa of the Kālikā P. (ch. 77) and is situated to the west of the river Tista in the Jalapaiguri dist. of Bengal. Kālikā Purāṇa locates it to the northwest of Kāma-rūpa and the five rivers forming Pañca-nada are Jātodakā, Trisrotā, Vṛṣadvanī, Svarṇodakā and Jambunadī. But KP. hints (v. 29) that it is near the sea. In that case Pañca-nada must be taken as the land of five-rivers (Punjab) where the five rivers meet. But the Tīrtha must be near the sea where Sindhu falls in the sea as Nandin went near the sea (v. 29) for his Japa.

2. For the story of Śilāda cf. L.P. I. chs. 41-44. But according to L.P. I. 42. 11-15, it was god Śiva who was born as Nandin.

Kumāra (Kārttikeya). With a grave tone Nandin repeatedly said to Śilāda "O father, O father."

26. On seeing that son born, Silāda embraced him. He showed him to the sages who resided in the hermitages there.

27. He performed the post-natal and all other rites for him. After investing him with a sacred thread in accordance with the Śāstras, he taught his son the Vedas himself.

28. Holy lord Nandin, after the study of the Vedas came to an excellent decision. "After seeing lord Maheśvara, I will conquer Mṛtyu (death)."

29. Endowed with faith and concentration of the mind, he went to the holy ocean and continuously performed the Japa of Rudra with his mind attached to Maheśa.

30. When he had completed a crore of Japas, Śaṅkara, favourably disposed to his devotees, came there accompanied by all his Gaṇas and said—"I am the granter of boons."

31. He requested lord Mahādeva the supreme God. Please grant me the boon. I shall perform again a crore of this Japa, which will completely consume worldly existence.

32. After saying "So be it" the lord vanished from the scene. The holy one (i.e. Nandin) performed a crore of Japa with his mind centred on him.

33. When the second crore was completed, the bull-bannered lord came there surrounded by the groups of Bhūtas (goblins) and said—"I am the granter of boons".

34. (Nandin said) "O Śaṅkara, I wish to perform the third crore of Japa too" The Ātman of the universe said—"So be it." and vanished alongwith the goddess.

35. When the third crore of Japa was completed, the lord was much delighted in the mind. He came there surrounded by the Bhūtas and said—"I am the granter of boons".

36. (Nandin said), "I shall perform a crore more of the Japa with thy brilliance". When this was said the lord said :— You must not perform the Japa further.

37-38. You shall be immortal and devoid of old age. You shall stay at my side forever. You shall be the great chieftain of the Gaṇas, the son of the goddess. You shall be a great lord, the lord of Yoga, a great Yogin and the chief lord of Gaṇas.

You shall be glorious and the overlord of the worlds. You will be the benefactor, identical with the Yajñas.

39. The perfect knowledge pertaining to me and named after me shall be accessible to you as easily as the fruit of the myrobalan in the palm. You will be alive till the dissolution of all living beings. Thereafter you shall attain my region."

40-41. After saying this, Mahādeva Śaṅkara called the Gaṇas together and got Nandīśvara duly crowned and consecrated. The Pināka-bearing lord himself made him marry the blessed daughter of the Maruts (Suyaśā according to Śivapurāṇa). He himself attained Viṣṇuhood.

42. This Japyeśvara is the abode of the trident-bearing lord of Devas. The man who dies here is honoured in the Rudra-loka.

CHAPTER FORTYFOUR

Description of sacred places (contd.)

Sūta said :

1. Near the holy centre Japyeśvara there is another excellent Tīrtha named Pañcanada.[1] It is sacred and destructive of all sins.

2. One who observes fast there for three nights and worships Maheśvara gets his soul purified of all sins and is honoured in the Rudraloka.

3. There is another excellent Tīrtha pertaining to Indra (king of gods) of unmeasured splendour. It is called Mahābhairava[2] and is destructive of great sins.

---

1. Vide note 1, p. 597.

2. Though KP. calls this Tīrtha as 'pertaining to Indra', it is one of the eight Śiva Kṣetras (HD. IV. 775), but Kane's reference to Mt. 181.29 is about a Tīrtha of the same name at Vārāṇasī.

4. The great river Vitastā (mod. Jhelum) is the holiest of all holy tīrthas. It is sacred and it removes all sins. Itself it is born of the king of mountains.

5. There is the Tīrtha belonging to Śambhu of unlimited splendour. Its name is Pañcatapas. It is here that Bhava (Śiva) was worshipped by the overlord of Devas (?) for the purpose of being mighty.

6. Offering of Piṇḍas etc. at that holy centre is the bestower of pleasure and happiness after death. One who dies there as a result of observance of holy rites, is honourd in the Brahmaloka.

7. There is a splendid shrine of Mahādeva called Kāyāvarohaṇa[1] where holy dharmas or religious doctrines pertaining to god Maheśvara have been promulgated by the sages.

8. The Śrāddha, the charitable gift, the penance, the Homa or the fast there is of ever-lasting benefit. He who abandons his life there goes to the Rudraloka.

9. There is another excellent Tīrtha called Kanyā-Tīrtha[2] than which there is no better holy centre. One should abandon one's life after going there, whereby one attains eternal worlds.

10. There is the splendid holy centre of Rāma, the son of Jamadagni and of unimpaired activity. On taking bath there in the excellent holy centre, one shall attain the benefit of gifting away a thousand cows.

11. The Tīrtha well-known as Mahākāla[3] is famous in the worlds. After going there and abandoning the life, one shall attain the chieftainship of Gaṇas.

12. The Tīrtha of great mystic efficacy is the excellent Nakulīśvara[4] Tīrtha. Lord Nakulīśvara, the glorious deity is present there.

---

1. Kāyāvarohaṇa is modern Kārvān, 15 miles South of Baroda in the Dabhoi Tehsil. The promulgation of 'dharma' special to Maheśvara probably refers to the Pāśupata doctrines propagated by Na (La) kulīśa (in the 2nd cent. A.D.). Mathura inscription of Candragupta II dated A.D. 38. (Gupta era year 61) mentions Lakulī.

2. This is near the sea and as such is different from one of the same name but under Narmadā (Supra II. 42.21).

3. Probably refers to Mahākāleśvara of Ujjayinī.

4. Nakulīśa, the founder of the Pāśupata sect probably finally settled in Himālayas. Hence, his dwelling place came to be regarded as a sacred place. Its exact location is uncertain.

13. On the beautiful peak of Himavān in the splendid (spot called) Gaṅgādvāra, lord Mahādeva is present for ever along with the goddess and accompanied by his disciples.

14. On performing the rite of ablution there and after worshipping the bull-bannered Mahādeva one is purified of of all sins. On death, one shall attain the perfect knowledge.

15. There is another abode of the lord of Devas. It is extremely meritorious and splendid. It is well-known as Bhīmeśvara.[1] On visiting it one eschews sins.

16. There is another confluence of river Caṇḍavega.[2]
It is destructive of sins. On bathing there and drinking the waters, one is freed from the sin of Brāhmaṇa-slaughter.

17. The great city named Vārāṇasī is very divine. It is a ten thousand times, nay, a hundred million times more auspicious than all these holy centres.

18. Formerly, its greatness had been narrated to you by me. Nowhere else does one attain salvation in a single birth even by means of Yoga.

19. These sacred places that remove sins of men have been mentioned in view of their importance. By visiting holy centres, one should wash off one's sin (accumulated) at least in hundreds of births (?)

20. The holy centres are not fruitful to him who forsakes his duties and goes on pilgrimage to various holy centres. The holy centres do not benefit him either in this world or in the other world.

21. A person performing expiatory rites, a widower, a wandering mendicant, or a householder or a person of their ilk should go on pilgrimage to holy centres.

22. One may go on a pilgrimage alongwith one's wife as well as the sacrificial fires. If he assiduously performs the pilgrimage, he shall be freed from all sins. He shall attain the goal as mentioned before.

23-24. A person desirous of going on pilgrimage shall wipe off the threefold indebtedness (viz. to gods, sages and one's

---

1. One Bhīmeśvara in mentioned under Narmadā (*vide Supra* II. 41.20). This is probably a different Tīrtha.

2. Mt. p. 22.28. There also it is regarded sacred to Pitṛs.

manes). He shall assign proper means of livelihood for the sons and entrust his wife to their care.

In the context of expiatory rites the greatness of the holy centres has been recounted.[1] He who reads this or listens to this is freed from all sins.

CHAPTER FORTYFIVE

The description of four types of Dissolution[2]

Sūta said :

1. After hearing these words or wisdom uttered orally by Nārāyaṇa, the sages asked the lord who had assumed the form of a Tortoise.

The sages said :

2-3. Dharma[3] has been recounted by you. The perfect knowledge (leading to) salvation has been explained in detail.

1. VV. 20-24 give instructions about eligibility to go on a pilgrimage. Pilgrimage to sacred places is a sort of atonement for sins. Hence these chapters followed the section of expiation.

2. Description of the dissolution of the world and recreation (*Pratisarga*) is one of the main characteristics of a Purāṇa. The KP. anyhow forgot to include it in previous chapters. So before ending the KP. this chapter was included. The description of the dissolution of the universe is found in the Mbh. Śānti, chs. 233, 312 and most Purāṇas e.g. AP. 368-1-27, Bh. P. XII.4.1.-43, Va. P. 100-118-199. As usual there are common descriptions containing some common verses.

3. The word *dharma* in this verse implies Smṛti chapters in KP. I, and *Mokṣa jñāna* implies the so-called *Īśvara-gītā* according to Hazra, and hence *Vyāsa-gītā* is an interpolation by Pāśupatas. The topics in the *Vyāsa-gītā* can be called *dharma*, as they deal with expiatory rites, pilgrimage etc., but that does not meet Hazra's objections. *Vyāsa-gītā* is an interpolation in the strict sense of the term.

The detailed explanation of the worlds, the genealogies of kings and sages and the Manvantaras have been explained. O lord of the chief of Devas, it behoves you now to describe the dissolution of the living beings, as narrated by you before. O lord of the past and the future.

Sūta said :

4. On hearing their words, the lord who had assumed the form of a Tortoise, the great Yogin, recounted the *Pratisañcara* (dissolution) of all living beings.

Kūrma said :

5. In this Purāṇa the dissolution mentioned is of four types viz.: *Nitya*, *Naimittika*, *Prākṛta* and *Ātyantika* (each type is described below).

6. The destruction of the living beings that is witnessed every day in this world is called *Nitya* dissolution by the sages.

7. The dissolution of the three worlds at the end of the Kalpa (a day of Brahmā) caused by Brahmā (due to his sleep at the end of his day) is called *Naimittika* dissolution by learned men.

8. When the ultimate causes of the universe (i.e. beginning with Mahat and ending with Viśeṣa) undergo dissolution it is called *Prākṛta* Pratisarga (dissolution pertaining to Prakṛti) by those who ponder over Kāla.

9. The final absorption of the Yogin into the Supreme Ātman as a result of the realisation (*Jñāna*) is called *Ātyantika Pratisarga* (ultimate dissolution) by those Brāhmaṇas who ponder over Kāla.

10. The *Ātyantika Pralaya* achieved through Jñāna has already been recounted. Now I shall tell you the *Naimittika Pralaya* succinctly.

11. At the end of the thousand sets of four Yugas, when the time of dissolution arrives, Prajāpati sets about to stabilise all subjects within his Ātman (i.e. withdrawing them into himself).

12. Then for a period of hundred years, a severe absence of rain takes place. This terrible draught destructive of beings destroys all living beings.

13. O lord of the Earth, those beings of deficient strength are dissolved at the outset. They attain the state of *Bhūmi* (become one with the Earth).

14. Then the sun rises up and begins to blaze with its seven refulgent rays. His rays become unbearable. Through them he drinks up water.

15. The seven rays of the sun drink up the water from the great ocean. Thanks to this intake, they become brilliant and change themselves into seven suns.

16. Then those seven rays (the seven suns) dry up the four quarters. Like the fires, they burn the four worlds entirely.

17. Those seven brilliant suns spread up and down by means of their rays. Brightened up by the fire at the end of the Yugas, they blaze forth.

18. Those suns become illuminated by means of the water (sucked up by them). They shed forth thousands of rays enveloping the whole sky; they scorch and burn the Earth.

19. Being burnt by their brilliance, the Earth alongwith the mountains, rivers, oceans and continents becomes devoid of moisture.

20-21. These blazing rays which have spread down, above and obliquely on all sides so powerfully and envelop everything that all these form one mass of flame mixed with solar fire and form one fiery unit.

22. The fire that crops up thus becomes destructive of all worlds. The fiery sphere immediately burns up the four worlds by its brilliance (burning capacity).

23. Thus when all things movable and immovable are destroyed, the earth being devoid of trees and grass looks like the back of a tortoise.

24. The entire universe appears like a frying pan. The rays completely burn everything down again and again.

25. Thereafter, the animals in the netherworlds as well as those in the great oceans become destroyed and dissolved. They crumble and get mixed into the earth.

26. Lord Fire, with seven souls, reduces everything to ashes—the continents, the mountains, the Varṣas (subcontinents) and the great oceans.

27. The flourishing fire drinks up the waters from the oceans and rivers. It blazes up resting on the Earth.

28. Then the great Saṁvartaka fire being ablaze and expanded by the power of the wind (*Māruteya*)* crossing over the mountains burns down the worlds.

29. After burning the Earth, it burns up Rasātala. After burning the Earth down below, it burns the heaven above.

30. The flames of that Saṁvartaka fire leap up hundreds, thousands and ten thousands of Yojanas.

31. Becoming more brilliant by being urged by Kālarudra[1] (Rudra, the destroyer) it burns the Gandharvas, Piśācas, Yakṣas, serpents and Rākṣasas.

32. The Kālāgni (the fire of destruction) whose body has been pervaded by Kāla entirely consumes Bhūrloka, Bhuvarloka and Maharloka.

33-34. When all these worlds are pervaded on the sides above by the fire, it shines and illuminates everything hidden. It enters the entire Universe. Then the terrible Saṁvartaka clouds rise up in the sky. They have the shapes of huge elephants. They are embellished with lightning.

35-38. There arise in the sky the terrible Saṁvartaka clouds of world destruction. Some are dark like the blue-lotus; some resemble the water-lilies; some are smoke-coloured; some are yellow, some have the colour of donkeys, and others resemble the red lac juice. Others are white like conch and the Kunda flowers. Some clouds are like the finest variety of collyrium. Others are like the red arsenic and a few resemble pigeons. Some appear like glow-worms and others resemble yellow orpiment. Some are like rainbows. Such clouds rise up in the heaven.

39. Some are like mountains; some are comparable to huge herds of elephants. Others are like heaps of burning coal and some like shoals of fishes.

---

*v.l. *rudra-tejo-vijṛmbhitaḥ* "expanded by the brilliance of Rudra."

1. Even in this chapter, the credit of destroying the world is given to Rudra, *vide* the next chapter for Rudra's *Tāṇḍava* dance. But in V.P. VI. 4, it is Viṣṇu who dissolves the world.

40. Then all these types of clouds of terrible form and loud report fill up the whole of the firmament.

41. Then those terrible roaring clouds of seven types born of the sun release torrents of water and extinguish the fire.

42. Like a flood water gushes out from them as rain. The terrible and inauspicious rain destroys the fire.

43. The entire universe is filled with water of enormous quantities. On being thus overpowered by water the fire merges itself into the water.

44. Due to the waters showered by the clouds the fire is subdued in hundreds of years. The flood envelops the entire universe with huge currents of water.

45. Impelled by the self-born deity, these showers fill the earth with huge floods of water like the flow-tide of an ocean.

46. The whole Earth alongwith the mountains and continents is slowly covered with water. The water drunk by the rays of the sun remains in the clouds.

47. Again it falls on the Earth whereby the oceans are filled up. Thereafter the oceans go beyond their shores everywhere.

48-49. The mountains become submerged. The earth too sinks under the water. In that vast and terrible sheet of water, all the mobile and immobile beings get lost. Lord Prajāpati adopts the Yogic slumber and lies down therein. Learned men say that a Kalpa consists of a thousand cycles of four Yugas.

50. The present Kalpa is the Vārāha. Its detailed description has been given. There are innumerable Kalpas pertaining to Brahmā, Viṣṇu and Śiva.

51. These have been recounted in the Purāṇas by the sages who ponder over Kāla (Time). The greatness of Hari predominates in the Sāttvika Kalpas.

52. It is said that (the greatness) of Hara (predominates) in the Tāmasa Kalpas and (the greatness) of Prajāpati (predominates) in the Rājasa Kalpa. The Vārāha Kalpa that is current now is considered to be Sāttvika.

53-54a. There are other Sāttvika Kalpas also. I (Lord Kūrma Viṣṇu) predominate in them. After acquiring meditation, penance and perfect knowledge, the Yogins propitiate Giriśa and attain that great region.

54b-55a. I am the wielder (master) of Māyā. I adopt Māyā and Yogic slumber in the whole universe as it submerges into the sheet of water.

55b-56a. At that time, during the period of my sleep the great sages of noble souls staying in the Janaloka see me with their Yogic vision.

56b. I am the lord and the ancient Puruṣa, the origin (creator) of Bhuḥ (the Earth) and Bhuvaḥ (the ether).

57-58. I am the glorious one with thousand feet, thousand eyes and thousand legs. I am the Mantra, the Brāhmaṇas, the cows, the sacrificial twigs, the Prokṣaṇīya (that which should be sprinkled), the Soma, the Vrata, (religious vow) the Saṁvartaka fire, the great Ātman, the great and sacred glory.

59. I am the intellect, the master of senses (the lord protector of cowherds), Brahmā's face, the infinite redeemer, the Yogin, the goal, the most excellent among those who afford the goal.

60. I am the Haṁsa (swan), the vital breath, Kapila, of universal form, the eternal one, the immanent soul, Prakṛti, Kāla (Time), the seed of the universe, the immortal nectar.

61. There is no mother, father or great lord other than I. Nārāyaṇa of the colour of the sun is the protector of the universe. I am the puruṣa of Yogic form. The Ascetics who abide by the Yogic practice see me. After realising the Ātman they attain my reality.

CHAPTER FORTYSIX

Dissolution and subsidiary creation

Kūrma said :

1. Henceforth, I shall explain the Prākṛta dissolution.[1] It is excellent. Even as I recount it succinctly, listen to it.

2. When the two Parārdha periods pass by (i.e. after the life time of god Brahmā), Kāla, the reckoner of the worlds, the dark fire of dissolution, sets out to reduce the entire universe to ashes.

3. After projecting the Ātman (his self) into Ātman, and having become lord Maheśvara, he (Kāla) burns the entire cosmic egg including Devas, Asuras and human beings.

4. Having entered into him (Kālāgni), lord Mahādeva, Nīlalohita, assumes a terrible form and annihilates the worlds.

5. Entering the solar sphere and manifesting himself in various ways, he assumes the form of the seven-steeded deity (i.e. the sun) and burns the entire world.

6. After burning the entire universe, he discharges the great miraculous weapon Brahmaśiras, that burns everything, on the bodies of deities.

7. When all Devas had been burnt, the goddess, the daughter of the most excellent of the mountains, stands by as the sole witness of Śambhu. So says the Vedic Śrutis.

8. The lord makes an excellent garland of the skulls of the heads of Devas and decorates himself with it. He fills the sphere of the firmament by the multitudes of suns and moons etc.

---

1. This concluding chapter deals with the dissolution of the universe after the death of Brahmā (*Prākṛta Pralaya*) and the table of contents of the Purāṇa.

The *Prākṛta Pralaya*—The involution of the universe till all the *guṇas* attain equilibrium, is based on the Sāṅkhya, all the credit of this Pralaya is given to god Śiva.

Ia. VV. 8-12 describe the Tāṇḍava dance of Śiva.

9. The lord has a thousand (i.e. innumerable) eyes and a thousand eyelids (v.l. thousand forms), a thousand hands and feet and a thousand rays of splendour. He is mightily-armed.

10. His face is terrible due to the curved fangs. His eyes shine like blazing fires. Holding the trident and wearing the elephant hide, he is established in his lordly Yoga.

11. Imbibing the great Bliss, the prolific effusion of the nectar, Īśvara glances at the goddess and performs a Tāṇḍava dance by himself.

12. The goddess imbibes the highly auspicious Nectar of dances of her lord. She adopts Yoga and becomes one with the body of the Trident-bearing Lord.

13. After burning the sphere of the cosmic egg, which is naturally fiery, the Pināka-bearing Lord enjoys the pleasures of Tāṇḍava dance out of his own will.

14. When Devas had been annihilated and Brahmā, Viṣṇu and the Pināka-bearing lord Śiva (are unified in a resting position), the element of earth gets dissolved in the waters alongwith its attributes.[1]

15. *Havyavāhana* (Fire) swallows the principle of water alongwith its attributes. The element of *Tejas* (fire) accompanied by all its attributes undergoes dissolution in the element of Vāyu (wind).

16. The wind, the sustainer of (livings beings in) the universe alongwith (its) attributes gets dissolved in the Ether. The Ether accompanied by its attribute gets dissolved in the Bhūtādi (Tāmasa Ahaṁkāra).

17. All the sense-organs become dissolved in the Taijasa (Rājasa Ahaṁkāra). O excellent ones, the Vaikārika (Sāttvika Ahaṁkāra) gets dissolved alongwith the groups of Devas.

18. The three types of Ahaṁkāra (ego) get dissolved in the principle *Mahat*. The *Mahat* (Intellect) principle gets dissolved in Brahmā of unmeasured prowess, alongwith these.

19-20. The unmanifast imperishable source of origin of the universe which is single and unchanging annihilates

---

1. VV. 14-21 describe the process of involution, the credit of which is ascribed to Śiva.

things. After annihilating the living beings and the principles thus, Maheśvara separates Pradhāna and the great Puruṣa, from each other. This is said to be the annihilation of the unborn Pradhāna and Puruṣa.

21. The dissolution does not exist by itself. It originates from the will of Maheśvara. When Pradhāna is in a state of equilibrium of guṇas, it is mentioned as unmanifested Prakṛti.

22. Pradhāna, the principle of Māyā, is insentient and the source of origin of the universe. The Ātman, the twentyfifth (principle) is stationed within the hearts of all. It is the pure consciousness and knowledge.

23. It is sung about by sages as the *Sākṣin* (cosmic Witness), the great Pitāmaha (grandfather). The power of Annihilation is certainly the Śakti of Maheśvara.

24a. The Śruti says that everything beginning with Pradhāna and ending with Viśeṣa is present* in the physical body of Rudra.

24b-25. God Śaṅkara brings about the eternal *Laya* (dissolution) of all Yogins whose hearts are dedicated to spiritual knowledge. In this way this self-controlled (or the controller of all) Rudra brings about the annihilation of the Universe.

26-27a. The Śruti says that the slumbering and the enchanting Śakti is Nārāyaṇa. Lord Hiraṇyagarbha, the twentyfifth principle, creates the entire universe consisting of the manifest and the non-manifest, through Prakṛti after identifying himself with it.

27b. (Defective) The Śaktis of Brahmā, Viṣṇu and Īśa, latent within the Ātman itself are weak** (?) [v.l. all-pervading, quiescent, and omnipresent. They are the bestowers of worldly pleasures and salvation.

28. They are all powerful, binding everything, (v.l. worthy of salute by all) perpetual and infinite in their enjoyments of pleasures. They form one imperishable principle in the nature of Lord Puruṣa, Pradhāna.

---

*v.l. *dahet* "will burn down" everything beginning with *Mahat* and ending with *Viśeṣa*.

**obviously a misprint v.l. *sarvataḥ*—all-round, all-pervading.

29-30a. There are thousands of other divine Śaktis therein. Āditya (Sun) and other immortal beings are worshipped through different kinds of Yajñas. For each of these Śaktis there are thousands and hundreds of physical forms mentioned. There is only one attributeless potency described variously due to its greatness.

30b-31a. Lord Maheśvara himself adopts that Śakti (in his activities). (With that Śakti) he creates many bodies. He is seen sporting about.

31b-32a. In all the Yajñas it is he who is worshipped by the Brāhmaṇas, the expounders of the Vedas. It is heard in the Vedas that Rudra is the bestower of all desires.

32b-33a. Among the Śaktis of the great Ātman the deities of Brahmā, Viṣṇu and Maheśvara are remembered as the most important.

33b-34a. It is sung (stated) that the Lord, the eternal great Ātman, the Ātman that wields all Māyās, the trident-bearing Maheśvara is beyond these three.

34b-36a. Some speak of Him as Agni (as the sole lord); others call it Nārāyaṇa. Some speak of it as Indra. Others speak of it as Prāṇa and still others speak of it as Brahma. (Really speaking) Brahmā, Viṣṇu, Agni, Varuṇa, all Devas as well as sages are glorified as the variants of the same single entity viz. Rudra.

36b-37a. Śiva bestows benefits after assuming respectively those forms by resorting to which they worship Parameśvara.

37b-38a. Hence, by resorting to one eternal form, one should propitiate Mahādeva. One attains thereby the greatest region.

38b-39. But you propitiate the eternal Lord Mahādeva, the omnipotent, lord Giriśa whether Saguṇa or Nirguṇa (with or without attributes). The Nirguṇa (attributeless) form of Yoga has already been explained to you by me before.

40. The devotee desirous of climbing (or attaining) to the Yoga of Saguṇa type should worship parameśvara (the supreme Ruler) in the Saguṇa form—the form with three eyes, bearing Pināka with matted hair and clad in elephant hide.

41. Or he should meditate on Rudra with golden lustre or shining like a thousand suns : So it is heard (mentioned) in the Vedas. O leading sages, this is pointed out as *Sabīja Yoga* (i.e. the Yoga with the seed).

42-43a. One who is incompetent to perform this should worship Hara as *Viśva* (the universe) or as Brahmā. O leading sages, if one is incapable of even this, one should devotedly worship Vāyu (wind), Agni (fire), Indra and others.

43b-44a. Hence, one should forsake all Devas beginning with Brahmā and propitiate Virūpākṣa (three-eyed) i.e. Śiva who is present at the beginning, in the middle and the end.[1]

44b-46a. He should be pure, devoted to his own Dharma or Karman. He should adopt the path of devotion. He shall ultimately approach Śiva of such a splendid form. This is pointed out as *Sabīja Yoga*. It is extremely sanctifying.

46b-47. One who practises Yoga in accordance with the injunctions shall attain the region of Īśvara. Two other pure *Bhāvanās* (meditations) have been mentioned to you. Moreover, the *Nirbīja* and *Sabīja* Yoga has been mentioned. The perfect knowledge which is the Nirbīja one has been mentioned to you before by me.

48. A sensible man should practise the worship of Viṣṇu, Rudra and Viriñci in the *Sabīja Yoga*, or he may worship Vāyu and other Devas with due attachment to them and with his self controlled.

49. He should worship Viṣṇu, Hari, who assumes the four Mūrtis (vyūhas) who has neither beginning nor destruction and who is the eternal lord Vāsudeva.

50. He should worship Nārāyaṇa who is the source of origin of the universe, whose greatest region is in the firmament.

---

1. VV. 43b-53 describe the *sabīja Yoga* path leading to *Brahma-bhāvanā* (meditation of Brahman). A synthesis of Vaiṣṇavism and Śaivism is attempted in this final discourse by Kūrma, as the worship of Viṣṇu, Rudra and Brahmā in practice of *sabīja Yoga* is exhorted therein (vide vv. 48-50). The final Siddhānta of Kūrma Purāṇa is the Upaniṣadic formula *Sarvaṁ khalvidaṁ Brahma* paraphrased by KP. : *tasmād Brahma-mayaṁ jagat* (V. 53a).

He should invariably wear his Liṅga (symbols), he should be devoted to him and resort to him.

51. The same procedure is to be followed in the final *Brahma-Bhāvanā* (meditation of Brahman). Thus the perfect knowledge related to Bhāvanā (meditation) has been explained by me.

52-53. It is this that had been narrated formerly by me to the sage Indradyumna. This universe of the nature of the manifest is born sentient and non-sentient. The Supreme Brahman is its Īśvara (Lord). Hence, the universe is identical with the Brahman.

Sūta said :

After saying this much Lord Janārdana stopped. Accompanied by Indra, the sages eulogised Viṣṇu the consort of Mā (i.e. Lakṣmī).

Eulogy of Viṣṇu

The sages said :

54. Obeisance to you, to Viṣṇu, the great Ātman of the form of the tortoise. Hail to Vāsudeva, to omnipresent Nārāyaṇa.

55. Obeisance, again and again to you, to Kṛṣṇa, and to Govinda, Obeisance always to you, to Mādhava, to the lord of Yajñas.

56. Obeisance to you with a thousand (i.e. innumerable) heads. Salutation to you with a thousand eyes. Obeisance to one with a thousand hands and to one with a thousand feet.

57. Om! Hail to Viṣṇu of the embodiment of perfect knowledge, to the great Ātman. Obeisance to you, the Bliss. Bow to you who are beyond the pale of Māyā.

58. Salutation to you of concealed body (or O Kūrma-Tortoise), to you the attributeless (Nirguṇa) one, to the ancient Puruṣa, of the form of only pure Existence.

59. Obeisance to Sāṅkhya; Bow to the pure Yoga, obeisance to you, comprehensible through the meditation on Dharma; salutation be to the unsullied one.

60. Hail to you the principle of Yoga; obeisance to the Īśvara of great Yoga; obeisance to the lord of the greater and

the lesser beings. Obeisance to you, comprehensible through the Vedas.

61. Obeisance to the enlightened one,[1] to the pure one; Bows again and again to you, the wielder of Māyā. Obeisance to Vedhas.

62. Hail to you Varāha; obeisance to you Narasiṃha; bow to you Vāmana; obeisance to you Hṛṣīkeśa.

63. Obeisance to the bestower of heavenly pleasures and salvation; salutation to one whose Ātman is un-obstructed. Obeisance to one attainable through Yoga; obeisance to the Yogin, to the bestower of Yogas.

64-65a. Obeisance to the lord of Devas. Hail to you, the suppressor of the distress of Devas. O lord, the perfect knowledge that is destructive of all worldly existence (Saṃsāra) has been acquired by us, thanks to your grace—the perfect knowledge on realising which one attains immortality.

65b-67a. By your grace different kinds of Dharma were heard, the detailed narration of the races and the Manvantaras, the Sarga, the Pratisarga and the detailed description of this cosmic egg—everything was understood; indeed you are the witness of all the universe; you are the cause of the universe; you are the great Nārāyaṇa. It behoves you the Infinite Ātman, to save us, who have sought refuge in you alone."

Sūta said :

67b-68a. O Brāhmaṇas, the whole of the Kūrma Purāṇa, that bestows worldly pleasures and salvation has been related to you. It is the same as was narrated by Gadādhara (Viṣṇu).

68b-69. In this Purāṇa,[2] at the outset, the birth of Lakṣmī has been narrated. In order to fascinate the living

1. *namo buddhāya,* though translated here as 'obeisance to the enlightened one, it can be taken as 'obeisance to Buddha'. Purāṇas did try (and successfully so) to accommodate Buddha in Brahmanism by regarding him as an incarnation of Viṣṇu.

2. VV. 69-118 give the main contents of this Purāṇa. It is not a table of contents in the modern sense but an enumeration of the main topics in this Purāṇa. Even understanding this summary is said to absolve one of all sins and secure honour in Brahmaloka (v. 119).

beings, her birth has been intended by Vāsudeva. The creations of the Prajāpatis, the duties of different Varṇas (castes) and their avocations have been described.

70-73a. The splendid characteristics of Dharma, Artha, Kāma and Mokṣa have been mentioned. The identity, the separateness and the special characteristics of Brahmā, Viṣṇu and the intelligent Maheśa have been recounted. The characteristics of the Devotees have been mentioned. The behaviour, the diet* and the characteristics of the castes and stages of life have been narrated precisely. O leading sages, the primordial creation, the seven coverings of the Aṇḍa (i.e. cosmic Egg) and the creation of Hiraṇyagarbha have been related.

73b-77. The period and units of time have been enumerated, then the greatness of Īśvara; the lying down in the waters by Brahmā; the derivation of the names; the uplift of the Earth by Viṣṇu in the form of a Boar; the narration of Mukhya and other creations, then the creation of the sages; narration of the creation of Rudra and Ṛṣis and of sages; the creation of the subjects by Dharma before the Tāmasa creation; the argument between Brahmā and Viṣṇu; the entry of Brahmā into the body of Viṣṇu the birth from the lotus of the intelligent lord and his delusion; the vision of Maheśa and the greatness of Maheśa recounted by Viṣṇu.

78. The granting of divine vision unto Brahmā, the supreme god (Parameṣṭhin); the eulogy of the lord of Devas by Brahmā, Parameṣṭhin.

79-80. The grace of Śiva and the granting of boons; the dialogue between Viṣṇu and Śaṅkara the great Ātman; the granting of boons at the outset and then the disappearance of the Pināka-bearing lord. O Brāhmaṇas, thereafter, the slaying of Madhu and Kaiṭabha has been narrated.

81. The incarnation of lord Brahmā from the umbilical lotus of Viṣṇu is described. So also the unification of the lord with Brahmā formerly has been narrated.

---

*This appears to be a misprint as the strangeness of the meaning shows. The v.l. *śobhanam* for *bhojanam* is better. With that v.l. the line means 'excellent behaviour of the devotees has been described'

82. The delusion of Brahmā and then the recognition of Hari has been described; the performance of the penance by the intelligent lord of Devas has been narrated.

83. The appearance of Maheśa from the forehead of Brahmā is mentioned thereafter; the creative activity of the Rudras and its prohibition of the same by Brahmā is told.

84-85. The glory of the lord of Devas, the granting of the boons and the instruction, the vanishment of the lord, the performance of penance of the egg-born; the appearance of the lord of Devas; Rudra's possession of half-male and half-female form; the narration of separation of the goddess from the Pināka-bearing lord of Devas.

86. Afterwards the daughtership of the goddess of Dakṣa as well as that of Himālaya is described alongwith the reality of the goddess.

87. The manifestation of the divine and the universe-form, the thousand names of the goddess are enumerated by the father Himavān himself.

88. The advice given by the great goddess; the granting of the boons; The creation of subjects by Bhṛgu and others; the detailed narration of the race of kings.

89. The *Pracetasatva* (the state of being the son of Pracetas) of Dakṣa, the destruction of Yajña of Dakṣa, the dispute between Dadhīca and Dakṣa is then narrated.

90. O leading sages, thereafter the imprecation of the sages (by Dadhīca) has been mentioned; then the arrival of Rudra, his grace and the vanishment of the Pināka-bearing lord.

91. Then the advice to Pitāmaha for the protection is described (*raṇāya** 'for fighting'), the creation of the subjects by Dakṣa and Kaśyapa, the great Ātman.

92. The slaying of Hiraṇyakaśipu and then that of Hiraṇyākṣa, thereafter, the curse to the dwellers of the Devadāru forest is mentioned.

93. Then the subjugation of Andhaka and the (granting of) the excellent chieftainship of the Gaṇas. The curbing of Prahlāda and the binding over of Bali.

*v.l. *rakṣaṇāya* instead of 'raṇāya' is accepted.

94. The defeat of Bāṇa and the grace shown to him by the trident-bearing lord; the detailed narration of the families of the sages; the races of the king are glorified.

95. The birth of Hari, Viṣṇu out of his own free will from Vasudeva, visit to Upamanyu and the performance of penance.

96. The acquisition of the boon after seeing the three-eyed Mahādeva accompanied by Ambā; the departure to Kailāsa and staying there by Śārṅgin (Kṛṣṇa).

97. Then the fear of the dwellers of Dvārāvatī, their protection by Garuḍa after conquering the powerful enemies are described.

98. The arrival of Nārada and the journey of Garutman (Garuḍa), thereafter the arrival of Kṛṣṇa to the hermitage of the sages.

99. The daily routine of Vāsudeva. His worship of Śivaliṅga. Thereafter, the questions put by the sage Mārkaṇḍeya have been mentioned.

100. The narration of the precise nature of the Liṅga and the Liṅgin as a sequel to the narration of the worship of Liṅga, the fear arising out of Liṅga.*

101. O leading sages, in the middle, the delusion of Brahmā and Viṣṇu has been described and their departure up and down the Liṅga has been related.

102. The eulogy of the lord of Devas, the grace of supreme deity Śiva, vanishment of the Liṅga and the birth of Sāmba thereafter.

103. O excellent Brāhmaṇas, thereafter Aniruddha's birth has been glorified, (then) the inclination of Kṛṣṇa towards departure (thence), and the arrival of the sages.

104. The laying down of precepts by Kṛṣṇa; the granting of the boons by the great Ātman, Kṛṣṇa's departure and visit of Pārtha (Arjuna).

105. Narration of the eternal characteristics of Yugas by Kṛṣṇadvaipāyana; the benediction to Pārtha and his departure to Vārāṇasī thence.

---

*Misprint for *āvirbhāva* 'manifestation of the Liṅga.'

106. (The departure to Vārāṇasī) by Vyāsa the saintly son of Parāśara, the worker of miracles, the greatness of Vārāṇasī and the description of holy centres.

107. Vyāsa's pilgrimage, vision of the goddess, his banishment and granting of the boons (have been mentioned).

108. The greatness of Prayāga; the narration of various holy centres, O Brāhmaṇas, and the enormous benefit therefrom and the going away of Mārkaṇḍeya, O Brāhmaṇas.

109. The nature of the worlds, the arrangement of the luminaries, the decisive position of the sub-continents and the rivers therein.

110. The enumeration of the mountains; the abodes of heaven-dwellers; the classification of continents and the description of Śveta Dvīpa.

111. The lying (sleeping) of Viṣṇu, the greatness of the great Ātman; the narration of the Manvantaras and the grandeur of Viṣṇu.

112. The classification of the Vedas into Śākhās (branches); the enumeration of Vyāsas; O leading sages, (the details) of non-vedas (Purāṇas etc.) and Vedas have been mentioned.

113. The story of Yogeśvaras and the glorification of their disciples. The various mystic Gītās of Īśvara have been glorified.

114. The conduct of life of the castes and stages of life; the mode of expiatory rites; the *Kāpālitva* (the state of holding the skull) of Rudra and his begging for alms.

115. The narration of the chaste ladies and the discussion (and decision) about sacred places, the restraint of Maṅkaṇaka. All these have been described.

116. O Brāhmaṇas, the killing of Kāla is succinctly mentioned. So also the entry of Śambhu as well as of Viṣṇu into the forest of Devadāru trees.

117. The manifestation to the sages of the six clans by the intelligent lord of Devas; the granting of boons by the lore to Nandin has been glorified.

118. Thereafter, the Naimittika dissolution has been described; subsequently the Prākṛta dissolution as well as the *Sabija yoga* has been explained.

119. He who is glorified in the Purāṇa after understanding its summary, thus, becomes freed from all sins and is honoured in the Brahmaloka.

120-121. After saying this and taking goddess Śrī (with him), Puruṣottama (lord Viṣṇu) abandoned the form of the tortoise and went; and then Hara (also) (v.l. *Hari* is relevant in the context). After saluting Viṣṇu, the Supreme person, and drinking the nectar, Devas and sages went over to their respective abodes, O Brāhmaṇas.

122. The whole of this Purāṇa was directly narrated by Viṣṇu who had assumed the form of the tortoise, who is the over-lord of Devas and the source of origin of the universe.

123. O Brāhmaṇas, he who regularly reads this (through) succinctly becomes freed from all sins and is honoured in the Brahmaloka.

124. Understand the merit accruing to the person who copies this and presents it to a Brāhmaṇa well versed in the Vedas, in the month of Vaiśākha or Kārttika.

125-126. He shall be freed from all sins. He will be endowed with every type of riches and glory. After enjoying the extensive divine and splendid pleasure (in the heaven), when he falls off from the heaven, he is born in the family of Brāhmaṇas. Thanks to the great efficacy of the previous impression, he attains Brahmavidyā.

127. On reading even a single chapter, he is freed from all sins. He who ponders over the meaning properly attains the greatest region.

128. This holy text should be studied by the Brāhmaṇas at every Parvan (festive occasion). O excellent Brāhmaṇas it should be heard also, as it is destructive of great sins.

129. If all the Purāṇas and the Itihāsas were placed on one pan and the greatest Veda* on another pan, the former alone is the weightier.

130-131. If this Purāṇa were to be excluded, there is no other means of dispelling sins. O sages of holy rites, in no

*This denigration of Vedas is unexpected. The v.l. *cedam* is better than *vedam* (probably a confusion between *c* and *v* in Devanāgarī script).

other Purāṇa is lord Nārāyaṇa, Hari, Viṣṇu glorified so much as in this. The Brāhmī Saṁhitā of this Purāṇa is destructive of all sins.

132-133. The greatest Brahman is glorified in this (*Purāṇa*) precisely. The greatest of all holy centres, the greatest of all penances, the greatest of all perfect knowledges and the greatest of all holy rites are glorified in this. This scripture should not be studied in the presence of a Śūdra.

134. If any one of deluded souls studies so, he falls into many hells, In the course of a Śrāddha or any other rites pertaining to gods, this scripture must be caused to be read by the twice-born.

135. Especially, at the end of a Yajña (it should be read). It wipes off all defects. This scripture must particularly be studied by those who seek salvation.

136-137a. It should be heard and pondered over. It explains and supplements the meanings of Vedic passages. After understanding it oneself, one should narrate it to the leading Brāhmaṇas endowed with devotion. He shall be rid of sins and shall attain identity with Brahman.

137b-138a. If anyone were to give it to one who has no faith and to one who is sinful, he will fall into hells after death. Thereafter, he will be born in the lowly womb of dogs.

138b-140a. Only after making obeisance to Hari, Viṣṇu the eternal source of origin of the universe, should this scripture of Kṛṣṇadvaipāyana be studied. This is the command of Viṣṇu, the lord of Devas of unmeasured splendour as well as of Vyāsa, the noble-souled Brāhmaṇa sage, the son of Parāśara.[1]

140b-142a. After hearing this from lord Nārāyaṇa, Nārada, the holy sage, gave this to Gautama at the outset. From him Parāśara obtained it. The holy lord Parāśara recounted this (Purāṇa) that yields the Puruṣārthas viz Dharma, Artha, Kāma and Mokṣa, to the sages, at Gaṅgādvāra, O great sages.

142b-144. At the outset, this was narrated to the intelligent Sanaka by Brahmā as well as to Sanatkumāra. It is

1. VV. 122-140a give the *Phala-Śruti* and other instructions regarding reading etc. of the Purāṇa.

destructive of all sins. The holy lord, the foremost among those who know Yoga, sage Devala got it from Sanaka. Pañcaśikha obtained this excellent (sacripture) form Devala. The saintly son of Satyavatī got this from Sanatakumāra.

145-146a. (From Sanatkumāra Vyāsa got this Purāṇa in which all topics have been brought together. I heard this (Purāṇa) that is destructive of sins from him and related it to you all. This should be given to the righteous people by you all.[1]

146b-147. Obeisance unto that sage, Vyāsa the great sage and omniscient son of Parāśara, the quiescent sage, a form of Nārāyaṇa.

Obeisance unto that Viṣṇu, lord of Devas, in the form of tortoise, from whom everything is born and in whom everything gets dissolved.[2]

---

1. VV. 140b-146a describe the three oral traditions of the KP as follows :

I Nārāyaṇa→Nārada→Gautama→Parāśara→sages at Gaṅgādvāra.

II Brahmā→Sanaka (and Sanat-Kumāra)→Devala→Pañcaśikha.

IIA Sanatkumāra→Vyāsa→Sūta→Naimiṣāraṇya sages.

2. The concluding verse confirms the original Vaiṣṇavite form of this Purāṇa.

INDEX

In the following Index, the 1st (Roman) figure indicates the number of the part (*Ardha*), the next (Arabic) figure, the number of the chapter and the next (Arabic) figure or figures the number of the verse or verses. In case no number is given after the number of the chapter, it shows that the whole chapter deals with that topic. For example on p. 623 the entry is *Aditi* I.17.14-42. It means that the story of Aditi is given in the I Part, 17th chapter and verses 14-42. *Agnihotra* II.24 means the topic of *Agnihotra* is dealt with in the 24th chapter of the II Part. If the topic covers more than one chapter, the abbreviation Chs. precedes the numbers denoting the chapter. Thus *Avimukta* I. Chs. 31-35 means the topic is dealt with in chapters 31 to 35 in Part I. When the reference belongs to the same Part, the repetition of the number of the part is omitted and simply the numbers of the chapter and the verse (s) are given. For example *Agni* (ii) A *Tīrtha* (a sacred Pool) I.35.7; 39.4 means that the second reference belongs to the same part (I) but is mentioned in the 4th verse of the 39th chapter.

A

Aditi—Mother of gods—performed penance to have Viṣṇu as son to punish Bali—I.17.14-42; mother of the Sun-god—I.20.1

Āditya—The Sun-god—Born of Kaśyapa and Aditi I.20-1—His progeny, a proginator of the Solar race—I.20-4 ff.—Description of the chariot of the Sun—I.41-27-33, —Movements of The Sun—I.41-36-41—The Twelve Ādityas I.41-44; 42.2-3—Functions of Ādityas—I.42—Seven rays of the Sun-god—I.43.3-4—Functions of the Solar rays—I.43.1-27—His Eulogy (*Sūrya-hṛdaya*)—II.18.35-45

Agni (1) The Fire-god—Identified with Rudra—I.13.14—Agni's progeny—I.13.15-18—Protected Sītā II.34.125 Eulogized by Sītā—II.34. 116-123—Destroys the universe as Saṁvartaka—II.45.27-33

Agni (ii) A sacred Pool (*Tīrtha*)—I. 35.7; 39.4

Agnīdhra—Original King of Jambūdvīpa—divides Jambūdvipa in nine Parts (*varṣas*) & gives one to each of his sons—I.40.30-35; Retires for penance I.40.36

Agni-hotra—Fire-worship— Rules and duties pertaining to—II.24

Ahalyā (i) Gautama's wife—II.41.44 —(ii) A *Tīrtha* II.41.43-45

Alakanandā—a sacred river—I.46.31

Amarakaṇṭaka—a mountain II.20.29 —II.40-32, 39; 40.9-13

Amarāvatī—a celestial city of Indra—I.46.10-12

Anadhyāya days (on which studies are prohibited)—II.14. 64-87

Ānakadundubhi—A king proficient in music—penance at Govardhana I.24.49-62

Andhaka—a demon I.16.95-96 —Fights for Umā I.16.131-193 —Surrenders and accepted as a Śiva-gaṇa—I.16.215—Accepted as a son by Umā I.16.219

Āndhras—N. of a people (Tribe)— I.47.41-44

Aṅgirasa—(i) Śiva's disciple—I.15-16. (ii) A Tirtha—II.41.31-33

Aparānta—N. of a people—I.47.42

Arjuna—A Pāṇḍava—After Kṛṣṇa's death meets Vyāsa and discusses I.29

Aruṇā—a sacred river—II.30.22

Arundhatī—(i) Vasiṣṭha's wife—I. 19, 20, 23—an ideal chaste woman X:I.12.223 (ii) Wife of Dharma— I.16.7-11

Āśauca—Impurity due to birth or death—Rules for—II.23.1-68

Āśrama—stage (s) in life—classification and duties of—I.3.2-28

Āsuri—Śiva's disciple—I.53-15

Aśva-tīrtha—A *Tīrtha*—II.35-38

Aśvina—N. of a twin god—II.7.38

Aśvinī—N. of a constellation—II.20.15

Avimukta (see Vārāṇasī)—I. Chs. 31-35; II.7.14

B

Badarī, also Badarīkāśrama—A sacred place beloved of Śiva—II.37.50-52 —Śiva imparted *Īśvara-gītā* to Sanat Kumāra and others here—II.1.18-31

Bali—A pious Demon-King— Story of—I.17
Bali's conquests—17.12 ff
Donates land to Vāmana—17.50ff
Established in the nether-world 17-63

Bāṇa (i) A demon-king absorbed as Śiva's gaṇa—I.18.1-7
(ii) A *Tīrtha* under Narmadā—II.41.9-10

Bhadrā—A branch of divine Gaṅgā in Uttara-kuru (Mod. Yarkand—De)—I.46.33

Bhadra-Karṇa—A Tīrtha under Narmadā (Mod. Karnali—De)— I.31. 46; II.20.35

Bhadrāśva—A Varśa east of Meru I.40.30-35; 45.20-21; 47.2

Bhārata-varṣa—India—I.47 Mountain-ranges and river-systems in—47.21-40; People in I.47. 41-44

Bhāvanā—A kind of meditation—classification of—I.2.93-96

Bhīmarathī or Bhīmā—a sacred river in Maharashtra I.47.36

Bhṛgu Tīrtha—a sacred place, (mod. Bhera ghāṭ)—II.42.1-6

Bhṛgu Tuṅga—A *Tīrtha* specially meritorious for *śrāddha*—II.20.33; 37. 33-34

Brahmā—The creator of the universe (sometimes identified with Viṣṇu and also with Śiva)
—Br. called Nārāyaṇa sleeps on cosmic waters I.6.1-5—Uplifts the earth as a Divine Boar (Varāha)—6.6-25;16.79-84
—Born from the lotus in Viṣṇu's navel—I.9.10-36; 9.25-36
—Eulogised by Vasumanas—E.—I.20.53-55
—Controversy with Viṣṇu about personal greatness—I.9.12-49
—Created nine Prajāpatis for world creation—I.10.88-89
—Proudly criticises Śiva—II.31. 1-22
—Challenges Śiva to fight—II.31. 23-28
—Bhairava cuts off Brahma's head—II.31. 29-31—Brahma's head sticks to Bhairava's hand—II.31. 65ff

Brahmā—Eulogizes Śiva—II.31.49-57

Brahmacārin—a religious (celibate) student—Duties of II.14—Duties in relation with the preceptor—II.14. 1-16; 22-27—with preceptor's family—II.14.28-37
Duties while learning—II.14.42-49
Japa of Gāyatrī—II.14.50-59
Anadhyāya days—II.14.64-87

Brahma Tīrtha : under various important Tīrthas e.g. under Vārāṇasī—I.35.9; II.37.28; under Narmadā—II.41-56

Brahmāvarta—The best (sacred-most)—land—II.7.14

C

Candra (i) The Moon (See under Planetary System in I.41, I-43)
(ii) A *Kula-parvata* in Plakṣa-dvīpa—I.49.3
(iii) A Dvīpa—I.47.7
(iv) Candra-Sthāna—I.48.53-54
(v) N. of a Tīrtha under Vārāṇasi I.35.11, Kāverī—II.37.23, Narmadā—II.42.15-16

Carmaṇyavatī—River (Mod. Chambal)—I.47.31

Chariots of Planets—
(i) The Moon—I.43.32—41
(ii) Budha—43.42
(iii) Śukra—43.43
(iv) Bṛhaspati (Jupiter)—43.44-45

Creation of the world—
(i) By Viṣṇu through Brahmā I.2.
(ii) By Rudra—I.10
(iii) Through Prakṛti—I.4
(iv) Different creations by Brahmā I.7 & 8 *vide* Intro. pp. xxii-xxv
(v) Mukhyādi creation (By Svāyambhuva Manu and Dakṣa)-I.8

Cyavana—(i) a sage—I.19.4
(ii) Śiva's disciple—I.53-19

D

Dadhīca—a sage, advocates Śiva's presence in Prācetasa Dakṣa's sacrifice—I.15.6-27—Curses anti-Śiva Brāhmaṇas I. 15.28-32

Dakṣa—(1) Prajāpati—God Brahmā's son and Satī's father—Insults Śiva —Satī's Yogic self immolation and Rudra's curse—I.14.54-65
(2) Second tirtha as son of Pracetas—I.14.53—Performs sacrifice at Gaṅgādvāra—Quarrel with Dadhīca on Śiva's Share—I.15.8-27

—Dakṣa's sacrifice destroyed at Devī's request—I.15.34-79
Dakṣa pardoned by Śiva and advised by Brahmā I.15.79-98
Progeny of Dakṣa's daughters—I.13 and 16 (chs.)
Dākṣiṇātya—People of the Deccan (of Bhārata varṣa)—I.47.42
Dāruvana and Deva-dāruvana—II. 37.53-61; Legend of Śiva's Liṅga dropping—II.Chs. 38 and 39
Dāna-dharma—Charity—Its four varieties defined—II.26.2-8 Qualifications of the donee and fruit of Dāna on specific days—II.26.9-74
Daśāśvamedhika—A Tīrtha awarding merit of Ten Aśvamedhas to the bather—mentioned under : Gaṅgā II.37.26; Narmadā—II.41. 104-107
Devī [Umā, Pārvatī] Śiva's consort
(i) Birth from Dakṣa—I.11.8-10 (For her self-immolation vide Dakṣa
(ii) Second birth from Himavān—I.10.11-13
One Thousand epithets of—I.12, 2-324
Eulogised by Andhaka—I.16. 216-218
Devikā—a river—I.47.29; II.37.25
Dharma-pṛṣṭha—A holy place under Gayā—II.37.38
Dhātakī-Khaṇḍa—I.40.15
Dhruva—(i) King, Son of Medhātithi—I.38-24
(ii) King, Son of Uttānapāda—I.14.2-3
(iii) a god—I.16. 11-13
(iv) The Polar star—I.41.5, 26, 31, 42—I.43. 30, 46
Dṛṣadvatī—River (Mod. Ghaggar?) —I.47.29
Durjaya—King. Descendant of Jayadhvaja
—Dalliance with Ūrvaśī—I.l23.4-47
—As per Kaṇva's advice expiates sins at Vārāṇasī—I.23. 41-44
Duties (Dharmas)—Cf. different Castes (*Varṇas*) and Stages in life (*Āśramas*)—I.2.38-74
Aśramas classified as per Trinity of gods—I.2.101-111
Dvārakā or Dvārāvatī—Kṛṣṇa's capital city—I.26.18-29; 47-35
Dynasties of kings I.20
of sages I.19

E

Eraṇḍī saṅgama—Confluence with Narmadā—II.43.31-32

F

Food-articles—Prohibited and permitted for eating—II.17

G

Gandha-Mādana—
(1) A division (*varṣa*) of Jambūdvīpa—I.40.35
(2) Forest to the south of Ilāvṛta—I.45.22
(3) a mountain (a part of Kailāsa-range)—I.45. 15, 31
Gaṅgā—(heavenly)—I.46.28-33—Four streams of—I.36.29-37
Gaṅgā—A River—I.37.33-36; I.39. 8-10; II. 20.29 etc.; confluence with Yamunā I.37.6-8
Gautama (i) A sage—Protects Brāhmaṇas in a draught—I.16. 97-103
—Death of a fake cow—I.16.104-105
—Curses ungrateful Brāhmaṇas—I.16. 109-110
Gautama—(2) One of the seven sages in Vaivasvata Manvantara—I.51.25-26
(3) Vyāsa in the 19th Dvāpara—I.52.7
(4) An incarnation of Śiva—I.53.7
Gayā—(1) A holy place—I.31.36—Greatness of—II.35.7-15—Pitṛs expect *śrāddha* at—II.20.30-32
(2) A *Tīrtha* under Vārāṇasī—I.35.5
Gāyatrī—Importance of—II.14.53.59
Godāvarī—River—Holy for bath and *śrāddha*—I.47.36; II.37.15-16
Gokarṇa (i) A sacred place—I.41.48, Uttara Gokarṇa—II.35.29-32
(ii) An incarnation of Śiva—I.53.8
Govardhana—a mountain—Place of king Pṛthu's penance—I.14.18

H

Harivarṣa—a sub-continent—I.47. 10-19
Hastināpura—Capital city of Kurus —I.36.6
Himavat (i) a mountain—I.45, 9, 30
King Suśila met Śvetāśvatara at—I.14.25-29;—Śveta, an incarnation of Śiva, lived on—I.53.1-3 etc.
(ii) A Tīrtha or Sacred place—I. 35.13

Hiraṇyakaśipu—A Demon king—Prahlāda's father—story of—I.16.21-75

Hiraṇyākṣa—A demon king—Hiraṇyakaśipu's brother—killed by Viṣṇu-Varāha—I.16.22, 60-63, 77-83

House-holder (*Gṛhastha*)—Duties of—II.15

Householder's dress—II.15.3-8

His marital duties—II.15.9-13

Other religious duties—II.15. 14-42

Etiquettes and Rules of Conduct——II.16

Prescribed daily routine of a *gṛhastha*—II.18

Rules regarding taking food—II.19

Hūṇa—A people in Bhārata-Varṣa—I.47.43

I

Ikṣvāku—Description of the race of—I.21

Ilāvṛta—A subcontinent (*varṣa*) I.40. 30-35; 45.14-16. 22-24—I.47.20

Indra (i) King of gods—I.1.123; 17.43 etc.,

(ii) Vyāsa in the 7th *Dvāpara yuga*—I.52-4

(iii) A *Dvīpa*—I.47.29

Indradyumna—The king—story of—I. 1.43-48—Born as a Brāhmaṇa—I.1-50—Propitiates Viṣṇu and is enlightened by him—I.1.51-122

J

Jaigīṣavya—(1) A sage—His hermitage—I.48.17-22

(2) An incarnation of Śiva—I.53.5

Jambūdvīpa—A continent of which India—Bhārata-Varṣa is a part. Description (e.g. Varṣa-parvatas—VV.6-10, people—vv.13-20 etc) in I.45.6-41. Also I.46 (for rivers etc. VV. 1-33, Boundary-mountains VV. 34-40 etc). See I. 48 also—Its divisions—I.40. 30-35.—Founder king Agnīdhra —I.40.10, 30

Jayadhvaja—A king, story of—I.22. 21-87 (e.g. killing of demon Videha—VV 51-65, adores Viṣṇu as per Viśvāmitra's advice—VV.74-87) Race of Jayadhvaja—I.29

Jaleśvara or Jāleśvara—A *Tīrtha* under Narmadā—II.40.22-23

Jamadagni Tīrtha—At the confluence of Narmadā and the Sea—II.43. 33-34

Jāmadagnya Tīrtha—II.44.10

Jāpyeśvara—Place of Nandī's penance (Story of Śilāda)—II.43.17-42

K

Kailāsa—Mountain-abode of Śiva—I.26.19, 14, 64 (Kṛṣṇa's stay at K. I.26) Indra's mansion on K.—I.48.3-12

Kāla—Time-calculation of—I.5 vide Intro.pp.xxv-xxvi

Kālañjara Kṣetra—Kāla killed by Śiva (see Śveta) and revival—II.36.11-38

Kaliṅga—(i) A deśa and people in Bhārata Varṣa—I.47-42; II.40.9

(ii) A hill east of lake Aruṇoda—I.45.28

Kāmarūpa—A people in Bhārata Varṣa—I.47.41

Kanakhala—A holy place-II.37. 10-12

Kapāla-mocana-tīrtha—story how Rudra's hand was freed from god Brahmā's skull—II.31.69-103

Kapardīśvara—A Liṅga and a Tīrtha under Vārāṇasī—I.33

Kaśyapa a sage—Description of Kaśyapa's race—I.18

Kāverī—a sacred river—II.37.16-17—its source—Candra Tīrtha—II. 37-23

Kāyāvarohaṇa—A sacred place—(Birth place of Nakulīśa)—mod. Karvan in Gujarat—II.44.7-8

Kedāra—A holy shrine in the Himālayas—II.37.5-6

Ketumāla—N. of a Varṣa (subcontinent)—I.47-1 ff

Kimpuruṣa—(1) King of Hemakūṭa Varṣa—I.40.30-35

(2) N. of a Varṣa—I.47.8-9

Kokāmukha—Varāha Tīrtha at Triveṇī in Purnea district—I.31-47; II.35-36

Krauñca-dvīpa—Founder King—Dyutimān—I.40.19-21; Description—I.49.26-32

Kṛṣṇa—Viṣṇu's incarnation—requested for a son by Jāmbavatī—I.24. 83-86—Kṛṣṇa's penance—I.25.1-50 (Śiva manifested and praised—Kṛṣṇa praised VV.51-77—Boon to Kṛṣṇa—VV.78-90—Kṛṣṇa accompanies Śiva to Kailāsa] Kṛṣṇa's stay at Kailāsa and return to Dvārakā—I.25.92 and Ch.I.26;Kṛṣṇa explained *Liṅga* worship I.26.50—109

Kṛṣṇa's retirement from the world—I.27

Kṛttivāseśvara—A Tīrtha under Vārāṇasī—I.32-14-29 (named after Śiva's killing of an elephant-formed demon)

Kubjāśrama—(also Kubjāmra as per De, p.105)—Sacred place near Haridwar—II.20-33, II.35.33-35

Kūrma— (1) Tortoise incarnation of Viṣṇu
—Supported Mt. Mandara while churning the Sea—I.1-29
—Guides spiritually Indradyumna —I.1.51-122—Narrates Kūrma Purāṇa to sage Nārada and others—I.1.126 ff
—Eulogized by sages—II.46-54-67
(2) N. of a Purāṇa narrated by Kūrma to Indradyumna and Nārada (vide above)—sections of the Kūrma Purāṇa.I.1.22-23—Contents of the KP.—I.1.23-25; II.46.67-119

Traditional reciters of KP—II.46.140-147
For problems in KP see Introduction, pp. xix-xxix; xli-xlvi

Kuru—A Varṣa (subcontinent) North of mt. Śṛṅgavān I.40.30-35; 47.6

Kurukṣetra—A holy place—Glory of—II.35-5-6

Kuru-jāṅgala—A Tīrtha—II.37-36-37

Kuśa-dvīpa—Description of—I.49. 19-26; Ruled by King Jyotiṣmān—I.40-12

L

Lakṣmī—(1) A daughter of Bhṛgu—I.13-1
(2) A daughter of Dakṣa—I.8.15
(3) Consort of Viṣṇu—I.1-123 etc.

Laṅkā—Rāvaṇa's capital (Location still uncertain)—I.21-37-38, 44—II.34.127

Livelihood—the means of:
—Rules regarding the L. of Twice-born house-holders—II.25

Loka—World(s)—Seven—I.41.2 Location of higher worlds—I.44. 1-8 The World of Viṣṇu—I.44.9-10 The world of Śiva—I.44. 11-14

Lokāloka—Mt.s demarcating the boundary of this world—I.50.14-16

Lunar race—The description of—I.22

M

Madhya-deśa (Āryāvarta)— N. of a region in India (Bhārata Varṣa)—I.47.41

Madhyameśvara Liṅga shrine (under Vārāṇasī)—The glory of—I.34

Magadha—N. of a people in Bhārata Varṣa—I.47-42

Mahābhadra—A lake in Ilāvṛta—I. 45.23-24; 31-35

Mahālaya (Oṅkāra or Amareśvara?) —II.37,1-4, 20, 30

Mahānadī—(1) A Tīrtha under Vārāṇasī—II.35.25,—I.35.5
(ii) A river rising from mt. Ṛkṣavat—I.47.32-33
(iii) A river rising from the Vindhyas—I.47-34

Mahātīrtha—A Tīrtha dear to Nārāyaṇa—II.37-12

Mahendra—A mountain (*Kula-parvata*) of Bhārata Varṣa—I.50.5

Maheśvara Yoga—A special Śaiva Yoga—II.46.30-51

Malaya—A mountain (*Kula-parvata*) of India—I.47-23

Mānasa—A lake (in the Himālayas) —I.23-29; 45.23-24; II.37-44

Mandākinī—A sacred river—I.14. 27-29—I.47.32; 48.4-8

Mandāra (i) A mount used as a churning rod for obtaining Amṛta from the sea—I.1-67;
(ii) A *Kula-parvata* in Kuśa-dvīpa—I.49-21
(iii) A mountain in Ilāvṛta Varṣa —I.14-25

Maṅkaṇa—A sage—Danced with elation at the achievement of his penance—Śiva subdued his pride—II.35.45-76

Manu-periods (Manvantaras)—I.51
(1) Svāyambhuva Manu I.51-6
(2) Svārociṣa (verses)—7-9
(3) Uttama—10-12
(4) Tāmasa—13-15
(5) Raivata—16-20
(6) Cākṣuṣa—20-23
(7) Vaivasvata—23-26
Manu Periods—(Future) Enumerated: (8) Sāvarṇa (9) Dakṣa-sāvarṇa (10) Brahma-Sāvarṇa (11) Dharma-Sāvarṇa (12) Rudra-Sāvarṇa (13) Raucya (14) Bhautya —I.53.29-31

Mārkaṇḍeya—a sage—meets Yudhiṣṭhira—I.36.6 ff
—narrates the glory of Prayāga—I.36.15-48; Chs. 37 and 38

Meru (or Mahā-meru): a mountain (mod. Pāmirs as per S.M. Ali)—Description—branches, lakes, lands around—I.45.6-40; Meru—Like a

Lotus—Border mountains—I.46. 34-40; Abodes of guardians of the world on Meru e.g. (1) of Brahmā-I.46.1-4; (6) of Śiva—VV. 5-9. In this way of (3) Indra—VV.10-12 (4) Agni (called Tejovatī) VV. 13-14 (5) Yama (N. of the abode—Saṁyamanī) VV. 15-16; (6) Nirṛti (Named Rakṣovatī)—VV. 17-18. Meru (Mahā Meru) (7) Abode of Varuṇa (called Śuddhavatī)—VV. 19-20 (8) of Vāyu (called Gandhavatī) —V.21-22; (9) of Soma (named Kāntimatī)—VV.23-24; (10) of Śaṅkara (V.25) and Īśāna (V.26)

N

Nābhi—King of Hima-varṣa, father of Ṛṣabha—His descendants—I.40 30, 37ff

Naimiṣāraṇya—Etymological Story—II.43.1-15

Naiṣadha—A *Varṣa* ruled by Hari—I.40.30-35

Nakulīśa—An incarnation of Śiva—I.53-9

Nakulīśvara—A Tīrtha sacred to Nakulīśa Śiva—II.44.12-14

Nandīśvara—Story of—II.43.17-42 (see Jāpyeśvara also)

Nara—(1) N. of a king—I.40-43
(2) N. of a god—II.1-30
(3) A divine sage—II.38-51

Nārada—(1) A divine sage—I.1-18
(2) A Gandharva—I.42-12
(3) A *Kula-parvata* in Plakṣa-dvīpa —I.49.3

Nārāyaṇapura (also Vaikuṇṭha)—city of Nārāyaṇa in Śveta-dvīpa—I.49.50-71

Narmadā—(i) A holy river—The glory of—II.Chs.40-42;Holy places under Narmadā are separately noted. Many names of such places under Narmadā e.g. Bhadreśvara, Bāṇeśvara, Kedāreśvara etc. are common under other places like Vārāṇasī, Prayāga etc.
(ii) Wife of Trasadasyu—I.21-26

Navaratha—A king—story of—Protected by Sarasvatī (and her Eulogy)—I. 24.12-28

Nīla—(i) A mountain North of Meru—I. 45-9, 37
(ii) The Haridwar hills—II.20-33

Nīlācala—A mountain in Ramya Varṣa—I.40.33

Niṣadha—A mountain south of Meru in Ilāvṛta—I.45-28

Nṛsiṁha—The incarnation of Viṣṇu —His story—I.16.23-77

O

Oceans—Seven—Names of—I.45.4

Oṅkāreśvara—A Tirtha under Vārāṇasī—I.32.1

P

Pañca-nada—A Tīrtha—near Jāpeśvara (near the mouth of the Indus?)—II.44.1-2 [See Jāpyeśvara]

Pāñcāla—A people in India (Bhārata Varṣa)—I.47.41

Pañca-śikha—(1) A disciple of one of the incarnations of Śiva—I.53-15
(2) A sage in the line of teachers (transmitters) of *Īśvara Gītā*—II.11-129 and of the *Kūrma-Purāṇa*—II.46-144

Parāśara—(1) A sage—grandson of sage Vasiṣṭha—I. 19-23
(ii) A disciple of Śiva's incarnation—I.53.16

Pāriyātra (also Pārijāta, Pāripātra) —A *Kula-parvata* (identified with Western Vindhya) in Bhārata-Varṣa—I.47.24; 48.39

Pārvatī (see Devī, Umā)

Pātāla—the netherworlds—the locations of—I.44.15-26; 50.15-16

Pativratā—A chaste lady—greatness of a Pativratā—II.34.110-141 (This covers the abduction of Sītā's shadow)

Payoṣṇī—A sacred river rising in the Vindhyas—I.47-34

Phalaśruti—The 'fruit' of listening to —Part I of KP—I.53.31-34—The whole of KP—II.46.122-139

Phalgu (or Phālgunī): A river (under Gayā) sacred for Śrāddhas—II.20-34

Piśāca-mocana—A Tīrtha—I.33-2, 16 (See Śaṅkukarṇa)

Plakṣa-dvīpa—A continent—Description of the—I.49-1-19—Its king Medhātithi, son of Priyavrata—I.40.26-27

Plakṣa-Prasravaṇa (On the Sarasvatī)—II.37.29

Plakṣāvatāra—The Source of the Sarasvatī—II.37.7-8

(The) Planetary system—The position, extent etc. of planets like the Sun, the Moon etc.—I.41.5-26

Prabhāsa (i) (Somanātha, the *Jyotirliṅga* in Saurashtra)—Comparable to Vārāṇasī—I.31-48; II.35.16-17
(ii) A Tīrtha under Vārāṇasī—I.35-12
(iii) A Vasu-god—I.16.16
Prahlāda—(also Prahrāda)—A saintly demon king—Son of Hiraṇya-Kaśipu—fights against Nṛsiṁha and gets discomfited—I.16.42-63 Dissuades Hiraṇya Kaśipu from fight against Nṛsiṁha—I.16.65-72 crowns Hiraṇyākṣa after Hiraṇya-Kaśipu— I.16.77-78 — Prahrāda rules after Hiraṇyākṣa—I.16.84 —Prahlāda fights against Viṣṇu—I.16.86-90—Converted as Viṣṇu's devotee—Performs Yoga Sādhanā —I.16.93-94
Pratisañcara (Pralaya)—End of the universe—Description of the—II.45; Prākṛta Pralaya—II.46.1-65 (Ātyantika—II.46.26) vide Intro. p. xxv
Prayāga—(Allahabad)—A sacred place—The glory of I. Chs.36-39—II.35-4
Area 5 Yojanas—II.35.4—Procedure of pilgrimage of—I.37; Suicide recommended at—I.38.3-14; Tīrthas under Prayāga—I.39
Prāyaścitta—(Expiation for a wrong or sinful acts)—Its need—II.30.1-3 The deciding authorities—II.30.4-7 Five great sins—The perpetrators and their associates are sinners—II.30.8-11
Expiation for Killing a Brāhmaṇa—II.30.12-26
—for Liquor-drinking—II.32.1-3
—for Theft—II.32.4-11
for defiling Teacher's bed II 32.12-24
—for Adultery—II.33.1-20
—for Killing men of different castes—II.33.21-2
Prāyaścitta (Expiation for Sins)—
—for killing different animals and cutting down trees—II.33.29-39
—for minor thefts—II.34.1-7
—for eating forbidden articles of food—II.34.8-39
—for miscellaneous sins—II.34.40-109

R

Rāma (Dāśarathi)—Story of—I.21.16-55
Rāmeśvara—A *Tīrtha*—II.30.23
Ramyaka—A *varṣa* (Sub-continent) to the north of Meru—I.45.12
Rasātala—Name of a nether-world (*Pātāla*)—I.47.3-4
Rāvaṇa—A demon-King killed by Rāma—I.21.18-45; II.34.113-127
Ṛkṣa or Ṛkṣavat—A *Kula-parvata* (identified with eastern part of the Vindhya mountain) in *Bhārata-varṣa*—I.4.7-23
Ṛṇa-mocana—A *Tīrtha* under Prayāga—I.38.14
Ṛṣabha—Son of King Nābhi and father of Bharata—a devotee of Paśupati—I.40.38-40
Rohiṇī (i) Vasudeva's wife, Balarāma's mother—I.24, 71,73, 77
(ii) A constellation—II.20.9
Romaharṣaṇa—Sūta, the narrator of the Purāṇas—recounted the K. P.—(I.12-4)—Derivation of the name—I.1.5; Born on *Sutyāha* day in god Brahmā's sacrifice. Requested for [—I.1-6 narrating the KP.—I.1.7, 9 ff. ; I.1.9 ff
Rudrakoṭi—A *Tīrtha* equal in merit to Vārāṇasī—I.31.47
Rudra-loka—The region of Rudra—I.36.47-48; 37.9-11; 49-14
Rudra-sāvarṇa (See Manus—future Manvantaras)

S

Sahya—The Western Ghats in India-A *Kulaparvata* in Bhārata Varṣa—I.47-23
Saindhava—A people (on the lower Indus) in Bhārata Varṣa—I.47.43
Śāka-dvīpa—one of the Seven island-continents (identified with ancient Scythia)—I.49. 33-39
Their founder king Havya—I.40.13
Śālagrāma or Śāligrāma—A sacred place equal in merit to Vārāṇasī—I.31-47; II.35.37; Place of Succhāya's penance—I.14.4
Śālmalidvīpa—One of Seven island-continents—Vapuṣmān, Their first king—I.40.11
Saṁvartaka—
(1) A Tīrtha—I.35.6
(2) N. of World-destroying fire—II.45.28-33
(3) Clouds deluging the world—II.45.34-35
Sanat Kumāra—(1) A divine sage—I.7. 20-21; 10.13 etc.
(2) Name of an Upa-purāṇa—I.1.17

Saṅgameśvara—A Tīrtha under Narmadā—II.41.36-37
Śani—Saturn—I. 43.8-9, 29; —I.41.11, 17, 19, 26
Śaṅku-karṇa—A Brāhmaṇa devotee of Kapardīśvara—redeems a ghost —I.33.15-49
A female deer becomes a chief of Śiva-gaṇas—I.33.4-6
Sannyāsa Āśrama—
When to adopt—II.28.1-4
Rules and observances for a Sannyāsin—I.28.5-31 and Ch. 29
Sapta-dvīpas—Seven Island continents of the World (with Priyavrata's sons enthroned on each)—I.40.10-13
Sapta-Mahālokas—Seven higher spheres or worlds—I.41.2
Sapta-Sārasvata—A sacred place—Place of Maṅkaṇaka's Penance—II.35.44-76 (see Maṅkaṇaka)
Sarasvatī—(i) a godders—Eulogized by Navaratha—I.24.17-20
Protects Navaratha—I.24.20-23
(ii) A holy river in Kurukṣetra—II.40.7; 37.29 etc.
Sarayū—A sacred river—I.47.28
Śatadru—Sutlej—a sacred river—a tributary of the Indus—I.47.28
Śatarūpā—Wife of Svāyambhuva Manu—I.8.7-10
Sauvīra—Inhabitants of Bhārata Varṣa (dwelling on the lower Indus)—I.47.43
Sāvastī (Śrāvastī)—A king, founder of Śrāvastī—Son of Yuvanāśva—I.20.18-20
Setu—at Rameśvara—Rāma established a Liṅga here—I.21.44-49
Śilāda—a sage, father of Nandin—The story of—II.43.19-27
Sītā—(1) Rāma's spouse—story of her protection by the Fire-god, sending out her shadow for abduction—II.34.112-140
Sītā prays to Agni (*Vahnyaṣṭaka*)—II.34.117-124
(2) The eastern branch of the heavenly Gaṅgā—I.46.29-30
Śiva—Born as Brahmā's son—I.9.71-87; 10.18-89
Eulogies of Śiva:
—by god Brahmā—I.10.49-73
—by Sky-dwellers—I.16.186-189
—by Andhaka—I.16.194-206
—by Vasumanas—I.20.66
—by Kṛṣṇa—I.25.60-77; 26.103-105
—by Brahmā & Viṣṇu—I.26.78-87
—by Vyāsa—I.30.44-52 (?)
—by Śaṅkukarṇa—I.33.36-45
—by sages—II.1-33-35
—by Vedas—II.31.13-16
Śiva—called Rudra 'The crier', after birth from Brahmā—I.10.22-25
Seven names of Śiva—I.10.26
Eight forms of Śiva—I.10.27
—Eight wives of Śiva—I.10.29
—Eight sons of Śiva—I.10.30
—Created deathless Progeny—I.10. 31-37
—Ten undiminishing attributes of Śiva—I.10.40-42
Creation of Trinity of gods by Śiva—I.10.75-87
Śiva incarnates to delude cursed Brāhmaṇas—a founder of Pāśupatism—I.16.111-125
—Wanders as a Kāpālika—I.16. 120-128
—Incarnations of Śiva—I.53
—Fall of Liṅga in Dāruvana—II.38. 1-83
—Repentant sages favoured by sages—II.39
Śiva and Pārvatī—Eulogised by Brahmā—II.31.49-56 (Somāṣṭaka)
—Eulogised by Śveta—II.36.29-32
— ,, by sages—II.39.21-36
Śrāddha-Kalpa—II.20-22
—Qualifications of invitees—II.21. 1-47
—Procedure of Performance—II. 22.1-107
—Articles of food and Meat
—recommended for Śrāddha—II. 20.37-47
—Fruits of Śrāddha performed under various constellations and days of the Week—II.20.1-17
—Fruits of Śrāddha on various Tithis—II.20.18-22
—Holy places for Śrāddha—II.20. 29-36
Śrī—(Generally identified with Lakṣmī)
—Churned out of the Ocean—I.1. 30-40
—Advises Indradyumna to propitiate Viṣṇu—I.1.58-65
—Identified with Māyā and Prakṛti—I.1.34-40
Śrī-Parvata or Śrī-Śaila (Mt. in Andhra)—A sacred place equal to Varāṇasī—I.31.46
—Holy for performance of Śrāddha —II.20.35; 37.13-14

Śuka—Son of Kṛṣṇa-dvaipāyana Śuka's progeny—I.19.25-26
Śukla or Śukra—A Śiva Tīrtha under Narmadā—II.41-67-83
Sūta—Purāṇa-reciter—The birth of—I.14.12-16
Sūrya—The Sun-god—*Sūrya-hṛdaya* (Eulogy of—)—II.18.35-45
Suśīla—A king—Son of Śikhaṇḍin—Story of—I.14.23-50
—Meets Śvetāśvatara & adopts Pāśupatism—I.14.32
Svāyambhuva Manu—Creation from half the body of Brahmā, The other half Śatarūpā, Manu's wife—'I' 8.6 ff
—The race of Svāyambhuva Manu—I.14
Śveta—(1) A king—Saved from Death by Śiva—II.36.12-38
(2) N. of a mountain—I.45.9
(3) An incarnation of Śiva—I.53.2
(4) N. of a disciple of an incarnation of Śiva—I.53.12

T

Tala & Talātala—Two nether worlds—I.44.20, 21; 24-25
Tāmraparṇi—A sacred river—efficacious for Tarpaṇa —I.47.37; II.37.21-22
Tapoloka—One of the seven Mahālokas—I.44.3
Traiyambaka—A sacred place (mod. Trimbak in Nasik Dist.)—II.35.18-19
Trikūṭa—A mountain east of lake Aruṇoda—I.47.30
Trivikrama (or Vāmana)—An incarnation of Viṣṇu—I.17
Tuṅga-bhadrā—A sacred river—A tributary of the Kṛṣṇā —I.47.36

U

Udaya—A mountain in Śākadvīpa—I.49-34
Upamanyu—A sage—initiated Kṛṣṇa in Pāśupatism—I.25.3-49
Upa-purāṇas—A list of—I.1.17-20
Urvaśī-pulina—A sacred place under Prayāga—I.37.26-27
Uśanas—
(1) The preceptor of Daityas—I.48-58-59
(2) N. of a king-descendant of Kroṣṭu—I.25.5
(3) A Vyāsa—I.52.3
(4) N. of a disciple of one of Śiva's incarnations—I.53-19
Uttānapāda—A king in the Solar race—Manu's son and Dhruva's father—I.8.12
Uttara-Kuru—
A Varṣa (Subcontinent) of Jambūdvīpa—I.45.12-13

V

Vaikuṇṭha (See Nārāyaṇapura) : Viṣṇu's abode—I.49.64-71
Vāmana—Incarnation of Viṣṇu—I.17.46-69
Vānaprasthāśrama : Forest-hermitship—Third stage in Life of a twice-born—
—When to adopt—II.27.1-3
—Rules and observances for—II.27.4-38
Varāha—A mountain West of Asitoda—I.45.38, II.20.32
Vārāha—A *Tīrtha* under Narmadā—I.35.6; II.42.14
Vārāṇasī—The Sacred-most place of the Hindus.
—The glory of—I Chs. 31 to 35
—Kṛṣṇa-Dvaipāyana's pilgrimage to V. described—I.31.
—Śiva glorifies Vārāṇasī or Avimuktaka—I.3 .22 ff.
—List of the sacredmost places—I.31.46-48
—Tīrthas under Vārāṇasī—I.35 (also I.31.46 ff)
Vāsudeva (Kṛṣṇa)—Incarnation of Viṣṇu—story of—I.24.70 ff. [For details, see Kṛṣṇa]
Vasiṣṭha—(1) A sage—I.2.22; 14.4 etc.
(2) One of the Seven Sages (*Saptarṣis*) in Vaivasvata Manvantara—I.51-25
(3) A Vyāsa—I.52-4
(4) A disciple of one of the incarnations of Śiva—I.53.18
Vasiṣṭhāśrama—Śiva kindly treated at—II.38.33-38
Vasumanas—A king—His Aśvamedha, penance & Sāyujya with Śiva—I.20.29-76
Vedas—Classification of—I.52.12-27
Vinaśana—The place of the disappearance of the Sarasvatī—Holy for Śrāddha—II.37.29
Vindhya—A Kula-parvata in India—I. 47.24
Vipāśa—The river Beas—I.47.29

Virocana—A demon king—The story of I.17.1-11
Becomes a Yogi as per Sanatkumāra's advice
Viṣṇu :
—Kills demons Madhu and Kaiṭabha—I.10.2-6
—Eulogized by Indradyumna—I.1.69-79
—Uplifts the earth in Varāha incarnation—I.6.1-10; 23-25.
Viṣṇu eulogised by the sages.I.6.11-21
—God Brahmā—I.16.28-31
—Aditi—I.17.19-23
—Prahlāda—I.17.32-39
Incarnations of Viṣṇu—I.5 .27-50

Y

Yadu—King—Dynasty of—I.24.1 ff
Yājñavalkya—a sage, composed Yoga Śāstra as per Śiva's advice —I.25-44
Yama—(1) God of death—I.20.3; 33.23; 41.34-35 etc.
(2) A *Tīrtha* under Vārāṇasi—I.35-6
,, under Narmadā—II.41.83-84
Yamunā—a very sacred river—I.47. 28
—Sister of Yama—I.20.3
—Her importance—I.36.23, 44-48
—Tīrthas under Yamunā—I.38. 14-15; 39.4-6 (cf. 36. 44-48)
Yaśodā—Nanda's wife—Kṛṣṇa's foster-mother—I.24.74
Yavana—A People to the West of Bhārata Varṣa—I.47-26
Yayāti—A king—The story of—I.22.6-11
Yudhiṣṭhira—Pāṇḍava king—His dialogue with Mārkaṇḍeya about the glory of Prayāga—I.Chs. 36-39
Yuga—Nature of the Yugas—I.29
—Yuga-dharmas (Characteristics of Yugas)—I.29.8 ff
—Conditions: in the Kṛta Yuga—I.29.16-18
—In Tretā-Yuga—I.29.19-41
—In Dvāpara Yuga—I.29.42-5
—Conditions in the Kali Yuga--I.30
Yogins—Duties of and classification of—I.2.75-85
Yuvanāśva—A king — Propitiated Nārāyaṇa for a Son—I.2 .12-19